taking space

HOW TO USE SEPARATION TO EXPLORE THE FUTURE OF YOUR RELATIONSHIP

robert j. buchicchio, LICSW, DCSW

CHARLER PUBLISHING

Published by CharLer Publishing,
2125 Brazier Road, Montpelier, VT 05602

Cover design by Greenleaf Book Group LP
Interior design and composition by Greenleaf Book Group LP

Submit all requests for reprinting to:
Greenleaf Book Group LP
4425 Mopac South, Suite 600
Austin, TX 78735
(512) 891-6100

Library of Congress Control Number: 2005937575

ISBN-10: 0-9774568-0-3
ISBN-13: 978-0-9774568-0-2

Printed in the United States of America

10 9 8 7 6 5 4 3 2 1 08 07 06 05

This book is dedicated to my mom, my first teacher and role model on how to empower others.

Acknowledgments

The inspiration for this book came as I sat on a beautiful southern New Jersey shore several years ago. I recall looking up from my reading material and blurting out to my wife, Harriet, a title for a ten-step problem-solving guide to help people cope and grow through a troubled relationship. She liked it and the rest is history.

I would like to thank Harriet for being my sounding board, cheerleader, and first editor. I will never be able to thank you enough for your support in this endeavor, both as a professional and in the lab of marriage. You've had to put up with my obsession with this project as well as all my initial resistance to your input and ideas, which were usually great! Thanks to the rest of my family, Stephany, Bill, and Beth, for your encouragement, support, ideas, and love.

Thank you to my very first editor, Rebecca Davison, whom I equate with my first-grade teacher. Rebecca got me started by helping me organize files and kept me on the task of rewriting my introduction until it really described what was in the following chapters.

Thanks to Marcia Hill, PhD, an established author and respected colleague for turning me on to my heroine, Caroline Pincus, book midwife, who took my dry, repetitive, clinical writing and made it into readable and interesting information for public and professional consumption. I would not have this book had it not been for Caroline. Thank you, thank you, thank you!

Thanks to my good old friend and colleague Michael Hollander for sharing his journey through life with me, along with some wonderful quotes and the inspiring meditation at the beginning of this book by Virginia Satir, a pioneer of the social work profession.

To Ruth Lehner, another trusted, long-time social-work colleague, thank you for having the patience to read some of my first-generation material and being kind enough to let me know the ideas were great, but my writing was, well, let's just say it needed some improvement.

Thanks to my good friends Jim Ritvo and Dave Raizman of 132 Main Productions for their great work in turning my educational materials into video works of art. Their professional eyes provided observations and feedback that allowed me to refine how I present information to people.

I wish to thank Edward Handy, a good friend and colleague, for his support and invitation to the martial arts, which have taught me to apply principles of self-awareness and defense to my own development and relationships.

For many years of working out together and discussing ideas from my book, I want to thank my good friend Steve Pitonyak for his support, feedback, and encouragement all along the way.

To my good friends and colleagues at Action for Child Protection, Wayne Holder and Michael Corey, who gave me opportunities to train internationally and learn about relationships and good times in our many travels together. Wayne and I did one of the very first role plays at Ohio State that demonstrated the importance and power of relationships as a foundation to everything. Michael offered a common theme for one of my couple situations: "If you love me so much, why are you always trying to change me?"

To those professionals who attended my Managing and Treating Couples Separations workshops, your feedback was invaluable and very much appreciated.

To the professionals throughout the country and world who have shared their knowledge and experience with me through workshops and trainings over the years, I thank you for providing the foundation of my ideas.

Katy Sudol, a natural and great artist who painted the first draft of a front cover and was an inspiration for the beautiful cover adorning this book. Katy's father, Joe, my life-long friend who left this earth too early, gave me a copy of *Games People Play* by Eric Berne in 1964 and said, "Here Bob, you might be interested in this."

I appreciate the staff at Greenleaf Book Group LP in Austin, Texas, who worked with my manuscript and made it into a polished product both inside and out with their sensitivity and informative guidance, communication, and consultation.

I also appreciate Herbert Benson, MD, and the staff at the Mind Body Institute at Harvard University, who provided useful information and great validation that helped me provide the finishing touches to this endeavor.

I especially want to thank the Transactional Analysis (TA) community for providing training and support throughout the years for a model applicable to individuals' and couples' growth and knowledge. As theories come and go, I have found that TA has consistently given me the tools I've needed to teach my clients ways to work on themselves and their relationships.

And finally, thank you to all of my clients who have entrusted me with intimate details of your lives and relationships throughout the last thirty-five years of my professional career. Without the stories of your journeys I would not have been able to share what I have learned from you with others.

Connectedness with Self and Others

Allow yourself to become
Intimately connected
With all your parts.
So free, to have options
Freely and creatively.
To know that whatever
Was in the past,
Was the best that we could do,
Because it represented the best we knew.
It represented the best in our consciousness.
As we move toward knowing more,
Being more conscious,
We also then become
More connected with ourselves.
And in connecting with ourselves,
We can form connections with others.

—Virginia Satir

Reprinted by permission of the author(s) and publisher: Reprinted by permission of the author and publisher, *The Satir Model: Family Therapy and Beyond* by Virginia Satir, John Banmen, et al, Science & Behavior Books, Inc., Palo Alto, CA, 0831400781.

Contents

List of Exhibits

COUPLE SITUATIONS	STEP									
	1	2	3	4	5	6	7	8	9	10
COUPLE 1: John and Mary: "He's Like a Third Child!"	14		87		137	164			240	
COUPLE 2: Tim and Margie: "Shutdown Spouse"	23		91		141					
COUPLE 3: Bill and Nancy: "We Fight About Everything. I Think We're Growing Apart."		41								
COUPLE 4: Sandy and Jeff: "The Affair"				113						
COUPLE 5: Dennis and Pat: "I Have Feelings for Somebody Else."						166		207		
COUPLE 6: Amy and Fred: "I Think I've Outgrown My Relationship."						168				
COUPLE 7: Ed and Beth: "When He Drinks Too Much, I Can't Stand Being Around Him."							182			
COUPLE 8: Stan and Jill: "If You Love Me So Much, Why Are You Always Trying to Change Me?"							194			
COUPLE 9: Steve and Jan: "I Married My Father!"								224		
COUPLE 10: Jane and Randy: "Romance Lost"									249	
COUPLE 11: Judy and Tina: "Mommies"									260	
COUPLE 12: Frank and Peg: "It's Either Me or Your Mother!"										274
COUPLE 13: Mike and Carol: "You Never Want to Have Sex!"										286

Introduction

Separations occur throughout the life cycle and are necessary to human development: at birth we separate from our mothers; at two years old we assert our independence and want to do everything ourselves; separation and independence describe the crises and risks of our teen years; and separations often continue through our adult years. In marriage or relationships, however, we consider the taking of space or separation as a sign of trouble with a capital *D* for "Divorce." In fact, temporary separations in a marriage can often be exactly what couples need in order to grow, develop, and renew their commitment to each other and themselves.

It has been my experience that people often choose divorce because they believe their marriages have become unbearable, they are desperate for change, and they don't know of any viable alternative. As I will show through stories and situations in this book, managed separation can be a viable alternative, offering a path that increases the chances of keeping your marriage together and your family intact. Separations, as defined in this book, are about taking both physical space and psychological space. I will show you how useful, healthy, and necessary such separations can be, and how you can make them work for you.

If your relationship is in crisis, a well-managed separation can help you regain much-needed balance and boundaries, and help you avoid a hasty move to divorce. This is a book about how best to figure out what you and your partner really want and whether the relationship can provide it.

This is not to suggest that separations are ever easy. They often stretch us way beyond our comfort zones and force us to find different ways of viewing life, but the self-growth we experience during the process of separation almost always leaves us better off.

In over thirty-five years of relationship, marriage, and divorce counseling, I have helped hundreds of couples sort through their conflicts and come to decisions about their relationships. Some did not want to work on their relationships, or for one reason or another simply didn't put in the effort. Others stayed together but continued to feel dissatisfied. Seeing so many couples in crisis, I began to realize that there are times in our lives when self-growth is more important than a relationship. Often we can't change, grow, and become satisfied in our relationships without periods of separation during which we have space to grow as individuals.

Thoughts of separating often pop up early in a relationship, shortly after the romance period. As a couple begins to settle into a routine and they come to know each other's "edges," they often fear they might be falling out of love. As they are adjusting to life together, they may start to feel disillusioned and disappointed. For this reason this period is often referred to as the disillusionment–compromise stage of the relationship. The couple is not falling out of love so much as reclaiming their original selves and shifting their expectations of each other.

This is a perfectly natural stage in any relationship, but it can be extremely traumatic. People often begin to show parts of themselves that their partners have not seen. It is about growing and separating into your *self*, learning to take care of your self, and meeting your wants in the relationship. But without realizing that separation can be a healthy thing, people often tend to fear that their marriage was a mistake. As you'll discover in this book such fears can be lessened by clarifying your wants and negotiating differences.

Another stage when thoughts of separation might come into a relationship is when women find themselves burnt out from performing the multiple duties of wage earner, mother, wife, and keeper of the household. Feeling unappreciated and unsupported, some women will begin to question where all the fun and romance have gone, and may even begin to question the solidity of their relationship with their partner. A temporary separation can be extremely useful at such times, helping both women and men evaluate the patterns that have developed in the marriage and how these patterns might need changing.

Perhaps the most familiar catalyst for separation is the midlife crisis, which can occur at any age. Usually, one partner starts to question his or her values, lifestyle, and direction, and the health of the relationship. These changes are normal and even predictable, but most couples lack a way of dealing with them.

Because people do not usually have a structure to follow during these challenging times, the conflict can become so difficult to manage that separation becomes a necessity simply to ease tension and survive.

I developed ten steps that provide individuals and couples with a starting point and a "map" to guide them. My approach essentially allows you to hit the pause button, which will give you an opportunity to develop yourself and learn more about your own patterns of relating to others. Even when relationships cannot be resurrected, this process helps people start new relationships on better footing.

There's simply no reason that a decision as major as whether to stay together or not—one that would permanently affect you, your children, and so many others—should be undertaken without the benefit of good information and the insight, knowledge, and experience gained by others who've already been through the process.

I wrote this book to share with you some of the ideas and methods I have used successfully with clients, and to share their experiences with taking space from each other. Whether you are considering a psychological separation (without a physical move) or a physical separation, my ten steps can help you gain control of the conflict, your feelings, and your self. Once you've given yourself that space or time, you will find that you are in a much better position to consider your full range of options. It is important to do this with great care because *how* you separate will have a lot to do with how easily and well the process goes, especially for your children, if you have any.

What people have found particularly useful about my approach is that it is not dependent on two people. Many of my clients have successfully used this approach even without any cooperation from their partners. That's because it is essentially about helping individuals face their fears and ask themselves such difficult and confusing questions as the following:

- Am I unhappy with myself or my spouse?
- Can I learn to be alone and deal with my feelings of rejection?
- What if the grass isn't greener on the other side?
- Can I fall in love again with the same partner?
- What's the difference between loving my partner and being in love with my partner?
- How do childhood losses and divorce affect my current conflict and separation?
- Am I depressed? What does my depression have to do with my relationship?
- What are my contributions to my relationship patterns?

I truly respect the power and resilience of the human spirit, and it is my hope that you will find in this book a path to guide you through your difficult time and the companionship and wisdom of others who have made the journey.

Take a quick look at the ten steps of Separation Management:

1. Managing the Crisis or Conflict You will learn how to answer questions such as the following: Is your conflict routine or are you in a crisis? Is your conflict aggressive and explosive, or passive and avoidant as in a cold war? You will also learn things you can do to control your anger and ease your pain.

2. Communicating in the Midst of Crisis You will look at how you currently communicate with your partner and yourself—if you communicate at all—and learn how to develop ways to communicate even during a crisis, with an emphasis on learning to communicate with your self.

3. Defining the Initial Goals of Separation (Both Yours and Your Spouse/Partner's) and Determining if Separation Is the Answer

4. Choosing the Type of Separation That Is Right for You

5. Deciding on Terms and Conditions, the Time Frames, and Ground Rules of Your Separation

Steps 3, 4, and 5 will help you determine whether separation is for you and what kind of separation might be best. You'll ask yourself why you (or your partner) are considering a change. This is probably the most important question you can ask. Determining *why* will give your separation the definition and purpose it needs.

Of course, things change. Sometimes people separate for one reason and then discover other reasons for separating. That's where the stories and examples that accompany each step become so valuable. They provide a kind of menu of different types of separations that have worked for different couples. Examples of different separation agreements will help you look closely at the various issues and problems couples wrestle with because of and during the separation.

These three steps will help you clarify your goals, motivations, investments, and commitments. You will also try to determine whether or not you and your partner should seek counseling, either together or separately.

6. Minimizing the Impact on Your Children You will learn the best ways to talk to your kids and minimize the impact of the separation.

7. Carrying Out Your Decision Here's where the rubber hits the road. How do you get started? What does an in-house separation mean in reality? How about an out-of-the-house separation? Numerous couples share their experiences.

8. Developing, Clarifying, and Changing Your Goals as the Separation Progresses After the crisis or conflict has eased, you may find your goals for yourself and your relationship changing. During a separation, with a bit of space and breathing room, many people find themselves asking big questions about what's important to them and who they are. Separation affects people at the very essence of their existence and many times the crisis becomes an opportunity, albeit often a painful one, to grow and stretch well beyond where we thought we could go. Some individuals and couples even go so far as to say that their separation was a spiritual journey that allowed them to develop deeper love and compassion for themselves and others. Often in the wounded heart one finds the courage to know, heal, and love oneself and others again.

9. Evaluating Whether Your Goals Are Being Met As important as it can be to separate, it is crucial to have ways to determine whether it's working. This step will help you evaluate your separation and changes and make new decisions and adjustments as necessary.

10. Determining What's Next: Getting Back Together, Staying Apart, or Getting a Divorce It's decision time. Sooner or later the separation will end. Do you need a trial union? More physical space? More time to work on the issues of separation? Is it time to file for a divorce, or time to make a renewed commitment? These and many other choices are presented through discussion and the experiences of other couples.

As you can see, this approach is circular. Each step is a building block that will help you move to the next step. For example, suppose your immediate crisis was that your spouse was having an affair. You successfully managed the conflict (Step 1) by having your partner agree to stop seeing his lover. Now you're working on your joint goal of reviving the romance in your relationship only to find a lot of old resentments surfacing. Every time there is a backslide into nonproductive conflict, you must once again gain control over yourself and the immediate conflict (Step 1).

This flexible structure and format also allows you to address the deeper goals, issues, and questions of separation, such as what you want and if the relationship will provide it. It will help you determine where your and your partner's responsibilities lie for the difficulties in your relationship, and your role in your own unhappiness and lack of fulfillment in the relationship.

I have found that insight and understanding into your self and your relationship often becomes overpowered by the intense feelings and conflict of change and separation. Your work, therefore, begins when you decide to control conflict for yourself and/or your partner and reestablish some basic communication. If you then decide to separate, either physically or psychologically, I give you a safe container for exploring your individual and relationship goals—one that allows you to use the separation to go as deep as you want to into understanding your self, your partner, and your relationship.

If I have one goal, it's to empower you so that you will be able to decide how things will go for you, whether you are the one initiating the change or the change is being forced on you. Each of the ten steps will be explored, in turn, in the following steps. For each step I offer you the coping skills, exercises, and methods that have been successful with my clients. Remember, however, that no two situations are alike. Even if you find yourself identifying with a particular situation, you may very well choose a different type of separation or make different decisions. The cases are not prescriptions, but they can be very good models when the going gets rough.

In these ten steps you'll find insights, knowledge, and coping strategies that my separating clients have used with success. From there, it's up to you.

Begin by looking at your conflict or crisis and see where to go from there. I wish you much luck and success on this separation journey.

STEP 1
Managing the Crisis or Conflict

Anger is a signal, and one worth listening to.
—Harriet Lerner, *The Dance of Anger*

People don't usually think about taking space unless there's a conflict in the relationship. Learning to manage that conflict is your first step. You simply can't make long-term decisions about the direction of a relationship without cooling the fires of conflict first.

Perhaps you and/or your partner fear that you've fallen out of love or even "like" with each other. Maybe you've already considered physical separation as a way to stop or ease the stress in your marriage and are reading this book to figure out how to do that. I urge you to look first at managing the conflict that got you to this point so that you will be in a better position to assess your full range of options.

Continual and escalating conflict, whether aggressive and explosive or passive and avoidant, is not only destructive to your emotional and mental health but to your physical health as well. It is one of the most common causes of stress to individuals, families, and especially children, and is often the best predictor of relationship breakup. Even affairs, which often seem to be a major cause of breakups, are often signs and symptoms of conflict within the marriage.

You could compare managing relationship conflict to taking a pain pill for a headache. While you're in pain (conflict) you simply can't concentrate on other aspects of life. But once you get some relief and you're out of immediate pain, you can begin to figure out what is really causing the headache/conflict in the first place.

Of course, conflict styles, or the ways couples express conflict, can vary widely, and for this reason I created what I call the Relationship Conflict Scale (See page 11).

Relationship Conflict Scale

"We Never Fight."

On the far left of the Conflict Scale are couples who would claim that they do not fight. The fact that these couples don't express conflict shouldn't be confused with their not having conflict. In fact, individuals in conflict-avoidant relationships may be very angry with each other; they just don't air their anger directly. In some cases, just one person is angry (and may or may not know it) and the partner may or may not know it, or may deny it.

In such relationships a decision, overt or covert, was made somewhere along the line that open airing of differences or difficulties is not permissible. People often learn this avoidant style in their families of origin, either because their parents also fought passively, or at the other extreme, because there was constant conflict and severe fighting. These individuals and couples learned that open conflict and disagreement are too uncomfortable, and they tend to avoid them at all costs.

It's very stressful to harbor unexpressed feelings, and people who shoulder such a burden often experience physical problems, such as headaches and digestive upsets, as well as worry, anxiety, and depression that seem to take up a great deal of their own and their family's energy.

Sometimes people aren't even aware of how upset they are with their partners, but they know that they're feeling beaten up by the relationship. Children may also act out their parents' unexpressed conflict through angry and rebellious behavior at home, school, or socially.

RELATIONSHIP CONFLICT SCALE

Passive (Avoidant, Aggressive)

I create an ice wall.

I never want to fight.

I internalize anger.

I avoid and withdraw from conflict.

I may be unaware of my anger or deny being angry.

My anger may be expressed physically, through headaches, tension, and digestive upsets, or through worry, stress, anxiety, or depression.

My children may express the anger I feel.

I may "act out" my anger through passive-aggressive behavior to get even, e.g., being late, forgetting to do things, giving silent treatment, or withdrawing sexually.

I take anger out on myself through unfair self-criticism, shaming, and guilt.

The silent tension in my relationship could be cut with a knife!

I have difficulty being me, being different, and expressing who I am.

Assertive-Expressive

I take responsibility for my anger.

I am aware of my feelings, including the negative ones, like fear, sadness, disappointment, and hurt, which underlie my anger.

I express my thoughts, feelings, and opinions.

I give my self permission to be who I am and to be different from my partner.

I do not act anger out physically or emotionally on my self or my partner.

I decide not to hurt me!

I stop destructive anger.

I communicate productively.

I get back to a power-balanced OK–OK place with my partner.

I communicate to express my wants.

I make it safe to express the free Child spirit within me.

Aggressive (Explosive, Abusive)

I engage in open warfare.

I get in fights all the time.

I say mean and nasty things.

I can become abusive physically or emotionally.

I use put-downs, threats, manipulations, criticisms, or power trips.

My fights with my partner can become loud, scary, and out of control. The neighbors must think we're crazy.

My children are scared!

I don't listen to my partner at all.

I try to hurt my partner in sensitive areas.

I'm angry a lot!

"We Fight All the Time."

At the other end of the conflict scale are those couples who are much more aggressive and sometimes explosive about their anger and conflict. In counseling sessions, I often hear how couples fight and argue all the time.

These couples often struggle with not being able to stop the conflict from escalating. In the extreme, their fights can become physically abusive and violent, or there can be emotional and verbal abuse. Other couples get locked into a series of angry and hurtful exchanges that can go on for long periods of time. These individuals and couples must learn to control conflict and fight fairly.

Everyone Else

It gets particularly challenging, of course, when one partner is at one end of the scale and the other partner is at the other, or when one partner is usually at one end but occasionally "flips" to the other. Just think of the usually passive person who stores feelings and then occasionally explodes and loses it.

Those who know how to express their wants, feelings (including anger), beliefs, and differences so they can be heard in an open and forthright manner would be at the center of the conflict scale, where the assertiveness quality lies. These folks are neither overly passive nor explosive. The goal in our work is to help you and/or your partner move from either end of the continuum toward the center, where you can express your wants and desires openly and have them heard without defense.

I always start by having people try to identify what they're feeling, and it's rarely an easy exercise. A list of feeling words follows, to help you get started. Needless to say, this list is not complete—you may well have your own words for describing your experiences—but many people find it helpful to have a list to refer to, and it always proves to be a good starting point as we begin to think about feelings.

FEELING WORDS

SADNESS	HURT	FEAR	ANGER	JOY
sorrowful	offended	fearful	resentful	festive
unhappy	distressed	frightened	irritated	contented
depressed	pained	timid	enraged	relaxed
melancholy	suffering	shaky	furious	calm
gloomy	afflicted	apprehensive	annoyed	satisfied
somber	worried	fidgety	inflamed	comfortable
dismal	aching	terrified	provoked	peaceful
quiet	crushed	panicky	infuriated	joyous
choked up	heartbroken	tragic	offended	ecstatic
mournful	despair	hysterical	sullen	inspired
dreadful	tortured	alarmed	belligerent	glad
dreary	lonely	cautious	irate	pleased
flat	pathetic	shocked	cross	grateful
blah	cold	horrified	bitter	cheerful
in the dumps	upset	insecure	frustrated	excited
dull		impatient	grumpy	cheery
sullen		nervous	boiling	lighthearted
moody		anxious	fuming	buoyant
out of sorts		dependent	stubborn	carefree
low		pressured	confused	surprised
discontented		worried	mad	optimistic
discouraged		doubtful	spiteful	spirited
concerned		suspicious	used	vivacious
sympathetic		hesitant	burned	hilarious
compassionate		dismayed	hateful	merry
embarrassed		cowardly	hot	exhilarated
shameful		threatened	pissed	jolly
ashamed		appalled	steamed	playful
useless		petrified		elated
worthless		gutless		jubilant
ill at ease		scared		thrilled
resigned		afraid		confident
disappointed		overwhelmed		up
abandoned		desparate		free
lost		tense		relieved
tight				helpless
empty				happy

Throughout the book I'll profile various couples who have reached some sort of crisis in their relationship and are considering taking action. As you read about them, think of how their situations and their conflicts and ways of addressing them may or may not apply to you and your relationship. Of course, you'll want to take only what's useful and meaningful back to your own relationship.

Couple Situation 1: Mary and John: "He's Like a Third Child!"

Mary and John have been married for five years. They are both in their early thirties. They dated for two years before they were married and have two children, three-and-a-half-year-old Denise and six-month-old Dan. Mary left her job in a large insurance company when Dan was born. She has since gone back to work. Mary has an associate's degree from a local college and has considered going back to school for a bachelor of arts. John is a car salesman.

For about a month after Dan was born, John seemed to be committed to helping out with the childcare and housework. Since the first month John has done less and less, putting most of the responsibility on Mary to pick up the children from day care, feed them their snacks, prepare dinner, bathe the children, and put them to bed. Usually, after all her work, Mary collapses from fatigue.

By contrast, John comes home from work, plays with the children for a while, reads the paper, eats dinner, and watches TV. He even has a weekly night out with the guys.

Mary has gotten increasingly angry as her workload has intensified. She has found herself constantly reminding John of the things that need to be done around the house, but most of the time John ignores her. To top it off, John also leaves his clothes lying around for Mary to pick up and put away. She says she feels like his mother.

Mary was able to handle her career and the housework with just one child, but when the second arrived she hit overload. At first, John tended to listen when she complained, and he promised that he would help. When he didn't follow through, Mary swallowed her anger, withdrew from him emotionally and sexually, and did all the work herself. No longer able to contain her anger, their fights have become open and aggressive.

This is certainly not what Mary imagined when they first married. She's tired all the time, angry and resentful at John, and thinks she has fallen out of love. At times she doesn't even like him anymore. She wants them to go for counseling, because she thinks that it would make John act more responsible for the work in their family life, but John refuses to go for help. Their fights have gotten worse, to the point where they find themselves screaming and swearing at each other, sometimes in front of the children. Both of them are aware that their fights scare the children. Denise has even started planting herself between her parents and telling them to stop fighting.

Mary is so unhappy that she is considering asking John for a divorce. She figures that being alone couldn't possibly be as frustrating as living with John, and besides, she is already doing all the work. The fighting is so stressful that it has become all she thinks about at work. It has started to affect her concentration and productivity.

Needless to say, Mary is unhappy and very confused. She is frightened by her feelings and does not know what to do. She often wonders if this is what the rest of her life will be like and what happened to their relationship.

When couples like John and Mary come to see me, the first thing I do, after hearing each partner's side of the story, is offer a time-out strategy (see Rules for Taking a Time-out, page 16) in which partners agree to disengage for a specific period of time. A time-out can be a necessary first step, especially when one partner won't agree to work on understanding and managing the conflict in the relationship.

Although it is best when both partners can agree to use the time-out strategy, it is quite possible, and sometimes necessary, for one partner, usually the partner looking to end the conflict, to use it alone. When one partner does not agree to abide by the rules of time-out, this could indicate the need for more physical space between partners in order to control conflict.

RULES FOR TAKING A TIME-OUT

1. When conflict becomes destructive or nonconstructive, either partner can call a "time-out."

2. When either partner calls a time-out, talking and arguing stop immediately!

3. The partner who calls the time-out disengages physically to cool down.

4. Communication stops—no last words and no following the partner who is taking space.

5. The partner who calls the time-out physically disengages for a period of time—ten minutes, one hour, before bed—but not more than twenty-four hours.

6. The partner who called the time-out is responsible for re-initiating communication within twenty-four hours.

7. When communication is restarted, partners agree to use a "share the floor" format, where only one person speaks at a time (see Ground Rules for Talking, page 17).

EXERCISE

Before reading further, take a few minutes alone or with your partner to imagine that you are experiencing this situation from Mary's perspective and then from John's perspective. Attempt to really "get into the shoes" of each partner.

If you are working through the exercises in this book with your partner, it can be invaluable to have some ground rules for holding meaningful conversations. We don't usually need ground rules for small talk, but when things are tense or emotional, these guidelines can structure conversation so everyone feels safe. Learning to

GROUND RULES FOR TALKING

1. **Take Turns** Agree in advance that only one person talks at a time, for at least three but no more than five minutes. The other person just listens. You can feel, think, and say whatever is on your mind. Your opinion is just that, *your opinion.* Your partner is also entitled to opinions, feelings, and thoughts.

2. **Don't Interrupt** You may not interrupt your partner except to ask for clarification.

3. **Try to Understand Your Partner** When you hear things that make you angry and unable to listen, call a time-out, and take a break. Attempt to listen to your partner's opinions, beliefs, thoughts, and feelings, and try to understand how your partner thinks and feels about the issues being discussed. You do not have to agree! Even though what you hear may be threatening or hurtful, it's important that you listen and acknowledge what your partner has to say. This does not mean that you are in agreement with what your partner is saying!

4. **Focus on Not Becoming Defensive, Blaming, Critical, or Sarcastic, or Withdrawing During the Conversation** Each element of your communication process—your overall attitude, nonverbal body and facial expressions, and what you say—is equally important. Own your own feelings; try to avoid blame statements, using "I" statements whenever possible. For example, "When you interrupt me, I feel angry." Avoid "you" statements such as "You make me feel angry." Others can deny "making you" feel anything, but they cannot deny that you feel what you feel.

5. **Limit This Exercise to Thirty Minutes** You can agree to extend the time, but having a limit in place is very important. Each partner should get equal time.

communicate in productive ways can also help prevent, replace, and repair conflict. Here and throughout the book, it's up to you to decide whether working through the exercise with your partner will help or possibly just intensify the conflict.

EXERCISE AND DISCUSSION

1. Who do you identify with more, Mary or John?

2. On what side of the Conflict Scale does Mary and John's conflict fall? Why?

3. Do you think Mary is justified in feeling so angry?

4. What does John do or not do that Mary allows to trigger her anger? Which of Mary's thoughts fuel her angry feelings?

5. From hearing mostly Mary's side so far, what are your first thoughts and feelings on whether John should be sharing more of the household and childcare chores?

6. What do you think seems to be making it so difficult for this couple to talk about and work out their issues?

7. What do you think either partner could do to reduce the conflict? What would you do?

Assessing the Conflict

The conflict between Mary and John is an example of the aggressive side of the Conflict Scale. Mary is stressed, tired, and angry, and she focuses her anger on John, who, she believes, plays a limited role in sharing the burden of family life. She blames John for the lopsided responsibility in their relationship and says she feels more like his parent than his partner. John often feels like a child and believes he must defend himself against her blaming and nagging.

Each passing week they grow further apart and feel less connected with each other in a positive way. They either ignore each other, or yell and scream. John is so angry with Mary that he doesn't like her much right now and has said some pretty mean things to her during their fights.

Such uncontrolled, escalating, and continuing conflict could easily destroy what is left in their relationship. Until each acknowledges and takes responsibility for the anger, frustration, and other feelings about the way their relationship is going, they will remain at an impasse.

For change to occur, Mary and John must learn to manage the conflict. Of course, this step alone will not solve their problems or reconnect them as a couple, but it is a critical first step toward better understanding the problem.

Perhaps you and your spouse are, like Mary and John, angry all the time. Even if just one of you decides you don't want to fight anymore, you can help cool the fires. You may find it useful to refer to the Anger Awareness Temperature Gauge. It can help you recognize when to keep talking and when to back off.

As you become more aware of how you become angry and what triggers your anger (a behavior, something said, a tone of voice, a facial expression, etc.), notice how the intensity of your feelings, your thinking, and your behavior changes as you "heat up" or move up the scale. Especially notice what feelings may lie under your anger (disappointment, sadness, hurt, fear/anxiety, loss of control, etc.). How are you seeing yourself being victimized by your partner or your situation? Anger, whether expressed or not, usually increases as our sense of having options shrinks.

Attempt to find out which of your beliefs and values are being threatened. Finally, learn to manage your behavior as you consider the consequences of your actions.

Twenty-five hundred years ago, Confucius said, "When anger rises, think of the consequences." The best any of us can do is to recognize our feelings, understand how and what triggers them, manage the strong emotions that emerge, and learn how we can express them in healthier ways.

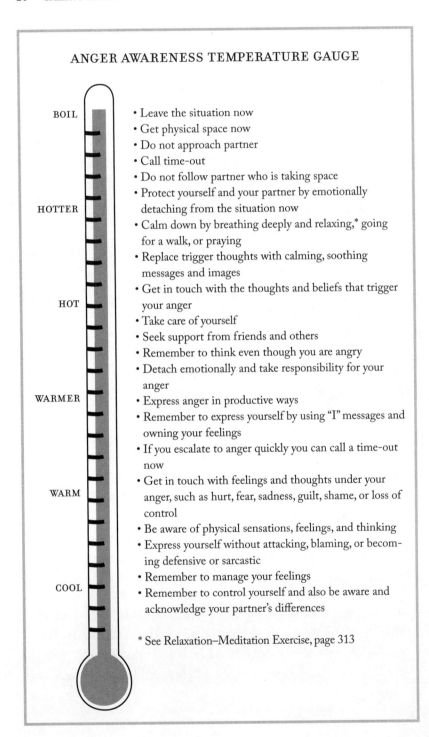

ANGER AWARENESS TEMPERATURE GAUGE

BOIL
- Leave the situation now
- Get physical space now
- Do not approach partner
- Call time-out
- Do not follow partner who is taking space
- Protect yourself and your partner by emotionally

HOTTER
  detaching from the situation now
- Calm down by breathing deeply and relaxing,* going for a walk, or praying
- Replace trigger thoughts with calming, soothing messages and images
- Get in touch with the thoughts and beliefs that trigger

HOT
  your anger
- Take care of yourself
- Seek support from friends and others
- Remember to think even though you are angry
- Detach emotionally and take responsibility for your anger

WARMER
- Express anger in productive ways
- Remember to express yourself by using "I" messages and owning your feelings
- If you escalate to anger quickly you can call a time-out now
- Get in touch with feelings and thoughts under your

WARM
  anger, such as hurt, fear, sadness, guilt, shame, or loss of control
- Be aware of physical sensations, feelings, and thinking
- Express yourself without attacking, blaming, or becoming defensive or sarcastic
- Remember to manage your feelings

COOL
- Remember to control yourself and also be aware and acknowledge your partner's differences

* See Relaxation–Meditation Exercise, page 313

What Mary Did

Mary realized that she was in a crisis and needed relief. By deciding to seek help and talk to friends and eventually a counselor, Mary began to stop blaming John and started taking charge of herself.

One day, after almost six months of continual and increasing conflict, Mary approached John and said she was tired of fighting and being so angry and needed to stop for her own survival (time-out). John couldn't believe what Mary was saying and at first did not trust that she would really stop blaming him. But since John was rarely the one to start the arguments, he decided to comply.

Every time Mary felt tired and overburdened with responsibility, she would take deep breaths and consciously and deliberately not focus on how John did not help. She started to notice how staying focused on John and her anger did not change the pattern but actually made her feel worse. She vowed to become aware of all the anger triggers in their day-to-day interactions and to try to control her feelings through deep breathing and working with her thinking and beliefs

---

THE FIVE STEPS OF ANGER AWARENESS

Be aware of your triggers. What feelings and thoughts are under your anger? Hurt, fear, sadness, guilt, shame, or something else?

Be aware of the intensity of your feelings. How intense are they, on a scale of 1 to 10?

Be aware of the thinking related to your feelings. Think things like, "I can take care of me"; I can control my anger"; I can learn to manage my feelings."

Be aware of the actions and behaviors associated with your anger. Replace thoughts that trigger these behaviors with calming, soothing messages and images.

Be aware of the consequences of your anger. What will happen if you let your anger get out of control?

(see Relaxation–Meditation Exercise, page 313). She knew she would eventually have to talk to John about their uneven workload, but she also recognized that this conversation would not happen while they were arguing so much.

Mary began to talk to friends about her situation and started to plan more time off for herself. This seemed to help manage her anger at John as well.

From working with so many couples, I have come to realize that anger is *always* secondary to other feelings and unmet wants. Mary was tired, scared, overwhelmed, and depressed. Her earlier expectations of marriage and family were not being met, and she felt she had no options. In other words, Mary felt trapped.

The decision to call a time-out in the fighting took a lot of courage on her part and was a good first step in an attempt to consider other possible solutions. Mary further decided that every time she found herself really angry at John and ready to attack him, she would leave the room either mentally or physically and use deep breathing to say to herself, "This will go nowhere except to get me more frustrated and upset."

The time-outs did not solve John and Mary's problems, but as Mary stopped looking to John for solutions, she realized that she had to stop making herself so angry and to stop feeling sorry for herself. It dawned on Mary that she was not a helpless victim.

Mary's decision to begin to control her anger did not magically make it stop altogether. At times, especially when she was stressed and tired, she would find herself slipping and becoming angry with John. But knowing when and how her anger was triggered and what that felt like helped her remember to use her strategy to control it. She frequently reminded herself that it was best for her and the children to control her anger and that it was only the first step to other options about her problem.

This strategy worked on a short-term basis and allowed them to proceed to Step 2, in which they attempted to communicate more productively. The second step would not have been possible without managing the conflict first.

You will meet up with Mary and John again as you (and they) move through the steps of separation.

Couple Situation 2: Tim and Margie: "Shutdown Spouse"

Tim and Margie are in their forties and have been married for about ten years. This is a second marriage for both. Margie has two children from her first marriage, Jane, fifteen, and Tommy, seventeen. Tim has no children. He works construction and experiences seasonal layoffs. Margie makes a good income as a medical office manager.

This particular afternoon Tim is lying on the living room couch starting to drink his fifth beer. He is depressed and feels sad and is thinking about what Margie told him the night before: *Margie wants a separation and has asked me to leave. She said she is tired of carrying me along. She said she cares about me and loves me, but I don't meet her expectations of what a relationship should be about. She says she is burnt out on trying to get our relationship to work. I guess I didn't listen all those times she said she wanted me to go for help. I'm tired all the time and pretty much want to be left alone after I come home from work. I like her to cook me a nice meal. Sometimes we have sex. I like to watch sports on TV and drink a couple of beers to relax. What's wrong with that? I guess I don't communicate well and don't really like to talk about myself much. My job is boring and not much happens, so I don't have much to say about work. She always wants to go out with friends or to the movies or dinner, and experiment with new things. She complains that I never talk or spend time with the kids. She expects too much from me. I can't leave; where would I go? I don't think I could go on without her!*

Margie is driving home from the grocery store and feels desperate about her relationship with Tim. She is angry and attempting to convince herself that she made the right decision: *I've had it! I've asked Tim for a separation. We haven't been acting like partners for such a long time. Tim is content with doing nothing. He works, comes home, eats, drinks beer, and falls asleep watching sports on TV. I want somebody who will be involved in my life. He's not interested in the kids either. He has a distant relationship with Tommy and hardly ever talks to Jennifer. I know he loves them, but he sure doesn't show it.*

He grew up with nobody caring for him and he has done the same with us. He depends on me for everything and gives nothing back. I've asked him to go for help. From what I have read, I think he's depressed and has been for most of his life. He won't go for help to a doctor or a counselor. I've asked him to see a marriage counselor, and he refused. I'm tired of being his mother and doing everything around here.

My life is empty. We have no dreams together. We hardly socialize and then it's because I push him to go out. I feel terribly guilty for separating from him, but it's self-survival. He isn't abusive to the kids or me in any way, but I feel emotionally starved and neglected. There is nobody else in my life, but I have these fantasies of being more connected to somebody. I become panicked just with the thought of staying in this relationship for the rest of my life. I've had it.

Tim's First Counseling Session

With the threat of separation hanging over him, Tim finally makes a counseling appointment. After introductions the counselor asks Tim to explain why he is there and what he wants.

TIM: (*in a soft, low voice, looking on the verge of tears*) My wife of ten years has asked me for a separation. I don't want one. I can't convince her that I'll change. She says I'm depressed and haven't been involved with her and the kids for a long time. I don't know what to do. I guess I need help.

COUNSELOR: Do you think she is right about you being depressed and about your lack of involvement with the kids?

TIM: I don't know? I do my best. I do know that I can't go on without her. She is all I have!

The counselor then asks Tim about

- sleep, weight loss or gain, how much he worries, his energy levels, his motivation on the job;
- how much joy and satisfaction he gets from life, including his sex drive, substance use/abuse, and social life;
- any self-destructive thoughts he may have;
- whether he or his family has a history of depression;
- his openness to medications.

TIM: I feel sort of flat. I sleep a lot but don't feel rested. I dread getting up in the morning. After several cups of coffee, I manage to do my job, but I hate it. When I get home I just want to drink a couple of beers and watch sports on TV. I don't have much of an appetite and I've lost a few pounds, especially since Margie told me she wants a separation. That's all I think about now. I haven't slept much in the last week.

After talking for a while, the counselor believes that Tim is depressed and has been for some time. With the marriage in deep trouble, the counselor expresses concern that Tim's depression may be worsening and that he may be at risk for self-harm or suicide. The counselor shares these concerns with Tim and inquires about any self-harm or suicidal thoughts he has had, or whether he has made any self-harmful gestures.

TIM: I never thought that I could end my life, but if I knew that it was over with Margie, I don't know how I would go on. I don't have any guns, and I haven't really thought much more than this.

COUNSELOR: Tim, I appreciate your sharing all you have with me. I would like to meet with Margie to get a sense of where she is at with your situation. Because we have met once alone, I would like to meet one time with her alone. Then perhaps you and I could meet alone once more and then we could all meet together. Meanwhile, I would like you to consider taking an antidepressant. If you are willing, we could talk about you seeing your personal physician or someone I could refer you to for a medication evaluation.

The counselor goes on to discuss medication generally and encourages Tim to consider it. The counselor also offers to talk to Tim's physician.

COUNSELOR: Tim, I know that things are feeling desperate right now. I need to know that you are going to be safe and not do anything self-destructive.

TIM: (*looking slightly more hopeful*) I'm glad I finally came here. I guess I should have come a long time ago, when Margie asked me to. As long as I know we have a chance, I have some hope. She's my whole life!

COUNSELOR: Tim, I can't say much about your marriage until I talk with Margie, but I can tell you that I work with marriages all the time, and I know that partners can get through the pain you are feeling now. Even in those situations when there is a divorce, people get through it, especially if they have good support. Tim, if you become desperate and feel like you are going to harm yourself or end your life, I want you to agree that you will call me. This is an agreement that I want you to make with yourself—that the part of you that wants to stay alive and feel better will help the part of you that wants to escape to relieve the pain. There are other ways to relieve the pain. If you can't reach me or anybody else, I expect you will continue to try, until you do reach someone. I call this a no suicide or self-harm agreement. This is important until you feel better. Are you willing to do this? Can you say this out loud and is there anyone else on that list besides me whom you can contact?

TIM: (*without much enthusiasm, nods his head yes*) I won't hurt myself and will call you if I get desperate. I guess I can't call Margie, although she's the only other person I can talk to about stuff like this. Also, I know I shouldn't be drinking while I'm taking medication. I've been thinking about going to AA.

The counselor gets the picture. He assesses how much Tim drinks and whether this might impede his judgment at any given moment. He encourages Tim to get involved in Alcoholics Anonymous.

The Counseling Session with Margie

COUNSELOR: As you know, Margie, I have met with Tim. He tells me that you have told him you want a separation. Can you tell me your version of events?

MARGIE: (*looking tired and run down*) I have lived with Tim for ten years. I now believe that except for the first year or so he has been depressed for most of our marriage. He has been emotionally unavailable to the children and me for at least the past two years. I'm starving emotionally and cannot go on this way. I need to save myself. I care for him and love him, but I don't think I could live with him any longer the way it is.

I also think he has a problem with alcohol. His dad drinks too much, too. I want a separation, and I've pretty much decided on a divorce.

I worry about him. He is depressed and has talked about having nothing to live for except me. You can't believe the pressure this puts on me. He gives nothing back to the kids and me. I'm not here to fix the relationship. I'm here to end it, but my guilt is tremendous. God help me, if he killed himself, I don't know how I'd cope. But I now realize that my emotional and physical health are at stake and I need to be apart from Tim. The resentment I feel is incredible. The only thing that keeps me going is the thought of being away from him. I'd rather stay in the house, but if I have to, I'll leave.

COUNSELOR: Sounds like you're pretty determined.

MARGIE: I am!

The counselor already has a follow-up appointment with Tim, so he makes a couple's appointment for a week later. Margie goes home and communicates little with Tim about the session. She chooses to wait for their counseling session. In the meantime, Tim puts forth a little more effort to engage with the family.

A Joint Session with Tim and Margie

The counselor opens the session by asking each for an update about how things are going. Both partners agree nothing much has changed between them. There is no overt conflict in the home. The children are fine. Realizing that Margie is here to get support for managing a separation, the counselor starts to introduce the tasks of the Separation Management process.

COUNSELOR: I have now talked to you both alone. I understand that Tim would like to work on keeping the marriage together and Margie wants a separation. I want to focus on helping you manage this situation. Margie, have you had any second thoughts about working on the relationship?

MARGIE: No, I just feel that I have to get space as soon as possible. (*glances at Tim*)

TIM: (*looks down to the floor, says nothing*)

COUNSELOR: Tim, do you understand that Margie is planning a physical separation?

TIM: (*after a long pause, nods yes*)

COUNSELOR: Let's talk about how to manage this with the least amount of stress to all of you, especially the kids.

EXERCISE

1. Who do you identify with most, Tim or Margie? Why?

2. On what side of the Conflict Scale does Tim and Margie's conflict fall? Why?

3. Until now, how has each of them dealt with conflicts in their relationship?

DISCUSSION

This couple falls clearly into the passive-avoidant side of the Conflict Scale. There are no heated discussions or arguments. Instead, an ice wall has slowly built up over the last few years. Margie appears to feel the pain most intensely, along with an increasing frustration over how her life with Tim is unfolding. She feels like she is going to explode if she doesn't take charge of her life. She has not communicated these feelings directly to Tim, with threat of consequences, as she is doing now.

Tim reacts as if Margie asking him for a separation is a total shock. He has coped with his stress and depression through alcohol and withdrawal.

Even though there is no open and aggressive conflict between Tim and Margie, this couple must learn to deal with all of their internalized and unexpressed anger. But the question remains whether too much damage has already been done. Tim needs to look at his alcohol use and depression. He must consider working on himself before even thinking about working on the relationship. Of course, at the moment he doesn't have the option of working on the marriage. Margie just wants out. She has a volume of stored hurt and anger and doesn't see any turning back.

You have just read about two couples in very different places with their conflicts. One couple's conflict could be described as aggressive-explosive, while the other couple's conflict could be characterized as passive-avoidant.

You may have identified more with one of these situations or individuals than the other, or perhaps with neither. It doesn't really matter. The point is simply that we cannot make clearheaded choices about the future of our relationships without first managing the conflict—a conflict that can sometimes *look* like no conflict at all.

Managing conflict does not mean reaching agreement. It doesn't even necessarily mean getting the cooperation of your partner. It simply means calling a cease-fire so that some clear thinking can happen. So many people, especially women (due to their socialization), believe that they can't put an end to their inner turmoil without the cooperation of their partners. No matter how independent we like to think we are, we often give our partners far too much power over how we feel, think, and behave. Endless battles go on between partners as we try to get one another to think, feel, and behave as *we* want them to. What often gets overlooked is our capacity to help ourselves. In fact, often the best or only way to change the dynamics in a relationship is to work to change oneself. Just getting out of the victim role can be a huge change. Even if you learned to be a victim early in life, you can unlearn it.

It is true that these internal changes alone won't cure your marriage problems. But they allow you to take some of the energy you've been expending in resenting your partner and refocus it on yourself. In so doing you may find a shift in the patterns that are undoing your relationship.

The bottom line is, while your efforts to fix and change your partner may not work, by working with yourself you open more options that can help heal you—and possibly your relationship.

In thirty-five years of working with couples, I have come to believe that the conflicts in relationships often challenge and confront parts of individuals that need to grow and develop. It can be hard to see this at first, and that is precisely why various kinds of separations can be so useful. They provide the context by which we look at ourselves and work on those neglected areas.

If this step has helped you call a cease-fire for yourself or your relationship, or helped you become aware of how you avoid conflict with obvious negative consequences for your relationship, then you have already taken a major step toward helping yourself. I congratulate you. Before we move to Step 2 and focus on communication and understanding, please try the following exercise to see how well you now understand your own conflict.

Step 1 Exercise: Assess Your Own Conflict

As with all the exercises, this one can be done alone or with a partner. It's up to you whether you keep your thoughts internalized, write them down, or perhaps even record them on a tape recorder. Depending on how much conflict there is in your relationship you may also want to discuss your thoughts and feelings with your partner (see Ground Rules for Talking, page 17).

1. How would you characterize the nature of your conflict in your current or past relationships: passive-avoidant/aggressive, aggressive-explosive, assertive-expressive or somewhere in between (see Conflict Scale, page 11)? Has the conflict been similar or different for you in other relationships?

2. How do you and/or your partner express your anger and conflict? Aggressively? Passively? Assertively? With sarcasm, blame, defensiveness, or withdrawal? How are you similar? How are you different?

3. What percentage of time do you think you are in conflict (expressed or unexpressed)? How do you each feel and what do you think during and after your conflict? How quickly do you make up, or do you not make up?

4. Do you feel like you control your anger, or does it get out of hand? Do you anger quickly, slowly, or save up your anger for a later explosion? If your anger is not expressed, where does it go? How do you think unexpressed anger affects your physical self, feelings, moods, behavior, sleep, appetite, digestion, work, productivity, concentration, stress levels, etc.?

5. Do you feel your anger is appropriate or destructive? Do you take your anger out on others in the form of criticism, blame, put-downs, or sarcasm? Have you been told or do you feel that you

become abusive physically, emotionally, or verbally? Is your partner or child afraid of your anger? Has your anger ever gotten you into legal trouble at home or elsewhere? Do your and your partner's perspectives on this differ?

6. How was anger and conflict handled in your family growing up? What did you learn and which parent or caretaker are you most like regarding your anger? Were you afraid of anyone's anger? What did you do when your caretakers expressed conflict? Was there any alcohol or substance use or abuse associated with anger and conflict?

7. What are your triggers for being angry? Stress? Specific things your partner says? Things your partner does or doesn't do that you allow to push your buttons? What are your thoughts and beliefs that fuel your anger? How do you behave when you become angry? What feelings do you think may be underneath your anger—hurt, sadness, disappointment, frustration, unmet needs, fatigue, hunger, others? What are the consequences of your angry behavior?

8. Do you have ways to calm yourself down, such as leaving the situation (disengaging), adjusting your breathing (see Relaxation–Meditation Exercise, page 313), self-talking, stating affirmations, detaching or letting go, humor, relaxing, doing yoga, meditating, praying, walking, or other physical ways? Do you refocus your thinking away from anger to something calming, such as calling or reaching out to friends or family or playing music? Do you think about solutions instead of feeling helpless?

9. If you have children, what do they do during your conflict times? How do you think they are affected? Have you asked them?

10. Are you ready to decide to take control of your anger and conflict?

11. Do you think you could use help from a friend, minister, counselor, relative, support group, or class?

STEP 2
Communicating with Your Self and Your Partner

Compatibility does not hinge on some personal inventory of traits.
Compatibility isn't something you have. It's something you make.
It's a process, one that you negotiate as you go along. Again and again.
It's a disposition, an attitude, a willingness to work.
—Hara Estroff Marano, *Psychology Today*, October 2004

Step 2 is about suspending blame and fault—the two most common words used during conflict—and recognizing the role you play in the creation of your relationship's patterns. Every one of us is guided by old beliefs, feelings, and patterns of communication established in our families of origin, and until we understand these patterns we cannot expect to change the dynamics of our relationships.

What You Say and How You Say It

As most of us know, communication is about more than just what you say; it's about how you say it. Many times a couple will come to me, one partner insisting that he has already said everything there is to say. Sure, he may have made his positions clear—on sex, money, kids, vacations, chores, the time he shows up for dinner, and his levels of investment and commitment—but often he is totally unaware of how he came across and how his behavior affected his wife. He may have said exactly what he meant (content), but his style—the volume and tone of his voice, his particular choice of words, body language, facial expressions, and inner feelings—made his wife unable to hear him.

Think of a person you do not particularly like. What if you were to find yourself standing next to this person at a party? You might notice yourself feeling critical and judgmental of everything he says and does. You might feel yourself tense up. You might not feel free to be yourself and express yourself openly. You might describe the climate between you and this person as icy, distant, and mistrusting. You will, in all likelihood, avoid talking with this person, or keep conversation to a minimum.

Now imagine yourself with a really good and trusted friend whom you enjoy being around. You know that you are liked and accepted by this person. Think of how you feel around this person. You probably feel relaxed and accepted, not judged or criticized. You can be yourself and say almost anything that is on your mind and expect to be heard and understood. This climate might be described as warm, caring, and accepting.

Of course, with your friend, you stand a far better chance of good, open, and relatively honest communication. No matter how well you communicate, communication with your good friend will flow better than it will with a person you don't care for.

The same goes for communication with your partner. When the relationship is working well or even during times of conflict, you will tend to eventually give your partner the benefit of the doubt and have empathy for your partner's negative behavior. For example, you may acknowledge that your partner had a bad day at work, didn't get enough sleep, or that the kids had been a handful all day. Recognizing adverse situations and giving your partner a hug or a smile reinforces a positive communication loop in your relationship and helps get you and your partner through conflict to making up.

When couples become stuck in a negative pattern, on the other hand, they are no longer able to empathize or extend benefit of the doubt. The simplest problems or topics might trigger anger, defensiveness, and conflict. Each partner might begin to view and perceive the other as judgmental, critical, not interested, uncaring, overly defensive, mean, an overly powerful bully, or perhaps not very "safe" to be open with. In short, their process has broken down.

A disabled process is difficult to repair, especially if your internal experience is negative, conflicted, depressed, anxious, confused, angry, etc. You simply won't be able to hear and accept what your partner has to say. It is only possible to open up your communication process by taking charge of your own inner process—how you think, feel, behave, and cope with change, stressful events, and conflict. Of course, starting to do this inner work can bring to light old fears and insecurities, and these feelings can be difficult to tolerate.

Slowing down, learning to breathe deeply, and managing anger and anxiety enough to reflect on what is being triggered inside will work for some people. Others may want to talk to a good friend, counselor, or minister to start the process of being honest about their inner feelings and thoughts. But regardless of *how* it happens, you *must* learn to express your feelings and innermost thoughts, even if it is just to yourself, before healing can take place.

Who's Feeling What

Every couple's process is circular, meaning that each partner's attitude, power in the relationship, and behavior affects the other partner in a continuous loop. Because of this, it can be confusing to figure out who is feeling what and who is contributing what to a conflict. A blaming, critical, and perhaps more dominant partner may trigger defensiveness and emotional or physical withdrawal in the other partner. This withdrawal could add to the frustration and desperation of the blaming partner who, in craving contact, may become more blaming and actually inspire more defensiveness in her partner. And so it goes on, and on, and on.

The Self

Throughout this book I will talk about working on the *self*, but what *is* the self? Who are we? We are obviously some type of energy that runs itself. We are made up of many different parts and subparts. We have our physical bodies with all of our senses. We have our unique beliefs, values, morals, and our perceptions about life and others. We have our own thoughts, feelings, and intuitions that affect the way we behave, adapt, and experience life.

The inner beliefs we hold about ourselves and others become our truth about life. Our caretakers pass onto us what they believe about life (their truths). We then spend the remainder of our lives developing and separating from parts of that borrowed program while attempting to discover who we *really* are, what we really believe, and how we want to be. Some of us like ourselves, some don't.

Some of us believe that our current life is all there is and when we die it is over, much like dreamless sleep. Others believe that we have a soul or spirit that may have lived forever and will continue through eternity and eternal experiences. Regardless of what we may believe happens before birth or after death, it seems clear that we develop from birth until death. Just look at our children and people we have known over time, and you can see evidence of how they have grown, adapted, and developed as a result of their life experiences.

I believe that we all have the inner resources to cope and develop, however much we may have to dig for them, and personal growth and change may be more about discovering or rediscovering who we already are rather than changing into somebody else. That inner core of willpower and determination is unique and available to each and every one of us!

Life Positions

Often we carry the general behavioral styles we learned in our family of origin into our relationships. Transactional Analysis (TA), a psychological model developed by Dr. Eric Berne in the 1950s and popularized by Thomas Harris in the 1960s, provides a very useful model for understanding our patterns of relating.

The TA model helps you understand how your inner beliefs—beliefs formed in childhood—determine how you relate and communicate with yourself, your partner, and others. According to TA, we each take one of four life positions as a result of what we are told, how we are treated, and how we adapt, cope, and survive emotionally in our families of origin. We then make decisions about ourselves and others based on those early experiences of childhood. Once our beliefs are established, our thinking, feelings, and behavior will shape our perception in accordance with those internal beliefs. In order to make new decisions based on the here and now, we must become aware of these old beliefs and grow and develop past the limits of what we were taught and what we decided as children before we had the maturity and ability to make informed decisions.

The first position, **I'm OK–You're OK**, is the most psychologically healthy position, in which people can find positive changes and satisfying outcomes and everybody wins. "Do unto others as you would have them do unto you" and "Love thy neighbor as thy self" come from this basic position.

From the I'm OK–You're OK position people are what is important. If I am OK and believe that others are basically OK, then I am in a position to feel good about others and myself. From this position, there is usually an abundance of positive strokes to share with others in a safe, accepting environment. Strokes are forms of stimulation between people (described in more detail later in the chapter). OK people believe that it's all right to have feelings. Feelings are OK. It's how we judge and think about our feelings that becomes Not OK.

I believe this is the ideal position from which to maintain a satisfying, intimate, and fulfilling relationship with ourselves and with others. This comes about by learning to accept yourself and learning to share this acceptance with others. Partners help to support each other's OK-ness from this position. People who are in this position want to maintain it. When they drop to another position, they attempt to get back to OK as soon as possible.

I'm OK–You're Not OK is the position of those who feel victimized or persecuted, so they in turn learn to victimize or persecute others. People in this position learn to survive, avoid, and protect their own hurt, wounds, guilt, or shame by assuming a false superior role with others. Guilt is often about feeling you have done something wrong or bad, whereas shame is about being a bad person whose worth is questionable.

Shame is often experienced as deep painful feelings that attack the core of our being and often originate in childhood. Addictive and acting-out behaviors, such as with alcohol, drugs, food, sex, and gambling, as well as criticism and abuse of others by this person may be an attempt to seek relief from inner painful feelings and a low assessment of self-worth. People in this position may have difficulty trusting, getting close to others, and getting in touch with their own feelings. Often, people in this position are well defended, self-righteous, and may have a chip on their shoulders. Their overcontrolling or critical Parent gets expressed or projected onto others and often hides an insecure and frightened little Child who does not feel very OK or powerful. This person may manipulate others, push them away, or get rid of them.

Mary, who you met in Step 1, feels like a victim to John. Early in their situation, she discharged those feelings onto John by being angry and critical with him. She basically views him as Not OK because of his lack of support with family duties and work around the house.

People in this position can discount others. When under stress, hurting, or threatened, this person will be controlling, critical, angry, and abusive of others. This person will have difficulty validating others and giving positive strokes. You may feel lonely and defensive around this person because it is not easy to be relaxed and yourself for fear of being criticized or put down. This person tends to persecute or rescue others by keeping them in the one-down, Not OK position. This can be seen in someone who discounts another's capacity to do for himself, for example, an overprotective parent; a partner who feels the other is incapable when he or she is simply different; or a partner who believes his reality of life is right and his partner's is wrong (and not just different). This person *must* begin to get in touch with his softer, vulnerable side underneath the part that is overcontrolling or critical and know what feelings fuel his projections onto others. He must learn to self-nurture, soothe, relax, and meet his own wants. He must begin to stop criticizing others or keeping them one down and realize that this will not make him feel genuinely OK. It is scary and will take courage to get in touch with the vulnerable Not OK Child inside. A person in this position is often attracted to people in the one-down position, who may view themselves as victims.

The third position, **I'm Not OK–You're OK**, is a position in which people feel powerless and victimized, but put themselves down rather than others. People in this position may withdraw from others and feel a lack of confidence. They may struggle with anxiety, self-doubt, guilt, shame, and low self-esteem, and have difficulty making decisions. They often feel others can "save" them and may become too dependent on others or expect too much. People in this position can become depressed and in extreme situations feel suicidal if left or rejected. They may have difficulty validating and empowering themselves or giving themselves positive strokes, because they don't feel they deserve them. They may accept negative or false strokes from others because they fit with what they feel and believe about themselves. Not OK people need to learn to think, build self-confidence, empower, self-validate, and to give and accept positive strokes from themselves and others. A person in this position will frequently be attracted to someone in an I'm OK–You're Not OK position.

The fourth position, **I'm Not OK–You're Not OK**, describes people who feel loveless, hopeless, and that life is not worth living. In extreme cases they can become suicidal, homicidal, depressed, addicted, or withdraw into their own world. These people often need a lot of hope, love, and protection from themselves. They need unconditional positive strokes to exist and live.

People will sometimes feel OK about some aspects of their lives and Not OK about others. For example, a person may feel she is a really good worker, but that she is a failure at personal relationships.

According to TA theory, the majority of us have a favorite life position where we may hang out more of the time. Some people will spend little time in Not OK-ness, while others will spend a lot of time there. I may feel basically OK when my life is going well, but fall to a Not OK position when stressed or threatened. I encourage you to become aware or mindful of how much basic OK-ness versus Not OK-ness you generally carry around. OK people tend to give themselves permission to have negative feelings, while Not OK people tend to judge what they feel and experience as Not OK.

The TA Model and Relationship Separations

Relationship separations can have a major impact on your basic life position and help you rework your inner self.

Once these beliefs take hold, they will shape your experiences, and you will create outcomes that make these beliefs come true.

For example, two people get divorced and one of them, an I'm Not OK–You're OK person, believes she is at fault and defective, and will never recover or meet another partner. Without validation from a partner, she may become depressed and hopeless. By isolating herself from others, she prevents new life experiences while reinforcing her old beliefs about herself. On the other hand, the person from a more I'm OK–You're OK position will—after a period of grief, adjustment and recovery, and feeling Not OK—find hope, learn from the experience, and make the necessary changes to go on with life and create new experiences.

The only position from which intimacy can grow and develop is I'm OK–You're OK. The first step in beginning to work on your OK-ness is to become aware and understand yourself. Assuming responsibility for yourself puts you on the journey toward self-help and growth. Beginning to challenge those old beliefs and the outdated thinking that keep you stuck in your current pattern can open the door to making new decisions about how you want to be. Practice self-acceptance! Of course, our relationships form around how we feel and what we believe about ourselves. As we grow, our relationships will be forced to grow as well.

Talking and Listening

Throughout this book, I demonstrate how various couples take or fail to take charge of themselves and their inner processes, and how this affects each partner and the future of the relationships. We'll start by looking at Bill and Nancy. Notice how this couple struggles to repair their damaged communication process and how this is the key to getting them out of their relationship stalemate.

Couple Situation 3: Bill and Nancy: "We Fight About Everything. I Think We're Growing Apart."

Bill and Nancy have been together for sixteen years. Bill is forty-one and Nancy is thirty-nine. They have two teenagers, a fifteen-year-old boy and a thirteen-year-old girl. They have always felt good about their marriage and family life and in many ways have been seen by friends and family as a model couple. Nancy is an elementary school teacher and Bill works for the State Transportation Department.

As their children have gotten older, they have spent increasingly less time together as a family. Both Bill and Nancy spend a lot of time at work and are also involved in their children's activities. Bill loves to golf and Nancy takes an aerobics class. Both spend regular time with friends and their own separate activities when they have the chance. In the past year, Nancy has begun to notice more distance between her and Bill. She has also noticed that they seem to differ in opinion more often. They disagree now about issues they used to agree on, such as curfews for the children and the amount of time the children spend with their friends.

In the last three months, Nancy has begun to question how much she still loves or even likes Bill. Bill seems to have similar feelings and also wonders if, over the past year, they have slowly fallen out of love with each other. It seems that in the past they were able to agree more and compromise. Now all they do is "dig in" and argue about everything.

During their arguments, each partner ends up blurting out how different the other has become and how they no longer seem to see eye to eye on anything. Even when they start out talking about something that seems easy and neutral, they somehow end up disagreeing. In recent months these disagreements have gotten worse and have turned into mean, escalating arguments, with yelling and name-calling.

Both are very frustrated with each other, and they are spending less and less time alone together. They had sex about two months ago and ended up arguing afterward, which ruined the whole experience for Nancy. She says they have stopped even being just plain nice to each other. Bill wonders how he could be nice when she is so critical and judgmental of him. He feels he receives no support. They have not touched or hugged since that "poor" sexual experience. In protest of how he feels he is being treated, Bill has even begun sleeping on the couch in the family room. Nancy has reluctantly talked about a physical separation. She says if this same level of conflict continues it will only damage their already poor relationship and escalate her negative feelings about Bill.

They have talked about going for counseling, but neither has taken the initiative. Each has begun to worry that maybe the motivation to repair the damage has gone. Nancy has talked to her best friend about their problems. On her friend's recommendations, she has started reading self-help books and doing online research to try to learn how to stop the fighting and improve their communication.

EXERCISE

See Ground Rules for Talking, page 17.

1. Can you identify with either Bill or Nancy?

2. Have you ever felt this way or do you presently feel this way in your relationship or in a past relationship?

3. What might you be thinking, feeling, or doing if you were in this situation?

DISCUSSION

What is happening to Bill and Nancy? The conflict in their relationship has worn down their process. Efforts at repair, by either partner, are quickly cancelled out by a flash of anger and disagreement, which fuels the fire of discontent even more. This has seeped into all aspects of their relationship and is beginning to affect their entire family life.

If either attempts to be nice, it is often met with resistance and suspicion. Like a blow to a wound that has not healed, every encounter seems to reinjure their bruised and hurt feelings. Anger can flare up as a defense to protect from further damage to each of their selves.

Bill and Nancy wonder if this is what happens before couples decide to separate and eventually divorce. Have Bill and Nancy fallen out of love and even like with each other? Are they going through some kind of a stage? Is there anything they or either one of them can do to correct or reverse what's happening?

> The hardest thing to give is in.
> —Albert Einstein

Suggested Coping Strategies for Bill and Nancy

1. First, Bill and Nancy must find a way to ease the conflict (Step 1). Their ongoing arguments reflect how frustrated and desperate each feels. I usually find unmet and frustrated wants and fears underneath anger. Each must realize that no one is winning! In intimate relationships, either both partners win or both lose. If there is one "winner," then both have lost! Either partner could begin to take the lead by acknowledging that the conflict is going nowhere and must stop, and by ending their part of the fighting or power struggle.

2. If even just one of them decides to stop their part of the conflict, this can have a positive impact on the relationship and on the other partner (remember the circular loop in relationship patterns). If the other partner agrees to look at his or her part, that will be a big step toward easing conflict and going on to Step 3, considering whether some kind of separation is needed. If one or both partners continue to battle, more physical space may be necessary.

3. Nancy must become aware of the triggers that she allows Bill to pull on a regular basis. She realized she let her triggers be tripped

by what she perceived as Bill's know-it-all attitude, which she feels leaves no room for her to be heard. Nancy reacts to Bill's parental tone of voice by digging in her heels and aggressively protesting his side of their argument. With awareness, Nancy can learn to detach and manage her reactions to Bill's behaviors.

EXERCISE

See Ground Rules for Talking, page 17.

1. Can you identify with Bill and Nancy's pattern of conflict?

2. How do you think each of them feed into the escalation of their conflict?

3. What seems to happen to their communication process after their triggers go off?

What Happened Next

In the following few weeks, Nancy decided to take the lead and call a time-out. "I'm done fighting!" she declared and refused to allow Bill to push any more of her anger buttons. As soon as she sensed her anger building (see Anger Awareness Temperature Gauge, page 20) she took physical and emotional space by disengaging and learned to calm herself down and temporarily lower or drop expectations of Bill as well as herself. Bill seemed ready to ease his anger and conflict as well. By disengaging from their arguments they found they were able to reduce the daily conflict in their relationship. They still didn't talk with each other in much depth yet, but they both felt better about the fewer arguments and lowered tension.

However, because relationships and family life require problems to be worked out and expectations to be met, just stopping conflict is often not enough to make a couple become better problem solvers, better communicators, or satisfied partners. By becoming more aware of their individual feelings and each taking responsibility for their parts in their arguments, Nancy and Bill were able to prevent and reduce conflict, but now they must begin to look at their communication process and the issues on which they have disagreed. For them to do this they must begin to develop their skills and a process of communication that works for them.

Communication Skills*

The following skills describe and offer examples of specific behaviors for both the listener and the talker to help build a positive communication process.

Listening

1. Attend Good listening always begins with paying attention to each other as you talk. Look at each other, give eye contact, face each other. Be aware of body language and nonverbal messages. Be as open as possible to listening and understanding. The need to be fully seen and heard is often at the heart of good communication.

2. Acknowledge and Validate Each Other This skill is probably the most important of all. Good listeners do this much of the time. Acknowledge the other person with a simple nod of the head and statements like, "Wow, you had a tough day!" or "You sound or look tired/sad/happy/scared/angry."

In satisfying relationships people give and receive an abundance of positive and validating strokes. Good listeners are able to temporarily suspend their own feelings and thoughts so they can listen with well-controlled judgments and defensive feelings. Of course, this is difficult to do when you are in conflict with your partner. You may hear your partner saying things that sound threatening and don't fit into what you believe to be true, and these things may trigger fear, sadness, hurt, disappointment, or anger.

* Credit for these ideas:
  Miller, Sherod, Phyllis A. Miller, Elam W. Nunnally, Daniel B. Wackman, *Talking and Listening Together, Couple Communication I* (Littleton, CO: Interpersonal Communication Program, Inc., 1992).

It may feel forced at first, but even attempting to acknowledge what your partner is saying, especially during periods of conflict, can begin to have a positive effect on the climate of your relationship. It is crucial to build on this by getting to know your partner's inner world. This kind of empathy forms the basis for love between people. It is important not to confuse this with agreeing with everything your partner is saying. You may understand but disagree with your partner. The point is to develop the ability to listen and tolerate someone who is different from you. This requires being aware and managing and controlling your inner reactions, feelings, and behavior even while you may be hearing things that trigger anxieties, hurt, and anger.

Being heard by your partner can similarly restore a basic sense of satisfaction in your relationship. Remember productive communication can also help prevent and repair fallouts!

3. Reflect, Summarize, and Paraphrase Reflecting, summarizing, and paraphrasing what your partner says shows that you understand and have heard what your partner is saying. This minimizes misunderstandings. To do this, repeat in your own words what you have heard to be your partner's points and ask for clarification and confirmation. Once you can do this comfortably, try acknowledging your partner's underlying feelings as well. Summarizing can begin with a statement like, "Let me see if I have gotten what you just said." If you are inaccurate, ask your partner to clarify so that you can understand. The talker can also ask the listener to summarize what has just been said. This skill will take practice and patience to acquire.

4. Ask for More Information Asking for more information indicates your interest in your partner. Ask for more information after a pause in the conversation and continue to ask for more until your partner has no more to say.

5. Ask Open Questions Asking open questions to gather or fill in missing information or to clarify confusing information allows an experience to be shared in the talker's words. Open questions encourage the talker to continue and show your interest in what is being said.

The following are examples of open questions: "Tell me about your meeting with your boss." "How did your lunch with Mary go and what did you talk about?" "What did you like about the movie?" "What did you feel when Joe started to get angry?"

Try to avoid too many why questions, since they tend to put the talker on the spot and force answers the talker may not have. Also, too many questions can limit the natural flow of the talker.

Talking

1. **Sharing Your Opinions, Feelings, or Thoughts About Something You Observe** The following are examples of this type of talking: "I noticed this morning during breakfast that when we were talking about having fun together you became very quiet and withdrawn." "You look like you were uncomfortable with my parents at dinner last night."

2. **Sharing Your Thoughts** Say what you are thinking, believing, interpreting, or expecting. Be careful to know the difference between thoughts and feelings. The following examples are expressions of thought: "I think I need to go to bed early tonight." "I think I'll go for a walk." These examples express feelings: "I feel sad and lonely when you leave." "I really enjoy laughing with you!"

3. **Expressing Your Feelings** Feelings are best expressed through "I feel" statements: I feel mad, sad, glad, scared. Feelings may also be expressed through descriptions: "I'm sad that John has left." "I have butterflies in my stomach before I get up to speak." "When you become angry, I get really scared." "You" statements can put others on the defensive and sound as if you know what their inner intentions are. "You make me so mad when you come home late"; "You know it upsets me when you leave dirty dishes in the sink!"

4. **Sharing Your Wants** It is important for you, your partner, and your relationship for each of you to share your wants.

For example, your wants could include the following: "I want to relax tonight"; "I want a hug"; "I don't want . . ."

Examples of your wants for your partner could include the following: "I want you to feel supported by me" and "I want you to relax and let yourself have some fun tonight."

Examples of wants for both of you or for your relationship could include: "I want us to have a good time together this weekend" and "I want us to stay in touch and talk about how each of us feels when we visit your parents next week." Attempt to separate needs from wants. They are often used interchangeably, but I define needs as food, air, water, and absolute necessities. Wants are optional, such as, "I want you to listen to me"; or "I want a hug." Stating wants to your partner does not mean you will always have them met, but you have made them known.

5. Make Statements About What You Have Done, Are Doing, or Intend to Do These statements are about actions that can be observed by others and are different from feelings and thoughts. Talking about what you will do makes intentions clear and understandable. It also lets others know you are aware of your behavior and what it means. The following are examples of these types of statements: "I will be at the recital on Tuesday"; "I will not hug you without being asked anymore"; and "When we talk, I will begin to tell you what I am really thinking and feeling."

> Listen
>
> When I ask you to listen to me and you start giving advice,
> you have not done what I have asked.
> When I ask you to listen to me and you begin to tell me why I
> shouldn't feel that way, you are trampling on my feelings.
> When I ask you to listen to me and you feel you have to do
> something to solve my problems, you have failed me, strange as
> that may seem.
> So please, just listen and hear me, and if you want to talk,
> wait a few minutes for your turn and I promise I'll listen to you.
> —Anonymous

Couple Situation 3: Bill and Nancy: "We Fight About Everything. I Think We're Growing Apart."

Bill and Nancy continued to manage their conflict relatively well, but they had been beaten down with conflict and were ready for change. Both had some fears about what would be left of their relationship once they stopped fighting. When either of their tempers flared from stress or fatigue or disappointment in the other, one or both would remind the other that there was a better way, that they didn't have to fight.

At times, an argument would start brewing and either Bill or Nancy would think that it wasn't worth a fight and manage to announce that they were withdrawing (time-out). This worked particularly well because both of them were taking responsibility for managing conflict and improving the circle of their communication process.

As the climate in their relationship improved, Bill and Nancy also discovered that they were beginning to share more of their underlying feelings, rather than just anger and frustration with each other. Both were learning to share feelings of loneliness, disappointment, fear, want, and other feelings that seem to be more associated with vulnerability and hurt than anger and apathy. At first, because Nancy was doing a lot of self-help reading and learning, this came easier for her. The climate in their relationship was becoming safer again!

Bill and Nancy were working on a psychological separation in which each partner assumes more responsibility for his or her feelings, thoughts, opinions, beliefs, and behavior. (Types of separations will be discussed in detail in Step 4.) Another part of learning to psychologically separate requires understanding the power balance in a relationship and how each person gives up more power to the other than he or she would like.

During their limited sharing with each other, Nancy and Bill began to realize that if either of them really attempted to talk to the other, at times the other would actually listen. Slowly their satisfaction with their relationship improved. By learning to talk, listen, and limit how threatened they felt by each other, Bill and Nancy began to realize how they were different and how they were similar. As each learned to really listen to the other, they felt closer and were better able to accept the other's differences.

Nancy decided she had to be the person she was becoming and was not going to always live up to Bill's "old" expectations of her. She also wanted equal power in the relationship. She realized that some of those old expectations were her own from how she was raised in her family of origin in which women were always second to men. She was beginning to see how some of her old beliefs were mixed up with what she thought were Bill's expectations of her.

Bill was beginning to enjoy his life more, especially with his children entering their teen years. Family life was still demanding, but because his children were more independent, Bill had more freedom. He felt some guilt about taking this freedom after many years of being so responsible. He and Nancy began to realize that they had made their marriage into a prison and each other into wardens. They needed to redefine what they wanted for their selves and from each other. Learning to be and share more of their truer selves, especially as they each became aware of those selves, became their new goal.

They further realized that they each had to be responsible for becoming aware and expressing their selves. They neither needed to ask the other's permission for expressing feelings nor could they blame the other for failing to express feelings. They came to see how what each did really affected the other, and how this at times would create conflict that would have to be worked out by both of them together. They paid more attention to their tones of voice and the way they spoke to each other.

Bill and Nancy decided to check in with each other daily. Check-ins involved some short discussions (five or ten minutes) to catch up on how each was doing individually and with the relationship. Bill and Nancy took turns talking and listening and made an effort to discuss what each was doing to control conflict and get along better. The following is an excerpt from one of their talks.

NANCY: I'm feeling better about us since I know we are working on not arguing so much. When I know you are at least trying, I get a sense of being in this together, and I don't feel so helpless or hopeless!

BILL: Yeah, I agree. It sure has felt better being at home in the last month since we're not fighting as much. I don't have the feeling that I don't want to be around you anymore. But I am concerned about how easy it is for me to dig my heels in when I feel you don't agree with me about anything . . . the kids, what to eat, what to do on the weekends, and even my own free time.

I have begun to realize that I have to be able to stand up for what I believe and want, and at least say it to you, whether you agree or not. Somehow I feel that if you disagree with me, I'm wrong, or I'm not allowed to do what I want or something like that. I have to realize that you are not my mother and I'm old enough (*laughs*) to have my own opinions. My mother would always second-guess me and then start to tell me the "right" way to do something. I always hated that and began to argue with her. Boy, I can see the same pattern with you.

NANCY: Wow, I feel the same way! I used to fight with my father like that and my older brother as well. I read somewhere that firing your partner as your parent and rehiring them back as your partner can help your relationship. I do believe that if I am listened to, I can be more understanding of your side of it. Do you think that is what we are beginning to do?

BILL: Maybe. All I know is that we are both adults and don't need permission to do things. I do realize that as a family we should share our plans just to be respectful of each other, but we must realize we both can stand up for what we believe is right. I shouldn't always have to feel like I have to ask permission to take space for myself. It feels so freeing to say this out loud. Maybe this is the prison we created from what we learned in our own families!

After Bill and Nancy had this interesting and insightful talk, they expressed how much closer they felt to each other and actually wanted to help each other more. They realized they weren't always going to be this accepting and open with each other, but feelings of liking and loving each other began to slowly return as their channels of communication reopened. This felt so good after such a long period of fallout and distance between them. I have seen hundreds of very stuck couples begin to repair their relational process simply by learning to talk to each other.

Functional Parts of People

Once again, I find the TA model very useful here and hope you'll bear with me as I explain some of its basic terms as I use them with individuals and couples.

The basic ideas of Transactional Analysis are based on three observable functioning parts of people: the Parent, the Adult, and the Child. They represent actual visible behaviors that can be observed and are useful in gaining awareness and control over how you communicate. Below are specific descriptions of these parts.

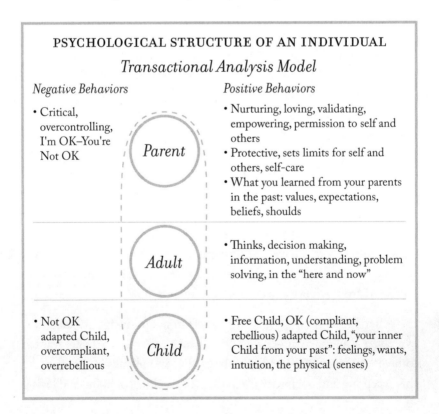

PSYCHOLOGICAL STRUCTURE OF AN INDIVIDUAL
Transactional Analysis Model

Negative Behaviors

Parent
- Critical, overcontrolling, I'm OK–You're Not OK

Adult

Child
- Not OK adapted Child, overcompliant, overrebellious

Positive Behaviors

Parent
- Nurturing, loving, validating, empowering, permission to self and others
- Protective, sets limits for self and others, self-care
- What you learned from your parents in the past: values, expectations, beliefs, shoulds

Adult
- Thinks, decision making, information, understanding, problem solving, in the "here and now"

Child
- Free Child, OK (compliant, rebellious) adapted Child, "your inner Child from your past": feelings, wants, intuition, the physical (senses)

Parent

As Eric Berne saw it, each of us internalizes the messages we receive from our parents or other primary caretakers, whether nurturing, loving, empowering, and protective, or controlling and critical.

We play the part of the parent in relation to ourselves: we are self-loving and nurturing, self-critical and controlling, or combinations of both. We also play the role of parent in relation to others (think of Mary's attitude toward John as a "third child"). Our values, expectations, and perspectives on life, as influenced by our community, society, and country (our culture) are passed on by this inner Parent. Our basic sense of shoulds, oughts, rights, wrongs, good, and bad often comes from this inner Parent, as does our sense of self-esteem and basic values. Our parents are necessary to our survival as humans, but in the process of growing up, we often get their unresolved baggage as well. TA helps us sort out what's ours and what's our parents.

Child

This is the part of each of us that feels, wants, and experiences life much as we did as children. The free Child (that free-flowing, spontaneous, uninhibited energy within ourselves) has imagination and creativity and loves to play and have fun. Our physical and emotional selves, including our senses and intuition, are part of this Child-self. The Child can be selfish and impulsive. It is the Child in us that feels the whole range of our innermost feelings and thoughts. This inner Child carries positive memories (assuming there are some) as well as the scars from what we had to cope with as children. Life events can trigger these memories for us.

Your inner Child is the part of you that is always on the lookout for compliments and strokes, positive and negative, verbal and non-verbal, from others and yourself, such as hugs, smiles, compliments, put-downs, and criticisms. All humans want and need strokes. Strokes can be viewed as food for our emotional diet and have much to do with how we feel about ourselves. Positive strokes help make us feel

OK about ourselves and negative strokes make us feel Not OK about ourselves. We may temporarily lose touch with parts of our free Child during stressful events and other life traumas. Lack of strokes has a lot to do with depression and lovelessness. Our families of origin are our first trainers on how to exchange strokes with ourselves and others.

As an adult you can challenge your old beliefs and make new decisions about the way you learned to give strokes to yourself and others. Learning to self-validate, by giving yourself positive and encouraging messages, affirmations, and strokes can raise and maintain your self-esteem. In *Scripts People Live* (pages 114–17*)*, Claude Steiner describes the rules from what he calls the "stroke economy" that can produce lovelessness: "Don't give strokes if you have them to give; don't ask for strokes when you need them; don't accept strokes when you want them; don't reject strokes when you don't want them; don't give yourself strokes."

Understanding what strokes you want, the strokes that make you feel good about yourself, and those you would like to receive from a partner can help you evaluate your relationship's health. Some people have strong parental messages about being too selfish. They have to work on learning to be OK about feeling good about themselves. This is not about being better than others, but simply learning to like and love yourself. Remember the type of stroke that we let in often reinforces how we believe and feel about ourselves and others (life positions). If we feel we're Not OK, our inner Parent may not let in positive strokes. We might, for example, carry negative messages, such as "You're stupid and will never amount to much!" and "You're a loser at relationships." Or, we might carry positive messages, such as, "You are a person who can grow, develop, and take charge of your life" and "You can learn to love and validate yourself." Our relationships can be evaluated by the quantity and quality of the strokes we give each other. A good and satisfying relationship has an abundance of positive strokes, enhances our sense of self, and allows us to feel good about our self.

We tend to create relationships that reinforce the way we feel and believe about ourselves. This is why we have to become aware of and challenge any outdated beliefs that have been programmed into us. We can begin to change our relationships by changing ourselves.

The Original Warm Fuzzy Tale by Claude Steiner (a must-read about strokes) is a wonderful story about the evolution of strokes in society.

Your inner Child is very important to your self-esteem. It has a free, natural part and a rebellious part. We all need to adapt to society by becoming somewhat compliant to rules and customs. However, many people become overcompliant and spend a lifetime pleasing others at the expense of self-care. The same is true of rebellion. The inner rebel can cause us to react in healthy, assertive ways, or to overreact and resist just for the sake of resistance.

I believe it is the energy and determination of the free and rebel Child along with Adult thinking and willpower that can help us make new decisions and changes in our lives. Mary's (He's like a third child!) decision to no longer be a victim to John's behavior and attitude and to take charge of her own life instead is a good example of this.

Adult

Just as the word suggests, this is the grown-up part of each of us, and often the most objective. Whereas your Child feels life and may be impulsive, and your Parent may be carrying lots of old messages from your actual caretakers, your Adult is the thinking (cognitive), objective, and here-and-now part of you. The Adult in you is able to see the big picture and think about options and outcomes.

Having an aware, informed, and engaged Adult can help us make changes and solve problems and make new decisions for our outer world and our inner selves. Think again of Mary. Instead of reacting impulsively to John, Mary decides on a plan of action to deal with her situation. Her inner feelings of frustration and anger (Child) fuel her new decision (Adult) instead of keeping her stuck.

Script*

A script is a life plan, whether conscious or unconscious, positive or negative. Most of the time we learn and decide upon a script in

* Steiner, Claude. *Scripts People Live.*

childhood and modify it as we move through life. If we were encouraged to pursue our dreams and got lots of reinforcement for doing so, we usually have a fairly positive life script; other times we get mired in old messages and behaviors that are rooted in past experiences and prevent us from moving forward in life. Life scripts can be loveless, joyless, powerless, or mindless.

Many different types of transactions can occur between two partners. Below are some of the basic transactions (using the TA model and language) that are necessary for a fully functioning and satisfying relationship.

Parent to Parent

Here is where we see whether our values and expectations and the messages from each of our family histories and cultures line up. Similarities will often make it easier to see our partner's side of things. Differences, especially extreme ones, will make it necessary for us to tolerate and stretch beyond what we have learned and believe. This is important especially in regard to parenting children and the type of lifestyle you envision and create with your partner.

Adult to Adult

Here we are able to share responsibilities, communication, empathy, problem solving, and decision making in all aspects of our relationship. The more equal the power, the better off the relationship will be, with sharing and fairness in regard to each person's wants and expectations. Two Adults are a must in a relationship or family. See the negotiation exercise in the Appendix. This exercise offers a good example of how two Adults can reach a win-win agreement.

Child to Child

Here is where all our wants, feelings, strokes, intimacy, play, fun, joy, sex, and sense of spontaneity come into play. Of course, we need our inner Child or life would be all business and no fun. Many couples have difficulties when there is a lack of Child fun and excitement in their relationship.

Parent to Child

When we relate to our partners in this way, we can give them support, care, nurturing, love, compassion, and empowerment when they need it. Of course, the reverse is true as well. When our Child is hurting or stressed, our partner can parent us with love and care. On the negative side, many relationship conflicts involve the critical, attacking, blaming, self-righteous Parent and the defensive Not OK Child. Some partners have to learn to express the nurturing, supportive Parent in the relationships.

Adult to Child

This label describes those interactions in which we help our partner develop more options to resolve situations and problems and not just react from a limited Child perspective and emotional state.

Problems can occur when one partner is more of a Parent and Adult and the other partner is more of a Child in the relationship. This was true of Mary, who believed that she was the only responsible grown-up and perceived John as mostly a Child. She suffered from burnout and depression. She felt her inner Child was emotionally and physically overworked. She was basically asking John to be a full grown-up and share in family responsibilities. Of course, John may not perceive himself as a Child in the relationship, and their conflicts and separation were about whether this could be worked out. Margie, in Shutdown Spouse, page 23, also feels she is emotionally starving in her relationship with Tim. She has decided she wants space from Tim so she can recover her creative, fun Child. Too much critical and overcontrolling Parent or Not OK Child in a partnership can lead to too many negative strokes, conflicts, and unsatisfying interactions.

Understanding how two partners' scripts interlock in a relationship can provide insight and options on how to make changes, or psychological separations, that result in more satisfaction for each and possibly for the relationship. Examples of these transactions will be discussed and demonstrated throughout the rest of this book.

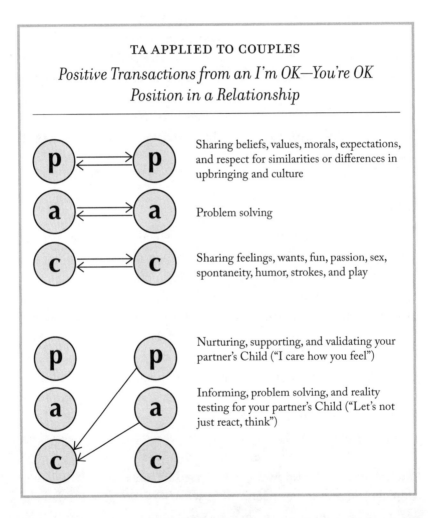

TA APPLIED TO COUPLES

Positive Transactions from an I'm OK—You're OK Position in a Relationship

Sharing beliefs, values, morals, expectations, and respect for similarities or differences in upbringing and culture

Problem solving

Sharing feelings, wants, fun, passion, sex, spontaneity, humor, strokes, and play

Nurturing, supporting, and validating your partner's Child ("I care how you feel")

Informing, problem solving, and reality testing for your partner's Child ("Let's not just react, think")

EXERCISE

See Ground Rules for Talking, page 17.

1. Regarding the concepts briefly discussed, how do you think your personality divides among the different parts?

    How much critical or overcontrolling Parent do you have with others and yourself?

    How much nurturing and protective Parent do you have with others and yourself?

2. What parts of your Parent need to develop? What parts need to shrink? Do you believe you have a well-functioning, thinking Adult? How well does it help you and your inner Child when you need it?

3. How much free or OK Child do you think you have as compared to Not OK Child? Is your adapted Child (that part of your child that developed based on your reaction to how you were treated by your parents and the examples they set) more compliant and pleasing to others, or rebellious, saying "no" and resisting being controlled? What do you think is the basic nature of your inner Child? Scared, worried, angry, sad, depressed, lonely, fun loving, carefree, loving, accepting, withdrawn, inhibited, always pleasing others and obeying, or rebellious and oppositional to the point of pushing others away?

4. What kind of strokes do you like and want? How were you shown love as a kid: physical affection, hugs and touching, verbal compliments? Did your family of origin give positive strokes and messages or negative ones? Can you remember which ones felt good and which hurt? How do you think this has affected what you believe and how you give yourself strokes now?

5. What kind of strokes does your partner like and want? How well do you exchange strokes with your partner? Are you starved and lonely, or fulfilled? Are your current relationship struggles about lack of strokes?

6. Think about how your partner's personality divides up among the different parts of Parent, Adult, and Child according to this model.

7. What life position, for example, I'm OK–You're OK; I'm Not OK–You're Not OK, do you think you live within? What position do you go to during times of stress or conflict? How about your partner? Do you move between two or more positions? Do you think this affects how you relate to your partner and others?

For now, try to be more aware of the different parts—Parent, Adult, and Child—within you and your partner, and how you think they are expressed in your relationship.

DISCUSSION

Both Bill and Nancy were beginning to challenge the Parent messages they had gotten as kids. When both realized that they were neither parents nor children, but partners, each began to relate to the other from the position of Adult. By using the conflict between them in a positive way, they began to stand up for their *selves* and to take responsibility for those selves. This worked especially well because each was becoming more communicative, cooperative, and accepting of the other.

> Remember: No one can make you feel inferior without your consent.
> —Eleanor Roosevelt

After a period of almost unbearable conflict and nearly deciding to break up, a psychological separation allowed Bill and Nancy to be more of who they really were and to slowly accept this in the other. Rather than physically separating from each other, they were separating from a pattern of relating that was no longer useful and fulfilling. Each became aware that the negative and Not OK feelings they thought were coming from the other partner were really coming from the internal Parent in each of their own heads. Learning to take responsibility and control over these messages and feelings was a way to fix their communication process and become more genuinely intimate. They knew that untangling this confusion about who made who feel what would have to continue over the life of their relationship.

EXERCISE

1. What do you think about Bill and Nancy's psychological separation?

2. Can you understand what they were separating from?

3. Can you relate to their experience? How?

Remember that Bill and Nancy were at a point in their sixteen-year relationship where all they did was argue and fight. The ongoing conflict had emotionally beaten them up so much that they were considering a physical separation to bring peace to their lives. They both had begun to feel that the love and like in their relationship was gone.

After exercising some new skills to stop the fighting, they began learning or relearning how to listen and talk with each other in deeper and more intimate ways.

Bill and Nancy spent the first few weeks just enjoying the improved climate around the home. They admitted that they were not really talking to each other as much as before, but they liked the fact that they were not fighting.

After a few weeks of peace, Bill and Nancy both felt like they were ready to try talking. Once they learned to share the floor and to listen, they were able to talk. Whenever they began to touch on difficult topics and become angry and defensive, they had some guidelines on how to call time-out.

After about three months of less arguing and more meaningful communication, Bill and Nancy felt closer to each other emotionally and seemed to be getting along better. They admitted that there were a few times they had begun to fight, but each time they were able to get back on track.

> When two people agree on everything, one of them is doing all
> of the thinking.
> —E.B. White

Making Room for Different Realities

Just about the time that Bill and Nancy were beginning to build some new confidence in their relationship, Nancy began to experience more work stress and often came home tired and depressed. She was questioning whether she should continue her current job or look for another. At night she would spend most evenings complaining about her boss, the school principal, and then fall asleep watching TV or reading, with Bill sitting next to her.

When this first started, Bill had more tolerance and support for Nancy's work problems. After all, they were beginning to listen to each other better and share more feelings. They had not done this for so long. But as time went on, Bill noticed that he was sharing less and less about himself and started to resent Nancy consuming all their time together. He noticed that she hardly asked about him about his life before the topic shifted to her and her work frustrations.

Bill was reluctant to share this insight because Nancy was already under enough stress and he didn't want to add to it, but what he secretly realized was that they had begun to fall back into their old pattern. The climate between them became cooler, and there seem to be less real sharing, at least from his side, and more anger, frustration, and short tempers flaring up between them. Bill became the frustrated one this time and started to feel helpless and hopeless. He started to forget how well the last three months had gone and now only remembered how unhappy and dissatisfied he had felt over the last year.

Bill and Nancy were just learning to talk and listen but all it took was increased stress from Nancy's workplace to hurl them into a backslide. With Nancy less available emotionally, Bill was struggling with how to care for himself. For some people, men as well as women, this deprivation, this lack of positive strokes, can breed anger and frustration, and help form power struggles and ice walls in the relationship. After about a month of listening to Nancy continually complain about her job and boss, Bill realized that he had been primarily a listening, nurturing, and supportive Parent to her with little returned to his Child. He decided to take a chance by trying to communicate his frustrations:

BILL: (*nervous and unsure*) Nancy, I have something to say that I hope you'll be able to listen to without getting defensive. I have begun to notice that we, or maybe I should say I, am falling back to where I was three months ago. Back then, you taught me how important it was to express how I feel. Well, I don't think that I have been doing this. I realize how stressed you are because of your work, and I think I have been trying to be helpful and supportive. But now I am noticing that I'm getting more and more frustrated and angry. All we talk about is you and your work. What about me and us? I am actually feeling guilty saying this.

　　We are beginning to argue more over small things and we seem to have drifted apart again. I need more from you, I don't know how to get it and I feel stuck in our old pattern. After we started to do better, I am now discouraged that nothing has really changed.

NANCY: (*While Bill talked, Nancy felt wounded by his words and defensive inside, and thought that Bill really didn't want to help her with her work stress.*) Bill, I'm starting to feel defensive and hurt about what you're saying. I know that I need to listen to your feedback so I can get my butt in gear. I thought it was great how we worked ourselves out of that hole last year, but the last thing I want is for my job to wreck us again. Even though it hurts to hear what you're saying, I'm glad that you are telling me this; you didn't have to wait so long. Remember, we agreed to share our real and truthful feelings. I have been so caught up in my work stress that I've neglected you! I *have* noticed that we are arguing more lately and we seem to be drifting apart again. This has actually made me worry in addition to all my work stuff. But with work problems and all, I guess I just went back to ignoring it. Hey, honey, do you know what we're doing? We are actually talking about how we really feel, and we're not arguing about it. We're both listening to the other!

BILL: (*Tears well up in his eyes, and he leans over to hug Nancy.*) I really appreciate you! (*They both start to laugh.*)

DISCUSSION

Bill and Nancy had again experienced becoming unstuck and making up. What they are just beginning to realize is that they need to learn how to get unstuck earlier on. Remember that each of them has a responsibility to their process. Their strengths lie in the fact that they have been together a long time, and each is able to accept a certain amount of influence from the other.

Bill's courage to express what he felt was a direct effect of their psychological separation. If Bill had remained stuck in his old pattern, he would have withdrawn angrily and his pent-up frustrations would have come out in their daily fights, or he and Nancy would have distanced themselves from each other. Nancy's ability to listen to him also stemmed from psychological separation and allowed their process to repair itself. What was new for Nancy was allowing Bill to be himself, even if she didn't like it or agree with him. This is not easy to do, but the stronger your sense of self, the more you can learn to tolerate and accept that your partner can be different without you losing who you are.

Nancy realized that they were different and separate people with different opinions, beliefs, thoughts, feelings, and ways of doing things, and she began working from this new premise. She was able to listen to Bill's feelings about her work stress even though she didn't like what he was saying. She initially became defensive, but after some understanding, thinking, and listening to Bill, she realized that he did care and just wanted more of an intimate connection with her. She also gave him the benefit of the doubt.

Nancy seemed to be so involved in her work problems that she needed Bill to tell her that he was becoming frustrated. She was so consumed by her work that she really didn't see this on her own. Her new strength showed itself in that after some initial defensiveness she was able to get herself back on track and hear Bill. With this valida-tion, Bill felt satisfied that he was heard, and Nancy actually felt closer and more supported by him. Once again, this was a nice breakthrough for them.

Bill and Nancy were learning how to repair their relationship pro-cess and were gaining some confidence that they could actually stop conflict and start communicating productively. Many couples enter marital or couples counseling just for a jump start on getting this pro-cess back on track. I believe that couples often fall in and out of like and love over and over again, but as with Bill and Nancy, must learn to communicate out of the stuck places repeatedly so the good positive feelings can reemerge and thrive.

Of course, their troubles were not over. Many couples experience a bit of peace in their relationship and improved communication and think they're out of the woods. The truth is that we often get stuck in the same muck over and over again. I view these stuck places as neces-sary for individual and couple growth and development. Sometimes, getting unstuck is simple and easy, other times it is hard and trying, and takes longer. The point is that it's a process. Without realistic expecta-tions, without addressing it and learning ways to correct it, however, people often decide their only option is to divorce.

Some couples learn little from a psychological separation except that they feel better and maybe a little closer after. Others have great insights and new understandings of themselves, each other, and the relationship. In order to really change the relationship for the long term, they have to be both invested and committed to a degree of psychologi-cal separation, and persistent in managing this change.

The Upshot

Bill and Nancy stayed together. Nancy eventually left her job for a more satisfying one. Bill and Nancy's pattern of getting along went well with fewer and fewer backslides into their old pattern. As time passed, they grew more aware of the pattern, each tolerated the fallout periods better, and each accepted the responsibility to not only take better care of him- or herself, which in itself reduced their conflict, but to confront and talk to the other as well. They developed persistence and also realized that their partner's first response—anger, avoidance, and defensiveness—was not always the underlying and truthful response. Each of them trusted that the other would come around, and if they didn't, the partner most frustrated would speak up. Both came to know that they would be heard, and this made all the difference.

If you and your partner are stuck in a pattern of blaming or setting each other off, I urge you to try the following guidelines.

First Response, Second Response

If one of you snaps or has a negative overreaction toward the other, instead of accepting this response as the final truth and responding in a way that keeps the conflict going, don't react. Either question this first reaction or call a time-out to cool down and take some space. Allow time for a more mature second response to come forth. This may take ten minutes, but should not go beyond twenty-four hours. If you were to immediately follow the first response, chances are you would head down a blind alley with a higher risk of escalating conflict. By allowing time for a second response, you can get back on track and hopefully continue your communication with greater satisfaction. This is a critical step toward fixing the communication process.

EXERCISE

See Ground Rules for Talking, page 17.

1. Do you and your mate fight about everything, like Bill and Nancy? Or are you, perhaps, locked into a cold war with each other?

2. What can you borrow from Bill and Nancy's psychological separation experience to help you manage conflict and regain intimacy in your own relationship?

3. What, in your view, were Bill and Nancy able to do differently once they controlled the conflict?

4. How important do you think this was to their evaluation and decision to stay together?

No one loves the man he fears.
—Aristotle

Fair Fighting

Many people want to know how to "fight" fairly. Many years ago, psychologist George Bach wrote about fair fighting in *Intimate Enemy: How to Fight Fair in Love and Marriage*. From Bach's work, I've developed a short list of guidelines that can be applied to heated discussions, conflicts, or fights. When these rules are violated, time-out should be called to explain how you believe you have been fouled. Fair Fighting Guidelines can help your communication process even during conflicts.

Couples can fight fairly only when the psychological power is balanced in a relationship. This means that one partner does not have an unfair amount of power over the other. If one partner is able to control the other with anger and threats, there can be no fair fighting. If one partner is afraid to argue because of physical assault or physical intimidation—for example, she is backed against the wall with a fist or finger in her face or chest—there can be no fair fighting. Often the one who uses threats of violence needs to learn some type of anger management. Classes, groups, and individual help are available through your local mental health organization. Unless the angry person (who often comes from the self-righteous position of I'm OK–You're Not OK) takes responsibility for himself, there will be no change.

If one partner has a history of being physically assaulted or abused in relationships, fair fighting will be very difficult unless the abused partner has really worked through the past experience and can trust

FAIR FIGHTING GUIDELINES

1. No hitting, hurting each other physically, or throwing or breaking of property.

2. No intimidation, threats, or power trips.

3. No "character assassinations" or name calling.

4. No making a case against your partner from history or claiming that everybody else you know agrees with you about how your partner is at fault.

5. No interruptions.

6. Take turns.

7. Stay on the current issue or topic; don't stray to other topics or issues.

8. Use "I" statements, such as "When you [fill in the blank], I feel [fill in the blank]." Take responsibility for your own thoughts, beliefs, feelings, and opinions as your truths and not the truth about your partner. Don't speak for others; speak for yourself. Don't try to destroy your partner. The point of arguing is to get your point across!

9. Don't make your partner the enemy!

10. Attempt to focus on the end result and avoid just going in circles.

11. Pick your fights! For example, instead of arguing about an issue before visiting with friends, save it for a later time.

that a physical assault will not happen again. Working with a third person, a counselor, for example, is strongly advised.

On the other hand, many couples learn to argue and express themselves loudly while still abiding by the rules, and no one feels taken advantage of. This is an ability best learned with a third person, a counselor, therapist, or mediator.

Conclusion

Working through Steps 1 and 2 (managing your conflict and restarting your communication process, respectively) will allow you to reduce conflict and examine your inner self and your communication process. This should allow you to begin to think about your situation and the available options before running to divorce court. Some calming and reduced stress gives you an opportunity to discover your own inner resources and power. This could also have an effect on your partner and relationship. Your problems are not permanently solved—there will always be new issues and crises in relationships that will test and stretch you and your communication process—but now you have some tools for controlling them, together or individually. As you practice Step 2, you may find that you are able to respond to the real issues beneath the conflict and not just react to your partner's style or process of communicating. Through this step, you are learning to regain your balance and create some stability for your self and perhaps your relationship, and to begin to gain insight into your self. It is about building in the necessary supports for you to continue examining your relationship; it is about regaining some of your power and getting the opportunity to think about what happens next.

Some couples find that focusing on Steps 1 and 2 alone puts them back on track to a more fulfilling relationship as they struggle through a tough period. They won't necessarily need to go on to Steps 3 through 10.

Other couples will want to think about taking some kind of separation. Step 3 has you consider what the purposes of a separation might be. This step should help you probe a little deeper as you begin to ask the following:

- Why is my relationship not working?
- What is the purpose of a separation at this time?
- How might more space help my situation?

You will also continue to develop Step 1 and 2 skills throughout the book, as you are exposed to how different couples understand, develop, and relate as they manage their various separations.

Step 2 Exercise: Reflect on Your Communication Process

See Ground Rules for Talking, page 17. This exercise can be done alone or with a partner.

1. In your experience, does your communication process encourage talking and listening to each other?

2. Realizing that you may be in crisis or intense conflict, how would you describe the "climate" in your relationship presently? How do you think your partner would describe it?

3. What are your current beliefs, feelings, and attitudes about your partner, yourself, and your relationship? What do you wish to believe? What do you really believe?

4. How do you think your current beliefs, perceptions, and feelings about yourself and your partner affect how you communicate and behave with him/her?

5. What happens with your inner self when you talk and interact with your partner?

6. How does your inner self change your behavior with your partner during conflict periods, breakdowns, or when you become stuck? What do you think your and your partner's contributions are to conflict periods?

REFLECT ON HOW YOU HANDLE CONFLICT:

7. How well are you and/or your partner managing your conflict?
   - How are you handling breakdowns and backslides?
   - Can you identify what triggers you allow your partner to pull?
   - When a trigger is pulled, how do you respond or react?
   - Are you able to use time-out to stop nonconstructive or destructive conflict?
   - Are you able to hold onto your sense of self during these times?
   - How do you end the cold war or icy, distant periods?
   - How and who makes up and how long does it take?

8. Do you fight fairly or not?
   - Do you blame, attack, find fault, withdraw, become sarcastic or passive–aggressive, hold grudges or get even, use power trips and threats, or look for allies (your children, relatives, or friends) to join you against your spouse?
   - Do you treat your partner the way you want to be treated?

9. How do you think your moods and stress levels from life demands such as work, childcare, illness, substance use or abuse, energy level, sleep patterns, etc., affect how you get along with your partner?
   - Does what you expect and receive from your partner change during these stressful times?
   - How well do you ask for what you want?

10. Evaluate your communication process.
   - Can you remember a time when your relationship process worked better and was more fulfilling?
   - What are your contributions to your relationship process when it is working well?
   - How safe and free are you to feel and express yourself with your partner? How can you make this safer?
   - Do you feel heard and understood by your partner?
   - How well do you really listen?
   - How well do you communicate your inner feelings, thoughts, wants, and expectations to your partner?

- Is your partner able to open up to you?
- Do you now understand how you contribute to the circular process of your relationship?
- Do you understand the difference between *what* you talk about (the issues and subjects) and the more underlying process of *how* you talk?
- Can you understand how your and your partner's contributions fit together to form your relationship process and pattern?
- Can you see how important this process is to problem solving and all other aspects of your relationship?
- Who do you believe is presently most resistant to creating a better communication process? Why?
- Can you see how fundamental and important managing conflict and being able to communicate is to deciding the future of your relationship?

11. What can you do now to reduce conflict and take charge in creating an improved climate for you that may also have a positive effect on your relationship or even help in deciding what kind of space you want while the future of your relationship is being considered?

STEP 3
Defining the Initial Goals and Purposes of Your Separation

It's not that some people have willpower and some don't.
It's that some people are ready to change and others are not.
—James Gordon, M.D.

Many couples turn to separation without first assessing their real goals and purposes. They believe it's their only option. Step 3 is about doing that assessment so that even if you do decide to separate, you'll be doing so with clarity on why and what your full range of options might be.

As you saw in Step 2, during conflicts, especially long-standing conflicts, your perception of your partner narrows. You may see your partner as overcontrolling, nagging, withholding, mean and angry, noncommunicative, uncompromising, uncaring, a betrayer, mistrusting, etc. In short, you no longer give your partner the benefit of the doubt. These perceptions then shape your behavior with your partner and become the norm of how you relate.

Without even realizing it, both partners often end up perpetuating the problem pattern and, regrettably, it becomes all too easy to forget what attracted you to your partner in the first place. If this is the case, all you may be able to see is a person who grates on your nerves, pushes your buttons, or worse.

Ironically, of course, it is often frustrated expectations and lack of a more loving intimate connection that leads to increased conflict and distance in the first place. In this situation, the negative way you begin to see and relate to your partner actually deprives you of the very thing you are hoping to get.

What's important at this stage is that you both find a way to come together, at least for the purpose of articulating your different dreams, expectations, perspectives, experiences, and inner truths with and for your partner and your relationship so that you can see how you have gotten so far apart. No matter how successful you have been at managing conflict (Step 1) and restarting your communication process (Step 2), if you have reached this step there are obviously still differences in wants, values, expectations, and compatibilities that are keeping you apart.

As you speak together, you will likely discover differences in how you each define the amount of space and freedom, emotional closeness, investment, and commitment you want and put into your relationship. You may discover that you've never really had a conversation (or series of conversations) like this before. You may find that you need to work out specific issues, such as how much time to spend together or apart, finances, sex and affection, child rearing, sharing family responsibilities, and decision making.

Some couples may be relieved to be renewing communication or notice real progress in how they are relating, while others will find at least one partner fixated on wanting a break from ongoing conflict or already gone from the relationship emotionally; perhaps they have even invested in a new relationship.

Some partners may not make themselves available to talk because the conflict and tension is too intense, and they feel emotionally unsafe or become easily angered when they are around their partner. Couples in this situation would be wise to separate simply to get the physical distance necessary to reduce the conflict. If being near your partner creates this much anger and negative feeling, then learning to manage at least your side of the conflict will be the first order of business and separation can give you both the space for doing that.

Step 3 challenges you in the midst of conflict, struggling communication, and disappointments to think about and explore some of the reasons your and your partner's expectations and wants are not being met.

EXERCISE

Take a few minutes to reflect on what you believe is not working in your relationship:

- What do you often say silently to yourself or out loud to others about your relationship?
- What do you complain about most?
- As you think about your relationship and communication pattern in a circular manner, what happens again and again that results in an unfulfilling or unsatisfactory process for you?
- From your perspective, what do you think you do and what does your partner do to contribute to this?

Level of Investment–Commitment

Every person's motivation to work on his or her relationship will be affected by his or her degree of investment and commitment to the relationship at any given time. By investment, I mean the amount of time, energy, and other nonmaterial resources you devote to your relationship. By commitment, I mean the pledge you make to involve yourself in your relationship and the decision to persist on working with your process.

When people are mired in conflict over a period of time, they can lose sight of how invested and committed they are. For this reason, I have developed a scale that partners can use to get a quick investment–commitment reading, and a gauge of just how much responsibility they are willing to take and how much work they are willing to do (or not do) to improve the relationship.

It is important to remember that partners and couples in crisis and continual conflict may initially rate themselves lower on the scale because they feel so beaten up and burnt out on trying. If one partner rates herself low on this scale but the other does not, this may then feel very threatening to the more invested, committed partner. As difficult as this may seem, it is important to really make an effort to listen to your partner and accept her where she is. This means you have already started to work on managing your anxieties and fears on your own. Invalidating a partner who is less invested than you are can only serve to push your partner further down the Investment–Commitment Scale. Listening to a less committed partner may actually result in the partner opening up more.

Take a look at the different levels along the scale and at the implications of having partners in different places.

RELATIONSHIP INVESTMENT—COMMITMENT SCALE

100%————75%————————50%————————25%————————0%

(Amount of Investment–Commitment)

1	2	3	4
"I'm invested and committed to you and our relationship, but going through a difficult time."	"There must be a change or I'm leaving the relationship! My investment and commitment are dependent on changes."	"I'm confused. I don't know whether I want this relationship or not. My investment and commitment are wavering and uncertain."	"I've decided to leave our relationship. I have little to no investment or commitment to our relationship." (disclosed or undisclosed to your partner)

Level 5 = Vacillation between any of the above

The Relationship Investment–Commitment Scale identifies five levels of investment–commitment.

Level 1: Invested–Committed

Level 1 describes people who are still very much committed to staying together as well as investing time, energy, and effort into their relationship. They may be stuck in a difficult period or passage in their relationships or their lives, but they at least say they are willing to work on their problems and issues to find a better solution. If both partners self-identify at this highest level of investment and commitment, the relationship has a good prognosis.

Such partners may still want space from each other and the relationship; they may want to work on changes and take a psychological separation, but their commitment and ongoing investment will often be enough of a glue to hold them together through these difficult periods. These couples can use psychological and physical space in a positive way for self-development and improved intimacy. Chances are good that these couples will cooperate through their separations and changes, attempt to manage conflict, improve communication, and work to make the relationship more satisfying for themselves and each other. Both individual and couples counseling can be very beneficial to these couples in helping them to achieve individual and couple goals.

It is important to recognize, however, that commitment alone does not ensure a satisfying or healthy relationship. There are some couples and individuals who may be very committed to harmful and destructive relationships. There are many reasons for this, such as being afraid to be on one's own, wanting children to have an intact home, finances, religious beliefs, fear of a partner's reaction (abuse), guilt, denial, and rationalizations for the destructive nature of your relationship. Taking some space during difficult periods, even just psychological space, can actually help overly dependent partners learn to take charge of themselves, increase their personal power, develop other forms of support, and thereby open new options and choices (anything that creates energy for change) in their lives.

Individuals who believe they are overly dependent or committed to unhealthy situations may want to seek individual counseling first to obtain an objective view of their relationship.

Both investment *and* commitment must be evaluated. A partner may be committed without necessarily seeing the importance of investing energy and time into working on himself or the relationship. Likewise, a person may be willing to invest heavily but have questionable commitment to how long he is willing to remain committed without seeing changes or experiencing increased satisfaction.

A more difficult situation, and the focus of this book, is when one partner is invested and committed (Level 1) and her partner is at a lesser level of investment and commitment. Mary and John were in this situation. Mary started out with a firm sense of investment and commitment to John. She was willing to work with him to make changes on how they handled the family responsibilities. John seemed to be committed to their relationship and family, but his level of investment fell below Mary's expectations. Everyone and every couple has to figure out for themselves how to strike the right balance between meeting one's own wants and meeting one's partner's wants and where the twain meet.

I remember working with a couple in which the female partner wanted more emotional and verbal sharing. Her partner responded by building a new deck and painting the house, which he thought would please her. He was surprised to see how little this meant to her as she still complained that they never talked. This is a good example of one partner giving the kind of strokes he wants and not those his partner wants. To really connect with someone, find out what they want and learn to give it.

Level 2: "There Must Be a Change."

At Level 2, one and sometimes both partners are still willing to work on the improvement but don't feel they can make a lifetime commitment without some changes in their partner or the relationship dynamic. Here a partner might be willing to invest time and energy into improvement for a specific period, such as three to six months, but can't foresee hanging in there beyond that.

If both partners are in Level 1 or 2, couples counseling can again be very effective. Even though these partners may be hurting, they will usually enter counseling with minds that are at least partially open to learning how to relate differently. If improvement occurs within either of them or the relationship, a new, more lasting commitment may be made, and these couples will have learned how to use problems and conflict to learn and grow. If improvements do not occur so as to satisfy both partners enough to recommit, more time and space may be necessary to rethink goals or work on individual issues.

Level 3: Confused–Ambivalent

Level 3, as its name suggests, describes the person who is confused and unsure as to whether he or she wants to be in the relationship any longer. I refer to this as standing at the door of your relationship. This partner may be resistant to working on the relationship while at the same time fearful of being open and honest about wanting out. This situation can lead to false hopes for the more invested–committed partner.

When I discover such ambivalence in one partner, I often schedule an individual session to explore that partner's confusion. Sometimes the confusion has to do with old resentments or hurts over an affair. Sometimes the confusion is not confusion at all but a kinder way of expressing a desire to get out of the relationship.

Ambivalence is also common in partners who feel that they have been putting all their energy into improving a relationship while their partner has not. One's sense of investment and commitment can also waver when one feels the need to devote more time to self-development or change. The point is, over the course of one's adult lifetime one's investment and commitment may continually shift from relationship to self and back again.

We are all subject to stressors from life, such as birth of children, physical problems or illnesses, emotional difficulties, the resurfacing of symptoms from past traumas, etc. Other times, grief (over the loss of a parent or child, for instance), work demands, finances, or unforeseen events might affect one's level of investment and commitment.

People at Level 3 can be greatly helped by counseling. Confusion and ambivalence can be frightening to the more invested and committed partner, but relationship health is not so easily restored when one partner is sitting on the fence. Until a decision is made, couples sessions may also be necessary to at least set ground rules over what each partner can expect, how each will relate to the other partner, and how they will operate as a family during a period of uncertainty.

The important thing here is to identify the difference. If one partner is at Level 3 while the other is at Level 1 or 2, agreements will be very difficult to make.

Living together in a situation in which partners are having such different experiences and expectations can be very difficult and painful. The more invested and committed partner can easily become excessively dependent or obsessed with trying to get her partner to change his mind. The partner at the door may view her efforts less as caring than as control.

In such situations it may be a real risk to continue to force the resistant or ambivalent partner into couples counseling or even individual counseling unless he or she has at least some motivation to go. Being forced may result in more anger, resentment and resistance.

Level 4: "I Want to End the Relationship."

Level 4 describes the partner who wants out of the relationship. Usually this partner has already made a decision, at least in his or her heart, but may or may not have been honest with himself or his partner until this point. This partner may be fearful of disclosing this decision or may be trying to let the other partner down easily. Sometimes he wants to show his partner and family and friends that he has tried to work on the relationship by going to counseling. An undisclosed affair may be behind this little bit of subterfuge. The partner has already left the relationship emotionally but is keeping up appearances. Here, couples work can be very difficult because there is not mutual agreement, investment, or commitment.

If, during counseling, the Level 4 partner discloses his or her affair or admits to having checked out of the relationship, dealing with the emotional crisis caused by the disclosure must take precedence over other issues. The counselor must also assess the physical and emotional safety and stability of the individuals within the couple. The more psychologically and emotionally dependent or Not OK a more invested and committed partner feels, the more desperate that person can become. Such a partner often requires a lot of support from other people until he can recover some hope and strength within himself again. In extreme circumstances, such Not OK people have been known to resort to violence, homicide, and suicide. These are very delicate matters that a professional must consider carefully.

Does a partner who has decided to end a relationship ever change his or her mind? Yes, of course, but usually only after a period of separation and some growth. Regardless of that potential, the hurting and left partner must be encouraged to grieve and let go.

Like those partners in counseling at Level 3, the goals of joint counseling need to be very clear so the partner still committed to working on the relationship can be helped to view goals realistically.

I have found that some couples will continue in counseling even after a decision to end their relationship has been made. Most often, this is done in order to learn as much as they can about their individual contributions and responsibilities for the patterns that developed in their relationship. This ongoing counseling can be very useful; the hazard is that it can also delay the grieving and coping process for the left partner. In fact, sometimes a left partner will use counseling as a way of hanging onto the relationship. It's up to the counselor to determine whether continued couples work will be helpful or detrimental in any given situation.

Individual counseling, on the other hand, is almost always beneficial to both partners. The leaving partner will benefit from working on his or her own growth, and the left partner will get some support as he or she grieves and attempts to move on. In both cases, the work can take some time.

Level 5: Vacillation

People at Level 5 aren't in one fixed place on the scale but move from one place to another based on changes in the moods, feelings, or experiences of one or both partners as well as other life factors. When this is the case, it's important to look at what lies underneath the wavering investment and commitment. Individual counseling may be necessary to assess the mental and emotional status of the wavering partner. If one partner wavers and the other partner is overly dependent on her mate's moods and behavior, her investment and commitment may waver, too.

If couple's counseling is undertaken, its focus must be on the process and patterns of the relationship and whether each partner is willing to look at these factors and take responsibility for them.

As well as an understanding of both partners' levels of investment and commitment, I have found that some knowledge of the stages of development that relationships experience has been very useful to couples and partners. These stages may be helpful so partners have some idea of what to expect during early and later stages of relationships. It is also important to measure partners' levels of investment and commitment as they relate to these different stages.

Stages of a Relationship*

1. **Romance/Fantasy** This is the first stage of a relationship in which partners bond to become a couple. Two separate selves merge into a *we* in which partners' similarities are highlighted. At this stage, you believe everything about your partner is great and wonderful. Partners are basking in a climate of mutual admiration and validation, sexual attraction, and infatuation. The inner Child in partners is feeling stroked, loved, and connected. When partners refer to being in love, they usually are referring to the feelings that come from this experience. At the biological level, hormones may be raging at high levels, which account for the feelings of bliss that partners experience. For some couples, this may not be a highly passionate state but extremely comfortable. Most individuals like how they feel about themselves around their

*Credit for ideas:
Rock, Maxine, *The Marriage Map: Understanding and Surviving The Stages of Marriage* (Atlanta, GA.: Peachtree Publishers, Ltd., 1986).

Bader, Ellyn, and Peter T. Pearson, *In Quest of the Mythical Mate: A Developmental Approach to Diagnosis and Treatment in Couples Therapy* (New York: Brunner/Mazel, 1988).

partner, which translates into, "You make me feel so good!" Many affairs start in the romance stage, which makes them so attractive and intoxicating. If an affair doesn't become a full-time relationship, it can remain in this infatuation period for longer periods of time. Movies and romance novels usually portray relationships in this romance stage. This period shifts between approximately six months and a year (depending on the amount of time together), usually leading to stage two, disillusionment.

2. **Disillusionment/Compromise** This period of time is characterized by a slow separation from "we" and a reclaiming of your self. Emphasis shifts to how the two partners are different. Some individuals feel as if they were deceived or betrayed as more undesirable traits of their partner begin to emerge. Increased conflict between two people often begins at this stage as they struggle to compromise on where there is disagreement: "You don't want to have as much sex as you used to." "You withdraw so much!" "You're a slob!" "You don't talk with me anymore." "You have a temper and say mean things." "You're moody." "You were so thoughtful when we first met, what happened?"

Some of the mutual stroking and validation from the romance stage eases, and partners may feel they have now fallen out of love with each other as the high of the first stage changes. Most experts and studies show that this period is more realistic as two partners show more of their real selves. Some of the hormones and chemicals that were present during the first stage begin to ease.

At least two problematic patterns can emerge at this stage as couples move from romance to disillusionment. First is an overdependence on each other and a fear of open conflict. This will tend to happen in couples on the passive side of the Conflict Scale. Couples may struggle with expressing their individual selves within the relationship. They may act as if "we" (the couple) is more important than "I" or "me" (the self). *Selfish* may be seen as a dirty word! Because of often natural differences between partners—especially men and women—learning to manage conflicts and communicate is very important to expressing who you are to your partner. A couple or a partner may attempt to hang on to the romance stage and suppress any conflict for the sake of keeping the peace. Tim and Margie (Shutdown Spouse) are an example of a couple that never fights. As a result, self-growth in their relationship was very stuck, with many wants and expectations going unexpressed and unmet.

The second problematic pattern also involves overdependence, but in this case the couple is engaged in open conflict at the aggressive-explosive side of the Conflict Scale. As the romance stage ends, this couple may spend a lot of time embroiled in arguments and power struggles as they react strongly to the differences they now see in the other. Here, the drama, turmoil, and tension of fighting prevent growth. Partners can burn out with the continual arguing and conflict.

Sometimes one partner is at the aggressive side and the other is at the passive side of the Conflict Scale, which can create very frustrating fighting styles and fear on the side of the more passive partner who doesn't like conflict. The more aggressive partner may be seen as over-controlling, a bully, or selfish. These power struggles are often attempts to change the partner into who we want him to be, often how he was in the romance stage.

Partners must learn to share power as their relationship develops. Your experience with power and control from your family of origin and prior relationships is included in the expectations you bring to every relationship. Power struggles can emerge over differences in taking space and time alone (autonomy), wanting more time together (intimacy), and how to deal with issues such as sex, money, and children. With all the demands of modern lifestyles most adults must grapple with ways to take care of themselves conflicting with just how much they can expect from a partner.

With more space between partners in the second stage, partners who miss the intense closeness and good feelings will long to return to the romance stage. How well partners adjust and cope with differences, give and take, and share and communicate with each other determines levels of intimacy and satisfaction in their relationship. Partners may begin to secretly or openly question their level of investment and com-mitment at this point.

3. Reality This stage in a relationship is born out of how well you adjust after getting to know and experience your partner over time. You get to experience your partner as he or she *really* is. This stage is where partners decide that their relationship is good, good enough, or unsatisfactory because it is not what was expected. Your choices become feeling that you can do nothing to change the relationship, believing that you can change your partner, believing that you can adjust and change, or realizing that you can end the relationship. What makes someone stay or leave a relationship is unique to each person and is judged by how well your inner picture of what you expect from your relationship matches what you actually experience. Obviously, your capacity to invest and commit can help a struggling relationship survive very difficult and stressful times. Since we are all unique, have different expectations, and started from different places from our early training in our families of origin, it is hard to compare relationships.

4. Ongoing Development The primary task at this stage, which can last for the rest of your life, is that each of your separate selves continues to emerge, grow, and develop into two interdependent whole people. It is this emerging sense of self that allows you to become more intimate and connected with your partner. Struggling with the balance between your independence and your connection to your partner defines many couples in this stage. Does your relationship foster self-growth? And does your self-development enhance your capacity for a more intimate, fulfilling relationship?

Common stressors that couples and families often experience include new babies, small children, the busy lives of active middle-school children, the struggles and conflicts of emancipating teenagers, children at college, an empty nest, aging parents, growing older, etc. These, along with job and career expectations, put enormous demands on the time and energy of couples. Relationships may become low priority during these demanding times. Nurturing intimacy must become a regular event. Just learning to stop conflict and begin talking can often start intimacy building again. But ways to spend time together must be built in to everyday life.

Remember that a partner will not meet all your wants and needs. Friends, hobbies, projects, sports, and other activities allow you to be you. Supporting your partner's individual interests will often bring your partner closer to you as that balance between being *you* as well as a *we* continues to develop.

Separation, as defined in this book, is about the process of strengthening a separate self so you can actually bring more of you to the intimacy you share with your partner. As you become more intimate with yourself, you can become more able to share this intimacy with your partner. Many individuals have experienced a breakup or divorce and have moved on to a second or third partner, and may also have blended families. Second and third relationships also usually start in the romance stage, but quickly move into the disillusionment and reality stages, where struggles begin. The extent to which partners are satisfied in these new relationships still depends on how much learning, wisdom, investment, and commitment is carried over to a new choice. Partners should think of themselves as a team, not as one carrying all responsibility like in Mary and John's relationship, in which Mary felt the responsibility of family life was hers alone.

Partners who can continue to manage conflict, listen to each other, express and share their changing wants, expectations, and power, and learn to share responsibilities have a better chance of maintaining and building mutual satisfaction as they grow and develop. The tasks and skills outlined in the ten steps of Separation Management are designed to help couples get started when they become stuck at any point in their relationship.

Remember people are different and not perfect. Learning from mistakes and experiences is crucial to growth. Although the stages of a relationship may be unique for each couple, they are often predictable. Therefore, conflicts and power struggles are often necessary for change, and you will need to continue to work on you and your relationship.

But all is not lost! After thirty-five years of working with couples, I am still surprised with how couples and partners can grow and change based on new information and experiences. People are resilient, dynamic, and forever changing their inner selves. Some of my main purposes for writing this book are to offer education, information, and the experiences of other couples so that those thinking about separating can see that, with willingness and some inner work, separation is normal and healthy if you use it to understand and develop yourself.

Let's revisit Mary and John from Step 1 to see how their investment–commitment levels affected their relationship.

Couple Situation 1: Mary and John: "He's Like a Third Child!"

Remember that Mary and John were engaged in heated open conflict with each other for a long period of time. Mary's anger would be triggered by John's lack of sharing in family responsibilities, and she was totally obsessed with getting John to change. When this did not work, she had to learn to let go of that expectation. Working on knowing and changing your expectations in a relationship does not necessarily mean decreasing your investment in that relationship. It may mean that the nature of the investment changes.

Mary continued to control her anger and criticism of John. John saw this as Mary backing off, and he seemed to relax somewhat. Mary realized that the only way she could keep her anger at John under control was to adjust or lower her expectations and detach from him. This did not come easily for her, and she had to remember to be mindful and focus on this new behavior. Mary accomplished this with much support from friends and a counselor.

Mary continued to practice deep breathing. She learned to calm and relax herself, becoming aware of expectations that would trigger anger and frustrations. She also used self-talk to reassure herself that she was coping and would resolve this problem. She also learned not to engage or focus on those situations with John that drove her crazy. Mary realized that she was able to cope as soon as she separated from the idea that the only way out of conflict was to have John do what she wanted. Working with the idea that John might or might not change, Mary freed herself from feeling like a victim to John or from having to control him.

"As long as you want power, you can't have it. The minute you don't want power you'll have more than you ever dreamed possible."
—Ram Dass, *Be Here Now*

By taking responsibility for herself and letting go of expectations of John that were not working, Mary was learning one of the most valuable lessons in her life. It became Mary's explicit purpose for taking a (psychological) separation to no longer give up the power to manage her own feelings to anyone else. This decision allowed her to invest less in her expectation that John would change. Mary's next dilemma was whether or not she could continue living with someone who did not seem to want to share the work and responsibilities of family life, or who at least had a very different picture of how family life should be. Through discussions with friends and her counselor, as well as self-help readings, Mary came to realize that she was trained to take on too much responsibility, whereas John had a big, free inner Child and could easily say no. Ironically, this was one of the things she had initially found so attractive about John—his ability to just let things go. What had seemed quite attractive to Mary about John in their romance stage turned into what bothered her most as their relationship moved through disillusionment and reality stages.

She still loved that free Child part of John, but now that they had kids of their own, she also needed an Adult partner to share the realities and problems of family life.

People are often attracted to an attribute or personality feature of another that they wish they had themselves. If they were denied that attribute or quality as a child, they will undoubtedly have some resentment as well, and the attraction can end up causing a lot of internal conflict. Mary had started out wanting some of John's relaxed, fun-loving, free Child qualities, but because she was not allowed that as a child, she found it hard to adopt this quality as her own. After a while, the overworked Child in her began to resent the fact that John could just say no to work and she couldn't. The critical Parent in her had a big attitude about too much play!

Feeling tired, worried, and obsessed with all the work she had to do in and outside the home was overwhelming for Mary. But the answer was not just to get help from John, though that was certainly important. Mary had to connect and resurrect her own inner Child.

The overcontrolling and critical Parent part of Mary that drove her so hard had also gotten into a habit of expressing her frustration as anger and criticism. Through counseling and reading self-help books, Mary realized that she would have to stop expressing feelings through demands and criticism, because these would only serve to make John defensive. She also needed to learn to shrink her own internal critical Parent and start to give herself new messages about how she wanted to be.

As Mary took more responsibility for taking care of herself (investing in herself), her anger at John eased. She also learned to use more of her Adult through thinking and developing options instead of letting John trigger her impatient, helpless, and hurting inner Child feelings.

Of course, none of this entirely resolved Mary's desire and need for a more equal partner. Even as Mary got clearer, John still didn't make any significant changes, and she came to believe that she wanted a partner who not only shared family work and responsibilities but also took her concerns and feelings seriously. She decided that only a physical separation would send John the message that her commitment was in question and that she would no longer tolerate the situation.

Mary's Separation Goals:

1. To Continue to Detach and Lower Her Expectations of John Regarding Sharing the Family Responsibilities Mary had to learn to accept that John was not going to step up to the plate on family responsibilities. Every time she slipped into higher expectations, she would have to work with her breathing, talk to herself, a counselor, or a friend, and adjust her expectations to reality.

2. To Develop a Better Balance Between Work and Play Mary realized that it wasn't John's fault that she didn't have a better work–play balance; overwork and overcontrol were part of her childhood script. She also realized that it was her responsibility to achieve it for herself. Although this was hard, she was learning to do it. It has been my experience that this particular childhood script leaves people particularly prone to anger and resentment, frustration, depression, and eventual burnout.

Mary came to realize that if she didn't challenge this joyless script now, it would only follow her through life and contribute heavily to her unhappiness and an increased stress level.

3. To Let John Know That She Would No Longer Live with a Partner Who Did Not Share the Burdens of Family Life On the Relationship Investment–Commitment Scale Mary moved down the scale from Level 1, fully invested and committed, to Level 2, requiring a change.

Mary's decision to separate made a statement to John that she was serious about change. She let him know that she expected him to be able to communicate better and to divide family responsibilities, including child caretaking. She told him she wanted a partner who would share the ups and downs of life with her, and she would no longer settle for less. While she knew she could not control his response, Mary felt he would continue to discount and disrespect her expectations and wants unless he experienced major consequences. Mary also needed time apart from John to decide whether she could recapture enough of the right feelings to make this relationship work.

Next Mary would need to have a serious conversation with John and decide what type of separation might address the problems in their relationship.

What Was Happening with John?

John, meanwhile, was becoming increasingly anxious from the lack of conflict in their relationship, an obvious sign of Mary's withdrawn investment. He knew something in their relationship had changed— she wasn't nagging him anymore—and he didn't know whether to celebrate or be fearful of what might happen next. Although John had picked up a few more household responsibilities, he still wasn't doing much, and he didn't seem to realize how important sharing was to Mary, or how little effort it would really require from him.

EXERCISE

See Ground Rules for Talking, page 17. You can do this exercise alone or with a partner.

Mary has learned to feel better by detaching from her expectations of John and taking more responsibility for herself.

1. Why do you think she still wants a separation?

2. What do you think might be accomplished through a separation at this time?

3. If you or your partner are considering a separation, what is the purpose(s) or goal(s) for you? What would you expect to happen as a result of a separation? Is your separation accomplishing this?

Couple Situation 2: Tim and Margie: "Shutdown Spouse"

You'll recall that Tim and Margie were stuck in a noncommunicative, icy-cold, distant relationship. Tim was depressed and had buried himself in alcohol, the couch, and the TV. Margie felt that her wants and expectations for the relationship and family life had not been met for a very long time. Unlike Mary and John, whose conflict was out in the open, Tim and Margie's was a cold war with little meaningful communication.

By the time a counselor met them, Margie's investment and commitment had dropped to Level 4, wanting to end the relationship. She just couldn't stand being around Tim anymore. She had denied and buried her feelings for so long that intense resentment had built up. She separated from the idea that she had to remain invested and committed to a relationship with little to no return.

Tim, on the other hand, didn't seem to have a clue as to how unhappy Margie was, or how unhappy he was, for that matter. He seemed really out of touch with himself, and had no energy or motivation to work on himself or the relationship. In many ways, Tim was committed and quite dependent on Margie. He had no plans for any changes.

Their conflict, unspoken as it was, seemed to have eroded whatever foundation was left in their relationship. The purpose of their trial or predivorce separation was simple: Margie wanted out! She no longer wanted to feel like a victim to Tim's "go nowhere" lifestyle. This is a good illustration of the fact that when there is little or no communication and feedback between partners, learning and change is very difficult.

Margie had moved from passive acceptance of things as they were to a firm decision to physically (and psychologically) separate from her situation. Her purpose was to reclaim the hope of a more satisfying life for herself. Tim was thrown into a crisis, but perhaps this was exactly what he needed to save himself from his aimlessness and addiction.

EXERCISE

1. What is your first reaction to Margie's decision to separate from Tim? Good for her? Poor Tim? She should have given him more warning? Other?

2. What would you do if you were Margie? Or Tim?

3. In your opinion, what is Margie's responsibility for her situation?

Conclusion

People separate for many different reasons, and one person's reasons would not necessarily motivate another person to separate from a partner in a relationship with a similar dynamic. This is why every relationship must be viewed as unique. I hope this step has helped you see the value in identifying some of the initial purposes of your separation. Before we turn to Step 4, please try the following exercise, which I designed to help you assess the purpose of your own separation. And remember: you may separate with only a preliminary understanding of your conflict. With time, however, with more information, insight, understanding, and experiences through the separation period, and especially through individual growth and development, these initial goals and purposes often give way to deeper reasons that can help you determine whether you are willing to make a deeper investment and commitment to your relationship or if it's time to move on.

Step 3 Exercise: Identify Initial Goals and Purposes of Your Separation

1. Now that you've read this step, think about your own purpose for separating in your current (or a past) relationship.

2. Envision what you would want to accomplish as a result of a separation and your expectations of what a separation would bring.

3. Which of the following do you expect or wish to be different or change in you, your partner, and your relationship? Should there be

- less conflict?
- improved communication?
- better stroke exchange?
- more cooperation?
- more fun and play?
- more intimacy as you define it: verbal, emotional, affectionate, sexual, etc.?
- more activities together or alone?
- more time for family life?
- more time and space for you?
- sharing responsibilities?
- being better friends?
- improved co-parenting?
- spiritual development?
- shared values?
- changes in the type and levels of investment and commitment you are making to yourself and/or your relationship?
- other?

Or, if you do not have a "vision" of what could change, think about why. Is it because of any of the following:

- the level of investment and commitment for one of you changed dramatically?
- this was not your decision?
- you or your partner believe you have fallen out of love?
- you or your partner believe too much damage has been done?
- you need a period of time to decide how you feel?
- one of you is involved in another relationship?
- you do not know or understand the purpose of your separation?
- you are already involved in a divorce process?
- you are making a statement to your partner?
- you are teaching your partner a lesson?
- you are punishing your partner?
- you (or children) have been abused physically or sexually?
- other?

4. Do you think that you and your partner are on a similar track regarding what you want changed?

5. Do you think that your purposes for separation are compatible and possible?

6. In what category would you each place yourselves on the Relationship Investment–Commitment Scale? Has this position changed over time?

- How would you measure or rate your level of investment–commitment?
- How would you rate your partner's level of investment–commitment?
- How do you think your partner would rate you?
- Do you know what your partner expects from you and whether and how your efforts meet those expectations?
- Do you feel that your efforts are misunderstood by your partner?

7. If you are currently separated, have you discussed the *purpose* of your separation? Is the purpose clear? Are you both in agreement on this purpose? Are you both able to manage the conflict and communicate about why you may want changes and space?

Now that you have given some thought to the purpose or purposes of your separation, take a look at the different types of separations that can help in your situation.

STEP 4

Choosing the Type of Separation That's Right for You

Don't be too timid and squeamish about your actions. All life is an experiment. The more experiments you make the better.
—Ralph Waldo Emerson

Once you have some understanding as to why you're considering space or a change in your relationship (Step 3), you can begin to think about what kind of separation might work best for you. Some people work on a psychological separation, without a physical move; some move into separate bedrooms but stay within the home. Others choose a very brief separation—a kind of time-out from the relationship to sort through difficult feelings and choices. Some utilize a trial separation so they can experience living apart before deciding on the future of the relationship, and others opt for a predivorce separation as a first step toward terminating the relationship.

In this chapter we'll look at the various options, including trial unions, with an eye toward helping you determine which is right for you. If you are already separated, this chapter can also help you clarify and define your separation and further options more carefully.

Remember, the steps of Separation Management are not necessarily sequential. Once you separate, new conflicts or crises may arise that require management (Step 1); with distance, communication can become strained all over again and need reestablishing (Step 2); or your purpose for separating may change (Step 3). As we look at the various types of separations, please remember that although some separations are mutually agreed upon (cooperative), more often they are initiated by one partner. We will look at separation from all the different vantage points.

Deciding the type of separation you will be working on helps to define and clarify expectations and responsibilities for each partner. For example, a predivorce separation often has very different expectations than a brief separation. As you choose which type of separation is right for you, you may also find that you start with one type and then

---

TYPES OF SEPARATIONS

PHYSICAL SEPARATIONS

In-house: partners remain in the same home with more space and adjust expectations for their relationship for a period of time.

Brief Separations or Time-outs: partners basically remain in the same home, adjust expectations for their relationships, and plan to spend time apart, usually less than three months (e.g., a weekend, week, a month).

Trial: one partner moves out of the home, expectations for the relationship are adjusted, and the future of the relationship is uncertain. Usually a time period for this type of separation is at least three months before a review time.

Predivorce: at least one partner physically separates, often out of the home, with the intention of ending the relationship.

Combination: of any or all of the above

PSYCHOLOGICAL SEPARATIONS

Individual Psychological Separation: focus on growth and development of your self (with or without a cooperating partner). This can be done with either a physical separation or with both partners remaining in the home.

Therapeutic (Relationship) Separation: *both* partners focus on self-growth and changing the patterns in their relationship. This can be done with either a physical separation or with both partners remaining in the home.

move into another. You may start with a very brief separation only to find that you need more time to learn and grow, or change existing patterns. As always, my greatest hope is that you are able to use the separation process, however it happens and whichever you choose, as an opportunity to look at your self and learn from it as much as you can before making lasting decisions about your relationship.

Physical Separations

When people say they're separating, they usually mean some kind of moving apart. Physical distance is often needed to sort out what's going on in a relationship. Physical separations can take many different forms. For example, these days, for reasons both financial and familial, many people are choosing to try a separation within the home.

In-house Separations

In-house separations are usually short-term and offer couples a cool-down period during a particularly intense time of conflict or crisis. An in-house separation usually works best when one or both partners simply need some space to sort out feelings and decide to detach or have minimal contact for a brief period of time but choose to stay together in the home. This kind of separation actually happens naturally in many relationships, during high-stress times, or when one or both partners want space for any of a variety of reasons. Sometimes during conflict periods, partners will detach and get space to cool down and regain perspective on the relationship.

What's important in an in-house separation is that each partner works toward completely dropping expectations of the other for the duration of the separation. With no expectations comes no disappointments! Of course, this is easier said than done.

I remember one couple I worked with who had simply become tired of having heated debates every night from the time each came home from work until bedtime. I suggested they think about an in-house separation that could be reviewed each week during our counseling session. This couple chose to take physical space by sleeping separately, eating meals alone, and doing other activities, such as reading and watching TV, separately. Reducing their contact and expectations of each other immediately reduced their conflict, much to their surprise. But it was a mixed bag. One partner felt immediate relief while the other felt lonely. The separation at least gave them both the opportunity to withdraw negative energy from their ongoing conflict.

In-house separations can be especially attractive to parents. Both parents can continue to be available to their children without major disruption, which usually means fewer negative effects on the kids.

Making It Work

I always caution my clients that it's important to establish clear guidelines and ground rules for an in-house separation. Otherwise, it can create unbearable tension within the home, which isn't good for anyone. The next chapter covers the specifics of guideline setting.

Some couples choose an in-house separation while they are waiting for a physical one. This can work, too, provided the ground rules are clear.

For an in-house separation to work, you must be able to stand at least seeing and occasionally being in the presence of your partner. You must also agree that you can act civilly around each other, as you must continue to take care of family responsibilities. If you agree to this sort of separation, however, you can use it precisely to learn how to handle the feelings that surface when your partner's behavior triggers a reaction in you.

The Risks

This type of separation is *not* advisable if you or your mate are so angry that you are not able to be civil and in control of yourselves.

If either of you is very emotionally dependent, in-house separation can be particularly challenging. But the challenge can be just what you need, to learn to rely more on yourself and to discover what it is you really want from your mate.

One of the downsides of in-house separations is that they can be used as a way of avoiding problems or of punishing your partner. For this and other reasons, I strongly advise getting counseling together during the separation period. The last thing you want to do in a separation is exacerbate an already negative pattern of distancing and poor communication. You must eventually learn to communicate with each other once again about wants, expectations, and whatever else is fueling the conflict in the relationship. You will also have to learn to reattach after periods of detachment. You can see how important it is to work on self-reliance, care, and management during periods of distance and fallout with your partner. During conflict time, you are often emotionally *on your own*!

Of course, an in-house separation is the least costly of separations because no one has to bear the expense of moving and financing two households.

In short, in-house separations are most effective if

- they are short-term with agreed-upon time frames,
- ground rules are established and agreed to so that family business and childcare can be carried out,
- both partners are able to distance, detach from each other, and learn to control anger and conflict while living under the same roof,
- both partners work on temporarily lowering and/or eliminating expectations of each other, and
- both partners are willing to identify and take responsibility for their part in the conflict and agree to manage it.

An in-house separation can eventually ease into other types of separations.

Brief Separations or Time-outs

A brief separation is short-term, meaning that it lasts no more than a few months—usually less than three months and sometimes as little as a week or so—and involves one partner temporarily moving out of the home.

A brief separation would best be described as taking space or a time-out. It means being on your own and having little or no contact or any type of physical connection with your partner for agreed-on, short periods of time. I have seen brief separations in which one partner volunteers to spend a weekend or week with his or her parents, other family members, with friends, or alone, or in which partners take separate vacations to get some space from each other.

If you and your partner are in the middle of a serious conflict, or have just agreed on how to resolve a conflict and one or both of you are still feeling hurt and wounded, or the risk of continued or escalating conflict still exists, a brief physical separation can cool tempers and soothe the pain.

As soon as partners separate, the conflict usually subsides. Brief separations will also give each of you a sense of what it feels like to be apart. In fact, one or both of you may discover that you like to be alone from time to time and can make brief separations a part of your marriage arrangement. These brief separations can be just what you need to get some psychological separation as well.

What to Expect

Being alone and separate often helps people become aware of how they feel, think, and behave independently of their partner. By taking a brief separation, you can become more aware of what you expect from your partner—and whether these expectations are reasonable. You can also learn—and are often forced to learn—ways to be alone, self-nurture, self-validate, soothe, play, fill your time, etc., all of which allow *you* to be and take care of your self. This in itself can be of great value.

You will discover just how comfortable you are on your own. You might ask yourself: "Do I feel sad, scared, angry, guilty, neglected, deprived, or relieved? How much do I think about my partner while I am away? What might my contribution to the conflict have been?"

> The psychic task which a person can and must set for himself is not to feel secure . . . but to be able to tolerate insecurity.
> —Erich Fromm

Making It Work

For a brief separation to work, couples must talk about what they want from it, and terms and conditions must be spelled out, even written down. Of course you and your partner may not agree on terms, and you must recognize that you can't control what your partner does during separation. Some couples will wrangle over where to stay and what to do during this time. Often one partner will use the wrangling as a stalling technique, a way to stay intimately connected.

The Risks

Of course if one of you is very dependent on the other, or is stuck on and invested in maintaining the conflict, that person will naturally resist this form of separation. One of you may feel that taking space really means the end of the relationship. Sometimes one partner will manage being away from the relationship better than the other. This can of course create conflict for the other partner, especially if he or she already feels threatened and insecure about the separation and they are at different places on the Investment–Commitment Scale.

Some people accuse their partners of using the separation badly, for example, spending the separation barhopping with single friends. Some partners may take more space to invest in an affair. How the additional space and time is used is important.

Trial Separations

If your conflict is destructive or very difficult to manage, or one that leads you to believe that the relationship is simply not working anymore, you might want to try a trial separation. Trial separations also involve a physical move, but tend to be more long-term than brief separations. I have worked with trial separations as short as three months and as long as a year or more.

Many couples choose a trial separation after revelation of an affair or recognition of long-term dissatisfaction in the relationship. Sometimes, a person will ask for a trial separation as a cover for an affair or to be free to date, or to soften the blow of asking for a permanent separation or divorce.

What to Expect

If you choose trial separation you must understand that the relationship is at risk to end. I would suggest that you at least not go into the separation expecting that you and your partner will automatically reunite. That decision has to be left open for future consideration, which can be very unsettling and painful for one or both partners.

During trial separations, your goal may not be to work on the relationship, but to work on yourself. So much will be revealed in the course of the separation. You will get a real taste of life without your partner and begin to see what it would be like to permanently separate.

Often one partner wants this type of separation more than the other. One partner may feel an enormous sense of relief at finally being free to be themselves, while the other partner feels fear, insecurity, anger, and rejection. But surprises happen, too. Sometimes the partner who chooses the separation discovers how much he or she appreciates and loves his or her partner. Sometimes the partner who is left is the one who ends up experiencing the greatest sense of relief. In fact, if you ask for a trial separation, be prepared to have your partner be the one to decide to call it quits. I've seen it happen many times. Of course just as often, trial separations may reveal what needs to change in the relationship to make it work again.

Making It Work

Trial separation works best if you really do go out on your own and see what it feels like to rely wholly on yourself (again or for the first time) to think, feel, reassure, and validate yourself. If you move in with a parent or relative, you may simply become enmeshed in another family system and not get the chance to flap your wings. Think carefully about this: you want to experience what it's really like to deal with stress and manage daily living, with or without children, on your own.

It is important to make ground rules and decisions on money, sharing and caring for children, boundaries regarding space, and what is expected of each other during this time. You might want a legal agreement as well (more on this later).

If the trial separation does not result in an improved process of relating and communicating, and you decide to come back together, you run a great risk that your old patterns will continue and the same conflicts will resurface.

One additional note: the idea of being alone for a time can be very frightening. Many couples already have conflict over negotiating alone time. Add the pressures of separation and the conflict can become very intense, triggering additional feelings of betrayal, mistrust, and fear. Whether you are planning to separate or not, I urge you to find ways to become comfortable with time alone. It's a part of life. Take small steps if you have to, such as a solo walk in the park, going to a movie, or eating in a restaurant by yourself. We'll explore this further in Step 8. Keep in mind that if you're feeling overwhelmed by the prospect of being without your mate, you're not alone.

Predivorce Separations

Sometimes it seems clear that you are headed for divorce, maybe because you want out of the relationship, as Margie did in Shutdown

Spouse. Sometimes both partners want out, but quite often one partner feels wounded or resistant to divorce, as Tim did in Shutdown Spouse, while the other appears more determined to leave. The wounded partner may feel unable to survive emotionally, financially, or otherwise without the other partner. In these situations the partner being left is at a much higher risk of emotional pain and hardship than the partner wanting out of the relationship. We could say that a separation has been *forced* on the resistant partner, who is often much more invested and committed than her partner.

If this is the case for you, it is especially important to be clear about decisions regarding caring, sharing and custody of the children, finances, ongoing family tasks, and work, as with all of the other forms of separation. You might need a lawyer's or mediator's help. Mediation can actually be just as effective, and far less costly than an attorney, which is not to say that attorneys cannot be very cooperative and understanding of the complex nature of an intimate relationship as well. It's just that the legal system, by its adversarial nature, can embroil couples for months and years prior to final settlement and divorce. This drawn-out process often delays and diverts work on the self, and sometimes intensifies the conflict. If there are large power imbalances in your relationship, however, mediation may not work.

Combinations

Combinations of separations can include a physical separation along with psychological separation. There may be an in-house separation along with a decision to spend more time away from each other, as in a brief separation. Many times separations can start out as one type (in-house) and change into another (e.g., brief or trial).

> Human beings, by changing the inner attitudes of their minds, can change the outer aspects of their lives.
> —William James (1842–1910)

Psychological Separations

Physical separations alone will not necessarily change old patterns, which require an in-depth look into your self, the relationship, and investment and commitment to change. Whether or not one of you actually moves out, there should be a psychological component to your separation. In fact, sometimes a psychological separation—a shift of focus back to yourself for a while—is all you really need. When we're feeling stuck in nonworking patterns or in the grip of some kind of power struggle with our partners, we often don't see our options anymore. We lose our ability to detach. This is when a psychological separation can be particularly useful.

Individual Psychological Separation

Psychological separation involves looking at and working with *your* part of the pattern. This means temporarily withdrawing the energy you've been putting into a relationship pattern that has not been working and being willing to disengage or let go of any sense of righteousness, the feeling that you've been wronged, or any other complaints you may have. This isn't easy, but it's necessary.

People often resist psychological separations because they're sure that it's their partner who needs to change and that they have no part in what's going wrong. They may also fear that if they withdraw their energy, the relationship will surely fail. They continue hanging onto a sinking ship in hopes that someone or something will save them. The fact is, we all play a part in the dynamics of our relationships, and it's very important that we turn our attention to ourselves from time to time.

What to Expect

What actually happens during the process of psychological separation? As one or both partners withdraw their energy from a pattern that has not been working, some new space and energy can open up for individuals and perhaps the relationship as well. Imagine that you are in a tug-of-war with another person. After near exhaustion and nobody winning, you decide to let go of your end of the rope. You are now free of the struggle and the other person is holding a limp rope. "Dropping the rope" is the first step in stopping the struggle in your relationship.

Many couples become so enmeshed that one or both believe that only their partner can provide what is wanted or needed. They've lost sight of their ability to validate and care for *themselves.*

Psychological separation involves strengthening your own identity and sense of self. It is a process of getting to know, understand, be, and express your inner self as well as understand your role in your relationship. It may be a time for looking deeply at how you were shaped by your family of origin, and how you are still acting from perspectives, expectations, beliefs, feelings, wants, and behavior that you learned as a child.

Becoming aware of how we relate to ourselves, learning better ways of meeting our own wants and expectations, and strengthening our sense of self can be very empowering. Ironically, realizing that you really can take care of yourself often allows your connection with your partner to change and even improve. At the very least, refocusing on *you* can help you gain insight and clarity into your wants and expectations and how your partner does or doesn't meet them. This, I believe, should be one of the goals of all separations: to become OK with your self, and only then evaluate whether your relationship is working for you.

In our very first couple situation, Mary decided to stop trying to get John to change. She was feeling so burnt out and frustrated from all her efforts to get him to be the type of partner she wanted that she decided to stop beating a dead horse. She chose to separate from the belief that she could make him change and that the only way she could feel better was by John cooperating.

By refocusing her energy on herself, Mary stopped settling for a situation she could not tolerate. Instead, she took the first step to solving her problem. She is working with her side of the dysfunctional pattern in the relationship. She has gotten in touch with her own power and can now decide what to do next in her relationship with John.

Mary is no longer playing tug-of-war with John. She realizes she cannot make John do what she wants and has let go of her end of the rope. Now John has to decide what he will do.

One can see Mary beginning to regain the power that rightfully belongs to her. Through her new decision, Mary has made a shift in her beliefs and behavior that in turn can begin to influence the patterns in her relationship with John. Mary has moved from a defensive position of "I'm OK–John is Not OK," which basically covers her underlying helplessness, frustration and Not OK feelings, to focusing on feeling a more genuine OK-ness with herself.

As I mentioned earlier, relationships can be more realistically understood as circular rather than linear. Seen from a linear perspective, John's behavior *causes* more work and frustration for Mary. But when looked at in a circular way, you can see that John's behavior is met by Mary's anger and critical comments, which in turn affect John's behavior again. Each partner's actions and behavior affect the other's reactions and continue the circle. As in a dance, one partner changing his or her steps will affect the other. The second partner's response will again affect the one who initiated the change.

If you decide to take a psychological separation, it is likely that even small changes in the way one of you behaves, thinks, believes, and feels will affect the circle and process of your relationship. You will see this in couple situations later in this book.

Therapeutic Separation

Therapeutic separation is a working separation that focuses energy back on changing the patterns in your relationship. Therapeutic separation could become a part of any of the types of physical separation, but it could also occur without either partner leaving the home, because the focus is on separating from outdated and limited patterns that are not working in the relationship. Therapeutic separation embraces the goals of a psychological separation, in which emphasis is placed on the individuals' responsibility to work on themselves as a precondition or simultaneous condition of working on the relationship. What distinguishes a therapeutic separation from a psychological separation is that in a therapeutic separation, the very purpose is to improve the relationship, and both partners must agree to undertake the work. Even though there's no guarantee of recommitment, the intention is to work toward improving the relationship as both partners take the opportunity for individual growth and change.

Usually a therapeutic separation is decided on when one person feels out of balance and realizes that he or she must become whole and healthy as a primary condition of improving the intimate relationship. For example, a partner with a substance abuse problem enrolls in a recovery program, and the other partner is in individual psychotherapy. Both partners then attend couples counseling to integrate the individual work into their relationship.

As with all separations, you must decide on ground rules and agreements regarding the care of children, finances, and managing the family tasks. In the next chapter, we'll look at the various issues and areas that should be considered during a therapeutic separation.

Therapeutic separations have the advantage of a mutual decision to work on the relationship with the awareness that both of you have contributed to the difficulties in the relationship and that there is no easy blame. Whether this contribution is 50–50 or 90–10 doesn't matter as much as the realization that both of you have brought the relationship to the place where it is.

Make no mistake, a therapeutic separation is not easy. It requires that you take responsibility and make a decision to grow and separate from the patterns that are not working. This kind of separation does not work when it is being used as a cover for other motives, such as an affair, or if it is an excuse for not being fully honest about wanting to end the relationship. Please understand that it is perfectly OK to be confused about a relationship that has not been working. What's not OK is not being open and up front about the confusion. Therapeutic separations often require a high level of investment even though future commitment to the relationship may be decided later.

Qualities of Separation

Separations also vary in *nature*. Some are cooperative, and others creative. Many relationship separations start out with resistance and a lack of cooperation. However, cooperative separations minimize conflict and proceed more easily for all, including children. Noncooperative separations can turn into high-conflict, contested divorces with increased stress. When partners decide to work together cooperatively, they can begin to listen to each other more and get creative on a separation design with increased options and experiences that can work for both of them. This can allow partners to do a much better job of discovering whether their relationship is working for them.

QUALITIES OF SEPARATION

• **Cooperative:** two partners cooperate on tasks of separation even though initially only one partner may want space or changes in the relationship

• **Creative:** partners use their imagination and vision to create and design the type of space or changes they desire in their relationship

• **Trial union:** partners plan to reunite after a period of consideration

---

Cooperative

Even though partners may differ on the pros and cons of separation, if they decide to work together, they are being cooperative. Any of the above separations except therapeutic separations can be cooperative or noncooperative. Some separations start out as noncooperative but change over time, as the resistant partner experiences some positive benefits of space and time. Other partners may remain resistant and noncooperative the entire time, and sometimes even well after the partners have divorced.

Creative

Partners in agreement about any type of separation can get very creative and experimental about physical time apart and newer ways of relating. They must still decide on terms and boundaries, however. Sometimes partners have no desire for permanent separation or divorce, but simply value "space" in their relationship. Some have agreements about occasionally spending time apart. Some take individual adventures or life pursuits with their partner's blessing. Sometimes taking off for work projects or humanitarian efforts in another community, state, or country, or quests that challenge you mentally and/or physically such as Outward Bound or the Peace Corps, can offer natural space and opportunities to grow and develop. Of course, military personnel and their families are all too familiar with such time apart. Some relationships thrive when given space, and others may be strained by the disconnection. Getting creative about establishing new patterns in your relationship can offer energy and excitement to a struggling relationship, but only if both partners have a solid sense of themselves and agree to experiment with new boundaries, space, and rules.

Maybe you like to go off alone or with friends for a while, just to get a break. Some couples even have an understanding that allows for the formation of other intimate relationships. People may question the commitment in such relationships, but if such arrangements work for the couple, who's to say they're wrong? On the other hand, partners working out "open" relationships of any kind have to be careful that they really do *both* agree to the arrangement.

My point is, pretty much any arrangement can work as long as it is mutually agreed upon and is evaluated from time to time to allow for adjustments.

Trial Unions

After making any of these separations, you and your partner may choose to reunite, and it's important to have a plan for that as well.

Separations temporarily throw the system of your relationship out of balance, and you must handle reentry carefully.

I chose to include trial unions in this chapter because it is usually unrealistic to expect reentry to go smoothly. Even if you are both fully committed to reuniting, one or both of you is probably feeling some hesitation, or the conviction that you will no longer tolerate the type of relationship from which you separated. Making the conscious choice to formalize a trial union gives you the chance to see how well the two of you can manage the old conflicts, communicate, and provide feedback on whether your expectations are realistic or not and whether the trial union is working or not.

I have worked with numerous couples who, after a separation, had differing desires. For example, one wanted a renewed commitment and the other was not yet ready. This difference, of course, creates additional conflict and strain. That's why I suggest that if you do undertake a trial union, you make it time limited and agree upon a date by which you'll make a firm decision to recommit or not.

If you have children I want to caution you against treating the trial union too casually. You may be willing to risk the emotional upheaval and potential disappointment of breaking up again, but your children may be more at risk of developing emotional and behavioral problems if they have to reexperience the breakup of their parents repeatedly. A lot depends, of course, on your children's ages, their degree of understanding of what's been going on in your relationship, and your assessment of how they've coped with the changes thus far.

I suggest that all trial unions start slowly, while you are still physically separated. You might decide to start spending more time together (weekends, overnights, day-long events) in a variety of situations to test new ways of being with each other. Some couples decide to live with each other again, but work on new agreements regarding identified problem areas such as communication, sex, parenting, time apart or together, shared responsibilities, expectations, commitment to counseling, etc. I suggest that you also talk openly about continuing to work on yourselves and the relationship after the novelty or second honeymoon of reunification wears off.

I hope this list of separation types has been useful to you. The way you choose to separate will be unique to you and your partner. Be creative. See what works best, and remember that once you decide on separation things will continue to change. You may need more or less time. New conflicts may arise over the kids, schedules, and logistics.

> Grass may be greener on the other side of the fence—but it still needs mowing.
> —Billboard, Twin City Equipment, Berlin, Vermont

Couple Situation 4: Sandy and Jeff: "The Affair"

Sandy and Jeff are each in their early forties. They have been married for fifteen years, and this is a first marriage for each of them. They have two children, twelve-year-old Sara and fourteen-year-old Paul. Sandy and Jeff have had a fairly good relationship for the first thirteen years of marriage. In the last couple of years, especially as the children have gotten older, Sandy has slowly gotten more involved in her work in a large insurance company. She loves her work and finds less and less time for Jeff. Jeff realizes that he wants more from Sandy, but has difficulty asking her. His resentment to her builds as the distance between them grows.

(Home of Sandy and Jeff)

SANDY: (*with a raised, angry, and shocked voice*) Jeff, what the hell is this? (*throws a greeting card at him*)

JEFF: (*looking embarrassed and reluctant to answer*) What?

SANDY: Are you having an affair with this . . . this Jen?

JEFF: She's just a friend from work.

SANDY: (*becoming really angry and agitated*) A friend doesn't write love and kisses or reminders about the next "get-together." You're having an affair, go ahead and admit it, Jeff!

JEFF: Well, you're never around, and I need *somebody* to relate to.

SANDY: (*starting to cry*) So it's true! (*Jeff tries to comfort her, but she pushes him away.*) You bastard! How could you do this to me?

JEFF: You don't understand . . .

SANDY: (*yelling loudly*) No, Jeff, I do understand. Do you know what this is going to do to the kids, and believe me they are going to know everything!

JEFF: Maybe I should move out.

SANDY: Sure, go move in with your new girlfriend . . . you fucking asshole! Do you know what you're doing to your family because of your selfishness?

JEFF: Sandy, I need you to calm down a little. You know as well as I do that my needs have come in last place with you for a long time now.

SANDY: It's always about your needs, isn't it? What about me and the kids?

Jeff exits the room, leaving Sandy shocked. She thinks, *What do I do now? Oh my God. This feels like a bad dream!*

As Jeff scrambles to figure out what to do, he also feels shocked and numb. He had never intended for this to happen. He believed that Sandy was so busy in her own world of work and the children that she wouldn't care if he had an affair. He thinks about how distant they have been, how their sex life is a joke, and how he's always at the bottom of Sandy's list. He wonders, *How could anyone blame me for this? But they will. Oh God, did I fuck up! What now? I'll get out of here for today and wait until things cool down, then try to talk to Sandy again. What a mess!*

Later that evening, Jeff returns home after being gone for the day.

JEFF: (*mumbling and struggling to find the words*) Sandy, if you want I'll move out.

SANDY: Sure, go move in with your mistress. That will be just great!

JEFF: Can we talk about this?

SANDY: What is there to talk about? (*with a raised and angry voice*) Do you have any idea what you've done?

JEFF: (*also with an angry voice*) Sandy, I know I've hurt you.

SANDY: (*starts to cry, then gets angry and paces the room*) Maybe you should have thought about that before you got involved with that whore from work.

JEFF: (*in a loud voice*) C'mon, Sandy, is that necessary?

SANDY: (*yelling out of control*) What, are you protecting her now? You really don't give a shit about me and the kids, do you?

JEFF: I love you and the kids and don't want to hurt anybody.

SANDY: It's a little late for that.

SARA: (*suddenly yelling from another room*) What's wrong mom?

SANDY: Ask your father.

JEFF: (*stumbling for words and giving Sandy an angry look for involving Sara*) Your mother and I can handle this.

SANDY: What's the matter, Jeff, afraid to tell her the truth?

Jeff leaves the room and begins packing some things to spend the night away from the house. The next day he arranges to move in with a male friend from work for a little while. He occasionally stops by the house to get his things when no one is home. He has had phone contact only with his children. Sandy refuses to talk to him. The children have been told that Mom and Dad are not getting along and that Dad is living with a friend for now. Both children are very upset and keep asking when Dad is coming home. The children can see that Sandy is stressed, not sleeping, and very irritable, which multiplies their fears.

On urging from his male friend, Jeff decides to contact a counselor. At their first session, he tells the counselor the whole story to date. The counselor acknowledges that Jeff seems pretty confused as to what he wants (Level 3, confused–ambivalent).

Jeff tells the counselor that his relationship with Sandy has been distant, without much intimacy or physical contact for some time, and that he has been involved with Jen for about six months. He explains that Jen is a woman at work who has always been very friendly toward him. She's about ten years younger than Jeff and seems to understand him, he says. Jeff explains that Jen has had some lousy relationships with men and sees him as a nice, sensitive guy who really listens to her as well.

Over the months they have spent more time together, but they became sexually involved only recently. Jeff admits that Jen has become important to him. "Right now, she's the only one who is not angry with me."

The counselor asks Jeff if he wants Sandy involved in his counseling. Jeff says it might be important to have Sandy involved because they are not talking, the kids are very upset, and the entire family is in crisis. The counselor encourages Jeff to invite Sandy to the next session. Sandy does not respond immediately but then decides to attend.

A Couples Counseling Session with Jeff and Sandy

At their first session the counselor acknowledges Sandy and Jeff's crisis. He especially validates Sandy's hurt and anger at being blindsided by Jeff's affair.

Sandy is desperately hurting and feels her life suddenly falling apart. When she sees Jeff, she can hardly control her anger and tears, attacks Jeff verbally, and threatens a divorce to get even. Jeff had not told the counselor how worried he was about Sandy's mental and emotional health. She has lost ten pounds in two weeks and does little sleeping. She looks distraught and depressed. Sandy's response to Jeff's concern was, "Bullshit, worried about me! Do you think about me when you're fucking her?" Near the end of the session Sandy says she's had enough and plans to talk to a lawyer.

The counselor suggests that they maintain the physical separation, since he doesn't hear either partner wanting to work on the relationship. He offers to work with them together and individually to help manage the separation and deal with family matters, the children, finances, etc. (Step 5, Terms of Separation). He encourages Sandy to find her own counselor and possibly some medication to help her sleep and cope.

Amazingly, Sandy agrees to come to more sessions. The counselor then works with them on an agreement to set up times for Jeff to see the children. They both spend some counseling time listening to how the children may be struggling and what they as parents can do. He also helps them decide how they will deal with issues such as finances and other family business obligations. They cannot agree on what to tell others, with Jeff wanting to keep things private between them and Sandy wanting to tell everyone, especially close family. The counselor emphasizes how important it is to use their sessions for managing their conflict and not expose the children to their angry exchanges.

DISCUSSION

Jeff and Sandy are in a crisis. Sandy's feelings are so strong that she and Jeff cannot be in each other's presence without fighting. The purpose of their separation is to get physical space because being together is too painful and difficult. Their physical separation was not planned, but happened spontaneously during their initial crisis, the stimulus being Sandy's discovery of Jeff's affair.

Theirs is a predivorce or trial physical separation. They have not yet agreed on its length, but at this point it looks like it will last until a divorce is finalized. Even though Jeff and Sandy are in a crisis and their separation was not planned, they can now begin to think about how to manage their conflict.

They should begin by focusing on themselves, especially Sandy, who is sinking to emotional and physical lows. They can also work on managing the children and family. Jeff has to decide what he will do. Will he stay involved with Jen or end their relationship? Or will he attempt to reconnect with Sandy, if she will allow this, to see if they can reconcile their broken relationship?

Jeff is not without ambivalence. He is involved with Jen, but he is also extremely worried about the effect this has had on Sandy, the children, and many of their extended family members who now know what has happened.

Sandy is experiencing a major depression, as loss of weight and sleeplessness has stressed her physically, emotionally, and mentally. She has difficulty functioning at work and home. She must take care of herself no matter what Jeff does.

The children are at risk for the emotional fallout from their parents in crisis. They are frightened and know what divorce means since several of their friends live in two households with divorced parents. Who will take care of them with their parents so involved with their own problems? Will Jeff and Sandy be able to manage themselves and their family?

Jeff's Next Moves

Jeff decides to talk to a different male counselor alone to help him decide what he wants. He begins to understand even more about why he chose to have an affair and to learn more about his family of origin. He is learning more about his wants, expectations, options, and ambivalence.

Although Sandy and Jeff have not spoken, Sandy wants to believe that Jeff has ended his relationship with Jen. Meanwhile Jen now knows that Jeff has been seeing a counselor with his wife, and she has begun to express her fear that her relationship with Jeff will end. Jeff feels the heat and realizes things were fine as long as Jen didn't put any demands on him. Although his situation was self-created, Jeff is now feeling trapped and responsible for two very unhappy and angry women.

As the weeks go by, Jeff continues to struggle with what he wants and where to invest his commitment. He has wavered from thinking that perhaps he wants a life with Jen, to wanting to rebuild his relationship with Sandy, if she is willing and if it can even work. Jeff is now at Level 5 on the Relationship Investment–Commitment Scale, vacillating between wanting to commit and wanting out.

Sandy's Next Moves

Sandy continues to deteriorate by losing more weight, not sleeping, and having fleeting thoughts of self-destruction to relieve her pain and humiliation, which she has only shared intimately with her mother and a sister. She feels intense anxiety, helplessness, and hopelessness about her future. She worries about whether she will be able to work and care for her children. She obsesses about her future and Jeff and Jen.

After discussions with her couples counselor, she decided to start taking an antidepressant. She secretly wants Jeff to know how badly she is doing so as to punish him and make him feel sorry for her. She struggles with mixed feelings of hating him and never wanting to see him again, and wanting him to hold her and tell her he loves her and is sorry. She obsesses about whether she will ever trust him again. She secretly blames herself because she became so involved in her life and work and neglected Jeff. Her life is in turmoil.

What Happened Next

After about two months Sandy began to take better care of herself emotionally and physically. She reached out to a couple of close friends and family for support and to her counselor and physician for medication and emotional healing. As she began to feel somewhat better, she had to consider her options. Would she ever trust Jeff again? Would she ever get over her anger and hurt?

Three months into their separation, Jeff was still in therapy, where he learned a lot about himself. He realized that his most basic wants were not met as a child and that as an adult he tends to wrap himself up in work so he doesn't have to talk or focus much on his feelings and wants. He realized too that he has struggled with some depression this past year. In hindsight, he wished he had bitched and complained to Sandy about wanting more from their relationship *before* becoming involved with Jen, but it was too late. Would she have listened? He'll never know.

He realized how lonely and angry he felt about begging for close-ness and sex from his wife and remembered thinking to himself, just prior to becoming more involved with Jen, *Fuck you, Sandy, I'll find someone who cares.* Jeff was aware that through all this he really cared deeply for Sandy; in fact, his feelings for her grew once he saw how much he had hurt her. He also realized that things weren't the same with Jen once the affair became known.

With fallout affecting everyone, including the children, Jeff was plagued with regret and guilt over what he had done. He began to obsess over how much he wants to get back to normal.

Jeff decided to end his relationship with Jen and chose to focus his energy on his family. He and Sandy spent about a month being more civil with one another but not ready to talk about what happened or their future. He knew in his heart that this was the right thing for him and the kids, but he worried whether Sandy would be willing to give him a chance and whether they could learn to reconnect and meet each other's expectations and wants. He feared that she would never trust him again.

Jeff finally decided to approach Sandy about working on their relationship. He took a risk and asked her to spend some extended time together to talk.

> Experience is not what happens to you; it is what you do with what happens to you.
> —Aldous Huxley

Sandy was feeling better physically and emotionally after help from an antidepressant, counseling, and support from friends. She was beginning to believe that she could cope with Jeff wanting out of the relationship, but she would no longer beg him to come back or be a victim to his relationship with another. Remember that her inner Child was hurt badly. By coping with one of the most stressful events of her life, and grieving what had happened, she now knew that she could manage on her own. She realized that being rejected by Jeff was a deep, dark fear that she had never really admitted to anyone, including herself. She was unsure about what Jeff wanted. Up until this point neither of them had contacted a lawyer, but with little communication between them, her fear was that Jeff was ready to say that he wanted a divorce.

(At their home, alone)

JEFF: Sandy, I'm afraid to talk with you because I know you'll just get angry with me, but I want to try to work on us. I'm done with Jen and realize I still have strong feelings for you.

SANDY: (*starting to cry and struggling to speak through her tears*) You're such a bastard for what you did...(*long silence*) but I still have feelings for you, too. (*Jeff, also crying now, reaches over to hug her. After months of turmoil, it feels really good to be holding and hugging each other.*)

JEFF: I know I did something really wrong by getting involved with someone else. I feel horrible guilt especially now that I know how much I hurt you. I am sorry! Whether you believe me or not, all I wanted was time with you. I guess I didn't know how to ask. So I got mad. I detached and started to not care anymore. So when someone else showed me some attention, I realized how starved I was. I wanted you to know what I wanted without me having to keep asking. You were always so busy. I just stopped caring and looking to you for what I wanted.

SANDY: (*with tears streaming down her face*) Jeff, I know that I haven't been there for you, and even though I hate you for what you did, I feel it's my fault, too. Why didn't you just scream and holler at me to get my attention? You know how absorbed I get in what I do. But I felt my whole world ending when I found out about her. I've never felt pain like that before. I also realized that even though I didn't want it to happen, I could survive. Maybe I took you and us for granted and needed a wake-up call or something. I realize just how much I want us to work this out.

JEFF: I want the same. I know I have to help you trust me again. I know in my heart that working on us is what I want most.

Jeff and Sandy hugged, cried, and continued to talk. They realized how much they had neglected each other and let stress, work, the kids, and life get in between them. Their relationship had dropped to the bottom of the priority list. They both acknowledged that they had a lot of work to do, but that somehow they were reconnected and the energy they felt was the driving force to get them through this.

Their talk lasted hours, and they were more open, honest, and vulnerable with each other than they had ever been. They were able to listen to each other even though some of what each had to say was painful to hear. They realized that recovering from this crisis would take time and decided to stay separated. They would continue to work on themselves but start actively working on the relationship, too. They agreed they would only tell their children and others once they knew they were on solid ground again.

With the help of counseling they worked on the following:

- Learning to listen to each other and really express themselves. They realized that their real trouble had started a couple of years before, when they stopped sharing their inner selves with each other and connecting regularly.
- Learning to manage their conflict, especially when either of them started to become angry over what had happened. They realized that they hadn't picked up on the fact that there was conflict between them for quite some time. They now understand that being intimately connected to another person, someone who is different from yourself, means that there *will* be conflict.
- Realizing that trust had to be rebuilt. Sandy knew that Jeff still worked in the same building as Jen and wondered how she would ever really know the affair was over. Sandy needed continual reassurance from Jeff that he was reinvested in their relationship and in her. At times she would become overwhelmed with panic and anxiety and get that sinking feeling in her stomach that her

world had just collapsed. This would happen if Jeff was late getting home or took off on a business trip. Jeff was sensitive to this and freely told Sandy that he loved her as he gave reassuring hugs and words. Jeff showed his commitment through a renewed interest and energy toward his wife. He called her throughout the day, especially if he was late and basically accounted for time that he was not with her. He realized and accepted the responsibility for helping Sandy rebuild her trust and shrink her fears.

- Jeff moved from Level 3, confused, to Level 5, a combination, to Level 1, invested and committed. He demonstrated this through his behavior and openness with Sandy and his willingness to work on himself in both individual and couples counseling. It is absolutely necessary for any couple rebuilding after the crisis of an affair that the one who strayed invest and commit fully to working on the relationship and healing the wounds. If Jeff were to remain confused and ambivalent, it would be impossible for Sandy to relax and learn to trust him again. This is a critical process in reconciliations after separations involving affairs.*

Jeff and Sandy stayed separated for about another month. What had started out as a predivorce separation moved to a psychological separation, then a trial separation with an uncertain outcome. They then went through a therapeutic separation to work on themselves and their relationship. Finally, they had a brief trial union in which they spent more time together before deciding to move back in with each other.

Their real work came under the umbrella of recommitment and reinvestment after having decided to work on the relationship patterns that had led to unmet expectations and wants. They were psychologically separating from a dysfunctional pattern in their relationship. They had stopped talking to each other about what each expected from the other, and over time, Jeff, feeling ignored by Sandy, internalized his hurt and loneliness and turned to someone new.

*Credit for ideas:
Abrams Spring, Janis, *After the Affair* (New York: Harper Collins, 1996).

Perhaps there could have been a better way to break this pattern. Perhaps they would have fought if Jeff had pressured Sandy into really hearing what he wanted from her. Perhaps Sandy needed to be confronted about neglecting her own wants and the relationship. But that's not what happened. Instead, Jeff's affair and the crisis created renewed energy to rebuild their relationship.

What About Forgiveness?

When there have been violations within intimate relationships—affairs, in particular, or any kind of pushing away of one's intimate partner—the hurt partner must find a way to forgive before he or she can truly heal and move on. Forgiveness, of course, is more than just words; it means truly letting go of the ongoing anger, resentment, and hurt that have poisoned his or her heart. In *After the Affair,* Janis Abrams Spring discusses many types of forgiveness, two of which are most relevant—and healthy—for resolving intimate violations.

First is *acceptance.* When faced with an unrepentant offender, this is often one's only good choice. When someone's partner won't change, acceptance is the gift she can give herself. Acceptance means letting go of the grudge so it will no longer poison our minds and hearts, and also forgiving ourselves for our part in the situation that caused us harm.

The second type Spring calls *genuine* forgiveness, and it is something the offender earns, at least in part through performing certain acts of repair.

Jeff's active involvement in Sandy's grief and recovery from his affair puts him in the second category. Sandy was deeply hurt, but was able to rebuild trust with Jeff because he showed her that he was there for her and wanted things to change.

Spring outlines the steps the offending partner must take to aid the healing process. These include listening to the hurt partner's pain as she works through it, looking at why he violated his partner in the first place, making a deep, personal, and heartfelt apology, engaging in trust-building behaviors (i.e., deciding to not have contact with the third party and if it happens to let the hurt partner know about it) and calling the hurt partner when he is going to be late or unaccounted for.

She also advises the hurt party to look at how she may be blocking forgiveness from happening, to work on acceptance and letting go of the feelings that surround the violation, and to create opportunities for the offender to help her heal.

In regard to these measures, Jeff fit the bill, which might explain why Sandy was able to heal so well, and they were able to work on their relationship. Of course, many couples have a very hard time with forgiveness—they give lip service to it but don't take the necessary steps, or one partner won't accept the other's apologies. Later in the book you'll read about situations in which partners were unable to forgive and heal.

Jeff and Sandy are still together almost three years later, and both believe they have a good relationship and do a much better job maintaining what they have. Of course, their kids are ecstatic.

Conclusion

In this chapter you learned about the different types of separations. If you are the one choosing to take space, please realize that you do have a choice about how to do it. One type of separation or space does not fit all. Even if space and separation has been forced on you, you too have a choice: the choice about how to deal with the shock, hurt, wounding, betrayal, pain, and anger of what you've been dealt.

Separations force us to search our inner selves for hope, understanding, and strength. In the end perhaps the only control we have over life is taking charge of what is handed to us. After all, it is the inner selves of two people that make a relationship. By working on your self, you *are* working on your relationship. The sooner you realize that, the quicker you can take charge. You must start where you are! You cannot fast-forward. Sometimes you must go back to understand how you became the way you are. Sometimes you get stuck in your pain. The end result is always that you are stretched beyond your comfort zone.

Step 4 Exercise: Types of Separation

1. If you are currently separated or considering a separation, which of the separations I described makes the most sense for you?

2. If you have been separated in the past, what type of separation did you and/or your partner decide on?

3. If a psychological separation is the one you believe you most likely need, what are your goals? What would you like to see change in your relationship pattern or process or in you or your partner? Is your partner in agreement or not?

4. Does the type of separation you are in (or considering) seem to best fit the purpose and goals of your separation? Is this difficult to know at this time? Why?

5. How much does your partner and your level of investment–commitment have to do with the type of separation you decide to take? Is your separation cooperative or not?

It might be useful to revisit these questions again after you've read through the book and seen how the different couples manage their separations.

STEP 5
Deciding on the Terms of Your Separation

Being unclear about the terms of a separation
would be like holding an athletic event without ground rules.
—Anonymous

In Step 4 we looked at various types of separations that can help couples deal with relationship conflicts and enhance individual coping and growth. Step 5 is about adding structure and ground rules to those separations.

Regardless of your age or how much *self* work you've done, relationship conflict creates fear, confusion, and upheaval for all involved. The disruption can take a major toll on family functioning and stress levels. One of the best things you can do for yourself and your family is to give some structure to your separation and make some agreements on how you will run the family during a period of uncertainty.

Even if you are the only one doing the work on the separation, you can still decide on a set of ground rules and terms to help guide you. You can then offer these terms to your noncooperative partner, and many times he or she will come around. If your offer meets with total resistance or is disregarded, that's often your trigger to involve the legal system. Either way, you will at least have a structure that you can follow and you won't feel like such a victim to your noncooperating partner. This kind of disengaging from your partner and empowering of your self is itself a very important part of the work of separating.

As always, all partners, couples, and relationships are different, and the terms of a separation must be tailored to your situation. Some

---

TERMS OF SEPARATION

1. Type of Separation: psychological, physical, etc. (see Step 4)

2. Legal Involvement: whether to contact attorneys

3. Length of Separation: specified period of separation, including review time

4. Living Arrangements: which partner leaves the bedroom, moves to an apartment, etc.

5. Sharing and Caring for Children (or other family members, dependents, pets, etc.)

6. Finances: how each will deal with finances

7. Keeping the Business of Family Going: how household chores and responsibilities, extended family events, birthdays, holidays, etc., will be coordinated and attended

8. Expectations of Partners: how partners will communicate with each other, work on themselves or the relationship, attend counseling together or separately, etc.

9. Other: anything else that is a concern to either partner as the separation unfolds

---

couples use the structure of a separation very informally. They may need, for example, only to discuss or reinforce an existing schedule on how to share and care for the children. Other couples may need to write the terms of separation in some type of formal document. Others prefer some kind of middle ground between the two.

Let's get started by looking at the areas and issues that tend to be most important as possible terms, conditions, and ground rules of a separation.

Terms of Separation

Type of Separation

The first decision to make is what type of separation you will try. As you have seen, this decision cannot always be made to the satisfaction of both partners. Often the partner who has initiated the separation decides on the type of separation he deems appropriate. The left partner is often in a position of either going along or protesting the decision. A resistant partner's decision to cooperate, however, often bodes for a better chance at reconciliation.

Remember, too, that the type of separation you initially undertake may change. Even if you initially agree to one type, you can always decide to change to another.

Deciding on the type of separation you want will at least partially dictate what terms apply. For example, an in-house separation does not require a decision for someone to leave the home and might not even change your arrangements for children, family duties, and finances, whereas if one partner were to leave the home, all of these issues would have to be worked out.

If the partner wanting space insists that her partner be the one to leave the home (as Mary did with John in He's Like a Third Child!), she can expect some resistance and a barrage of angry feelings as well.

Legal Involvement

Most separations do not require legal involvement, unless partners simply cannot agree on terms. In fact, if you can work out basic terms you may not need to involve attorneys at the early stages of separation. I also feel it's best not to start divorce proceedings during this period of separation, nor make any long-term economic or financial divisions or child custody agreements. I have also seen couples draw up an agreement with an attorney that stipulates that leaving the home would not be used as grounds for a charge of abandonment. Though partners may not necessarily want to apply for divorce, they may want to contact an attorney for information.

My basic rule of thumb regarding legal involvement is that you should contact an attorney if

- you have any doubt, concern, or fear that leaving might jeopardize or affect your legal position regarding custody of your children, financial settlement, or any other issue related to a legal separation or divorce;

- your partner is threatening to contact an attorney;
- your partner is threatening to take the kids away, to kick you out, that you will lose all rights to the kids because of your affair, etc.;
- you are being physically, emotionally, verbally, or sexually abused or threatened in any way (in which case I also strongly suggest contacting a domestic violence hotline or battered women's or men's program);
- you have specific questions about what would happen should your separation become permanent;
- your partner files for divorce or legal separation;
- one of you wants to change the terms of the separation and you cannot reach agreement.

If you don't have an attorney, ask for referrals among friends, colleagues, or family who have gone through a separation or divorce. You can also contact your state Bar Association, family court, or legal aid. You can also check with these above agencies to find out your state laws regarding your options from cooperative to contested separations and divorces. Keep in mind that laws vary from state to state.

If you would feel more empowered knowing your legal rights, by all means go for it. You have the right to gather information; it's not the same as filing for divorce.

Length of Separation

I usually recommend a three-month period for a physical separation (trial separation) to start out. This is, of course, open to negotiation. I favor three months because it seems to be enough time to begin to work on stated goals but isn't so open-ended as to leave people hanging. At the end of the three-month period you'll want to evaluate or review the separation to decide whether the initial goals have been met and to discuss what changes you might want to make. At this point you will want to discuss extending or changing the terms of the separation, reuniting, or divorcing.

Three months is also a good period for in-house separations and for couples and individuals working on improving their communication and quality of intimacy (psychological separations).

Regardless of the type of separation you choose, you will want to establish some mechanisms for providing feedback to each other throughout the separation period. If, for example, one of you decides that your investment and/or commitment to the relationship has changed, you should be able to communicate this and discuss its implications for the separation. But one thing I strongly advise is that you not make any final decisions during this time period, even if one or both of you is not working on the relationship.

Sometimes, for example, the initiator of a separation will threaten to file for divorce. Having an agreement in place that you will not make such final decisions during the separation allows you both to go forward with the exploration of wants and differences without such a looming threat.

If your partner has already filed for divorce, of course, this won't be possible, but even with a divorce filed, you can decide to take a three-month separation to experience how it feels to separate and actually be apart. After all, no divorce is final until both parties have signed off on it.

Obviously this agreement on time is as good as the individuals who make it. If one of you realizes that you know what you want and decide to break the time agreement and end the relationship, then that's that, and you'll have to address new terms and goals around permanent separation.

Living Arrangements

If you (or your partner) have decided on an out-of-the-home physical separation, a further decision will have to be made about who goes and who stays. How this gets decided is up to the two of you. There's no magic formula. In my experience, men leave the home more often than women, but more and more women are also opting to move out.

Often the partner who did not initiate the separation wants the other one to leave. When there are children involved, parents may decide to take turns rotating in and out of the home, so the children do not have to suffer too much disruption.

The point is, living arrangements, just like the entire separation experience, seem to work best if they can be mutually decided and agreed upon. Sometimes a partner initially resists but still goes through with it. Sometimes arrangements change to accommodate children. If agreement simply cannot be reached, legal counsel or action may become necessary. Here again you may want to consider mediation.

Sharing and Caring for Children

Probably the most frequent concern regarding separations and/or divorce is how it will affect the children. In Step 6, Talking and Dealing with Children During Separation, I will discuss what parents can do to lessen the impact of separation on children. For now the important issues are that children need contact and continuity with both parents and to be protected from parental conflict. The existing family pattern will often determine how best to do this. The best things that parents can do for their children are

A. learn to manage and control conflict,

B. get children out of the middle, and

C. not use the children against the other parent.

The purpose of this term is to decide how much contact children will have with both parents, especially the one who physically leaves. If the family pattern is one in which only one parent is very involved with the children on a daily basis, you might decide to continue this pattern. Bear in mind, however, that it's never too late to establish a better relationship with children. In fact, sometimes leaving the home makes a parent realize that he or she wants a closer connection to his or her kids. Improved relationships with one's kids can actually be one of the positive outcomes of a separation. Yes, some hurt, angry, and resentful partners will use the children as a weapon in the power struggle or refuse to cooperate with visits. Or the left partner might construe the leaving partner's "sudden" interest in being a better parent as trying to gain an advantage with the children. If there is suspicion or rancor over time spent with the children, it is important to discuss this openly and with a third party (a counselor, mediator, or minister). The trauma potential for children lies precisely in these power struggles.

Other aspects of this term include the following:

- Who will talk with the children about the separation?
- What will be said and how will it be done?
- How will children's questions be answered?

Specific issues will have to be discussed and decided upon as well, such as

- attending children's school and after-school functions,
- sharing holidays and vacations,
- how parents will communicate with each other about their children regarding school, friends, what is happening in the children's lives that affects them daily,
- whether parents will support each other regarding discipline,
- what kind of schedules will work best.

As you can see, this term is also rehearsal for shared parenting should the separation become permanent. See Step 6 for more on sharing and caring for children.

Finances

How will finances be worked out during a physical separation? This will be determined largely by how it is handled in the marriage. As always, the more cooperation, the better!

Of course a physical separation is usually more costly, because it involves financing two living situations. As with sharing the parenting, this also gives partners and couples a rehearsal experience on what a permanent separation or divorce might be like. But, as with sharing children, managing finances can become one more issue with which to fight and have power struggles. Perhaps one partner is closer to the children and the other partner makes more money. You can see how each partner could use that to his advantage.

Trying not to play games or be manipulating during this difficult period could allow both partners to begin to cooperate in a new way. But again, remember, even if your partner does not cooperate, you can still attempt to be fair. Specific issues such as joint or separate bank accounts, new purchases, sharing vehicles, and any and all issues around finances must be considered. Here's a chance for the Adult in each of you to be in charge.

When agreement cannot be reached, you may want to consider mediation or legal involvement.

Keeping the Business of Family Going

If both partners are accustomed to sharing the work of family life, how will this work continue during a period of separation? Specifically, who will handle

- the household chores and tasks, such as housecleaning and outdoor work?
- all the daily, weekly, and seasonal maintenance that must be done to keep a household functioning?

This function could also include how partners will communicate and what will be said to friends, family, and others about the separation. With shorter, in-house separations, you might not want to tell anyone, but in physical separation it is often necessary. Who will attend school and family functions? If both of you attend, how will you handle it? Of course we can't cover every issue that will arise; the point is simply to be prepared to raise and resolve these "family business" issues as they arise. It may come down to decrees—"This is how I will be dealing with this issue during our separation"—but discussion and some cooperation always work better if possible.

Expectations of Partners During the Separation

This issue of expectations is very important and, if not discussed and clarified, can cause major problems. (I refer you to the Relationship Investment–Commitment Scale, page 76, which can help you gauge where each of you falls, as well as to Step 3, Defining the Initial Goals and Purposes of Your Separation, page 73.)

The type and purposes of your separation will often determine whether and how you and your partner choose to have contact during the separation period. If you and your spouse have been in conflict for some time, you can expect to struggle and disagree on these terms. Some partners may decide to have minimal contact. Others will want to continue to have involvement, even while they work on themselves, but sometimes their partner is feeling too blinded by hurt, rejection, and anger about the separation, making it difficult if not impossible to be in contact. In all cases, the best course is to be clear about your wants regarding space, even if you have to wait a bit until your partner's pain has eased.

You should also spell out how much and how often you would like to communicate, either by phone or in person, as well as such issues as what to do before entering each other's living area, even the family home. You should also be prepared to discuss how much, if any, intimate contact you will have, including affection and sex. Nothing must be taken for granted. Even small violations of space can turn into major conflict.

If a partner is angry and noncooperative and wants to continue the battle, violation of space is an area that is often targeted. Again I must emphasize that the purposes and goals of a separation often determine whether partners even spend time together at all.

The partner wanting more space will often be more in control of time together than the partner who didn't want to separate, and this can cause conflict. Sometimes a third party can help with this. When one partner chooses to physically separate so he or she can be free to date, there are always special challenges, and these can precipitate a breakdown in communication and difficulty cooperating on the other items of a structured separation. Whether this desire is kept secret or openly expressed, a decision to date others must be looked at in relation to overall investment and commitment to the primary relationship.

Sometimes the partner wanting space hopes that he or she will still have the option to return to the primary relationship after a period of separation. How the resistant or left partner learns to cope and grow will often determine what happens here. Sometimes the results are surprising. Abandonment can sometimes translate or transform into freedom. I have worked with couples in which both partners agreed that dating was necessary for any chance of future reunification, and I have worked with couples who decided that no dating was ground rule one. I have seen couples come back together who I never thought would reconcile, because both partners worked hard on themselves during the separation. I have worked with people who at first resisted separation and then blossomed when off on their own.

One other issue that requires some agreement is who and how much to tell about the circumstances surrounding the separation, especially if it involves an affair. How much should kids, other family members, and friends know? Sometimes one partner chooses to tell all, while the other hopes to contain the spread of information. A third-party mediator or counselor can be helpful here as well.

> There is more to be learned on one day of discomfort, poverty, and anxiety than in a lifetime of apparent happiness, security, riches, and power.
> —Anonymous

Other

Any issues particular to you that have not been covered above, as well as those that emerge as you go through the separation experience, fall here.

As you cope with the conflict, agony, and uncertainty of separation, creative energy deep within the human spirit can surface to enable you to grow and develop in ways you never thought possible. I believe in the resilience and willpower of human beings, and I know that there can be much growth from the hardship of a relationship separation.

Read the following couple situations to see how they managed through purposes, types, and terms of their separations.

Couple Situation 1: John and Mary: "He's Like a Third Child!"

Like many couples who have been engaged in ongoing conflict and seem stuck, Mary and John are not in agreement over whether to separate. Remember that Mary has actively worked on reducing her stress and her anger at John. In order for her to do this, she has had to separate and detach from her unmet expectations.

Mary is also working on self-care, such as learning to manage her anxiety and take more time for herself. Through all this conflict, she realized that she had the power to make herself feel better and no longer wanted to be so dependent on John for her happiness.

Considering the different types of separations, which do you think Mary chose? If you said psychological separation, you are right!

In realizing that she could separate from her belief and not have to be held hostage by John's lack of sharing the responsibilities of family life, Mary still had the work burden, but no longer felt so sorry for herself and let go of some of her anger at John.

Mary went one step further. She realized that she did not like John very much anymore. This realization concerned her deeply, but she wanted an active partner in her marriage and family life, and she wasn't going to settle. Mary decided that she needed time away from John.

Mary knew she would have to continue to work on herself, but with John not showing any signs that he was willing to do the same, her investment and commitment to John changed as well. She decided she wanted a physical separation. However scary it was at first, Mary knew this separation would be beneficial to her because she was already learning so much, but John felt forced into it and wasn't at all sure that the separation would be good for him.

The question Mary wanted John to consider during their separation was whether he was willing to rethink the way he had behaved in the relationship thus far. She let him know that she would not accept knee-jerk responses or false promises.

Mary believed that physical separation made a statement to John about the necessity of change. She knew that she could only work on herself and that she couldn't force John to change. It remained to be seen whether Mary could recover any positive feelings for John.

John was starting from scratch. He would have more thinking and feeling to do about himself, his marriage, and his family before any decisions could be made.

The following are some of the terms that John and Mary decided upon during their separation:

Type of Separation Mary referred to her separation as a trial separation because the outcome was uncertain. She was already in counseling and actively working on her own psychological separation from those frustrating and dysfunctional patterns she had developed with John. She was not ready to decide whether she wanted to leave the marriage permanently, and realized that she had more work to do to separate from the power she had given him to make her feel OK or Not OK.

John was clearly the resistant partner in this separation. He was angry and scared. He complained that Mary had made a unilateral decision and protested that it would permanently damage the kids, but underneath he was afraid that his relationship might be over. He loved his kids and did not want a divorce, but he knew he had to deal much more seriously with Mary's requests and the feelings newly aroused by the experience of separation.

Legal Involvement John and Mary agreed not to seek a divorce just yet and not to involve lawyers in their separation.

Length of Separation Mary decided that three months was a good initial separation period, and that no decision on divorce would be made until the three months had passed. She also decided that they would review their arrangement after the initial period.

Living Arrangements Because of the children's ages—three-and-a-half-years-old and six months—Mary decided that it would be best if she remained in the home. Even though John did not want a separation, he did agree that the children were closer to Mary and, at their ages, needed to be with her more of the time, so he reluctantly agreed to move out. He talked to one of his brothers and a single friend about moving in for a while. He decided to move in with his friend.

Mary asked that John work with her to set up the rest of the terms so they could continue to manage the children and household. Again, he reluctantly agreed.

Sharing and Caring for Children John and Mary both wanted the children to have as much time with John as possible, so they decided on a schedule in which John could see them almost every day after work. He would spend more time with them on weekends, and his daughter would spend at least one overnight a week with him.

Finances At least to begin with, John and Mary agreed to continue to share finances as usual. John knew it would be more costly for him to live outside of the home, but at least living with a friend or family member would not drain their finances too much in the short run.

Business of Family After John moved out, Mary made a list of all the household chores and responsibilities—yard work, housecleaning, auto maintenance, and paying bills—that she had been doing by herself and presented it to John. She noticed that although John had been resistant to the separation, he did cooperate with her on this list. Secretly she appreciated his interest and involvement, but she remained guarded, realizing it was too early to assess whether he had changed and careful not to set herself up for further disappointment.

Meanwhile, in taking on some of these tasks, John came to appreciate all the work Mary had been doing around the house.

Expectations of Partner Soon after he went to live with a close friend, John indicated that he wanted to start spending time with Mary. Mary decided that while it would be OK to see John when he came over to play with the children or to take care of household responsibilities, she needed to continue to have some distance from him and their conflict. John was frustrated and felt he was losing his connection with Mary, who now seemed to have all the power.

Mary, of course, felt guilty for forcing John out of their home, but she also liked the idea that he was beginning to feel the effect of her taking charge. She also knew that spending time away from John gave her the only real chance of reviving positive feelings for him.

Mary further decided and told John that they would have sexual or physical contact only if or when she felt better about him and the relationship. For this first phase of their separation, they would only talk about the children, family tasks, finances, etc.

Mary was clearly saying that she needed a break from John. She made it clear that other than at scheduled times she and John would spend no time alone together, though they discussed the possibility of going on family outings together. Both had no intention of dating other people.

John and Mary's extended families already knew they were having conflict, so it was not news that they were physically separating. Both families were worried that this would lead to a divorce. Mary tried to reassure them that divorce was not their intention, and that the separation was intended to help them reduce conflict and rethink whether they still had mutual goals and commitments. Another of Mary's goals was talking and listening to each other better. Whether this would eventually become a mutual goal would have to be looked at later.

Other: Telling Their Young Daughter Mary and John sat down with their oldest child, their daughter, and explained that Mommy and Daddy were going to take a time-out from each other for a while. They both reassured her it was not her fault, that she had done nothing wrong, and that both of them loved her a lot. With tears in his eyes, John continually hugged his daughter while they talked. He felt sad that he would not be at the home more of the time, but he reassured his daughter that he would see her every day and talk to her on the phone.

John was beginning to get in touch with how a permanent separation might feel, and he already did not like it.

The six-month-old child simply needed continuity of contact with his parents. He was too young for explanations about their separation, but he and his sister already benefited by the reduced conflict at home. Other than a schedule of sharing and caring for the children, and a list of shared responsibilities around the home, most of this agreement between John and Mary did not have to be written. What wasn't clear at this point was how seriously John would embrace Mary's requests to share the work. John knew he was on "probation" in Mary's mind and that some cooperation with Mary's decisions was his first test. Mary was impressed with how well John was cooperating thus far. Whether this would result in any permanent change was still unclear.

Later in the book you'll find out how John and Mary move through their separation experience.

EXERCISE

What are your thoughts about John and Mary's separation agreement?

Would you include anything different if it were your agreement?

Couple Situation 2: Tim and Margie: "Shutdown Spouse"

Remember that Margie was finally carrying out a decision to separate from Tim. Even though she felt terribly guilty about leaving, since she had taken care of Tim for so many years, she realized it was time to care for herself. They had avoided conflict, and meaningful intimate communication was nonexistent. At this point Margie appears to be at Level 4 ("I've decided to end the relationship.") Although Tim seems to be at Level 1, his actual investment has fallen far short of Margie's expectations.

Tim seems to be quite dependent on Margie and is obviously resistant to a separation. Let's pick up their situation where we left off, in the counselor's office. The counselor is attempting to get them to decide on the terms of their separation.

(Tim and Margie in their counselor's office)

COUNSELOR: Have you decided who will leave the home?

MARGIE: For the sake of the kids, I think Tim should leave, but he has not said he will.

TIM: *(Puts his head in his hands and starts to cry. Everyone is silent.)*

COUNSELOR: *(after a pause)* I know this is very sad for you, Tim, but for now let's focus on where you can go to live.

TIM: *(after a long silence)* I have nowhere to go.

MARGIE: Your brother or mother will gladly take you.

TIM: *(silent)*

COUNSELOR: Would you be willing to talk to them, Tim?

TIM: *(reluctantly nods his head yes)* I'm a burden to everybody.

COUNSELOR: When would you like to see this happen, Margie?

MARGIE: In a couple of weeks. We need to talk to the children right away. I know they'll be upset when they find out that Tim will be leaving.

Type of Separation Initially Margie was so ready to get space from Tim that all she wanted was a permanent separation or divorce. Her need for an immediate divorce seemed to ease after Tim left the home.

Legal Involvement Because children are involved, the counselor encourages Tim and Margie to contact a lawyer to get more specific information on each partner's rights before Tim leaves. Tim has no interest in contacting a lawyer at this point, and Margie feels the same.

Length of Separation The counselor suggests they separate for a three-month period and then review how things are going. The counselor knows that Margie is not planning to file for a divorce right away and is willing to wait to see how time and space will affect their relationship.

Living Arrangements Tim reluctantly agrees to call his brother to discuss staying with him for a short time, and his brother says it's OK. Margie and the kids will stay in the home.

Sharing and Caring for Children The counselor also helps them set up a schedule for Tim to see the kids. He realizes that Tim hardly spends time with them now but hopes that this might change. Margie welcomes having Tim spend as much time with the kids as possible, although she is concerned that he not dump his troubles on them or try to make them feel sorry for him, and that he not drink when he is with them.

Margie proposes a schedule in which Tim would spend some weekend time with the children and even see them after school at home, at Tim's brother's house, and at neutral places. This time will have to be coordinated with their natural father as well.

Finances Margie expects that she will have to get by on her paycheck and continued help from the children's (natural) father. She also realizes that she may have to work extra hours to make up the difference.

Tim will have to manage to survive on what he earns.

Business of Family Margie does most of the work around the home and will continue to do so. At this point she does not have any expectations that Tim will start to share responsibilities.

Margie also realizes it may be more difficult for Tim emotionally to visit the home and have to leave again and again, so it would be better if he not be there much for now.

Expectations of Partner Finally, they discuss their expectations about seeing each other. Margie does not want to see Tim outside of family matters that concern him. The counselor realizes this will be hard and very painful for Tim, who suddenly wants much more contact with Margie.

Margie proposes that they meet once a week to discuss any issues that come up. She agrees that they can call each other to share information or discuss any of the terms of their separation.

The counselor establishes a plan to continue to see them weekly through the separation process and to monitor all the terms of their agreement. He will also see Tim alone to work on individual goals. He is concerned about how Tim will cope.

Other: Talking to the Kids about the Separation

COUNSELOR: What do you want to say to the children about your separation?

MARGIE: The kids know that we have not been getting along. Both of them have asked if we are going to get a divorce. I think we need to tell them that we are separating to get space because we are not getting along. They understand this because they do the same with their friends and each other when they are having problems. I don't think we have to mention divorce until that's finally decided upon.

Margie's answer gives Tim a ray of hope, and he looks up at her.

COUNSELOR: It is best if you both can talk to them together, either each child individually or both at once.

TIM: (*with a low voice and sniffle from crying*) I'm afraid that I might break down in front of them.

COUNSELOR: This is a sad experience for everybody, and I believe it is OK to show feelings around the children. This gives them permission to feel whatever they might be feeling, too.

The counselor goes on to talk about how the children might react and the importance of keeping in touch with them emotionally during the separation process. Although he says this to both, he realizes that Margie will probably carry the ball.

They choose a date on which to separate, and the counselor talks about possible scenarios for Tim leaving. He encourages involving the children in the actual transporting of some of Tim's belongings to his brother's. He talks about how it would be hard if Tim's things were suddenly gone when the kids came home from school and encourages Tim and Margie to prepare the children by talking to them and providing information. It helps that the children already know Tim's brother and like to visit him and his children.

An Emergency Call Regarding Tim

The night after Tim moves out of the house the counselor gets an emergency call from Margie, who tells him that Tim is at his brother's, has been drinking, and is having an emotional—perhaps suicidal—crisis. The counselor is finally able to get Tim to speak to him on the phone.

COUNSELOR: Tim, tell me what's happening with you?

TIM: (*sobbing on the phone*) I can't do this. This is too hard for me.

The counselor determines that Tim's brother and his girlfriend are home in another part of the house. Tim says he cannot sleep and that he can't live without Margie.

The counselor talks with Tim, asks how much he has had to drink, and tries to determine whether Tim's at risk for self-harm by asking him straight out (remember, they had a no self-harm or suicide agreement).

The counselor then asks to speak with Tim's brother. After they talk for a while, the counselor feels assured that the brother is aware of the severity of the situation and capable of handling it. They discuss going to the local ER or calling 911 if Tim gets worse. Talking with the counselor allows the brother to think through options to help Tim cope through the night.

The counselor then gets back on the line and assures Tim that he can cope with his pain and that it will pass. He also makes an appointment to see Tim the following day.

Next Day, the Counselor's Office

(*Tim looks exhausted, sad, and passive.*)

COUNSELOR: Well, Tim, I'm glad you are here. Let's talk about how you coped and how you can continue to cope.

The counselor takes a lot of the responsibility for Tim's learning to care for himself. He does this by scheduling additional appointments for Tim and being available for Tim on the telephone during crisis times. He makes sure to reinforce the no-suicide agreement Tim made with him. He then discusses Tim's drinking and the negative impact this has on his ability to cope. He also arranges for Tim to attend an AA meeting. Tim complies.

The counselor sees Tim three times that week. When he next sees Tim and Margie together, he focuses on how the separation is going and whether the agreed-on terms are working. When Tim expresses anger at Margie for throwing him out of his house, the counselor acknowledges that it is a positive thing that Tim can express anger openly. He explains that this is part of his grieving process. (Remember, Tim's pattern is to stuff his feelings.)

The counselor continues to see Tim alone for the next three months. The crisis calls ease, and Tim begins to actively cry and grieve his separation. He starts taking an antidepressant that allows him to feel feelings and not just be numb and flat.

Three Months Later, at an AA Meeting

TIM: (*looking a little better, is able to talk more openly about his experience*) I guess I was very depressed for a long time. I'm beginning to feel some energy. I'm on an antidepressant. But I'm so sad about my family, and I miss Margie so much. I decided that I was not going to kill myself. My counselor says it will get better, and, slowly, it has. But the ups and downs aren't great. I'm tired of feeling so bad. I realize that I haven't been much of a husband or father. I feel so ashamed of myself. I come to AA meetings about three times a week and actually talk some about me. I haven't had a drink in three months. Six months ago, I would never have thought this was possible. I guess I needed my life to crash before I did anything about it.

I feel so bad about how I was. I don't blame my wife for dumping me. I think our chances of getting back together are slim, but in some strange way I feel like I have more of me back. I do more with the kids, and I am so happy I didn't take my life. I still have a long way to go, but I can at least see some light at the end of the tunnel. I've met a lot of nice people at meetings who seem to really care about me. My counseling has also helped me see how little I got from the family I grew up in. I guess I'm rediscovering that "inner kid" in me and learning how to "parent" myself. I still feel overwhelmed with anxiety, fear, and loneliness. But I am taking one step at a time.

Margie, Approximately Five Months Later, Sharing Her Experience with a Friend

MARGIE: I'm glad I did what I did. It helps that Tim's making progress, of course. I am rediscovering a life of my own. I am involved in dance classes, painting classes, and I have decided to take a course toward a bachelor's degree. At first the kids were very sad, and we had a period of time when Tommy stopped doing homework, and his grades fell. He almost jeopardized his graduation from high school. He started to see a counselor, and that really helped.

What was especially important was that Tim got very involved when Tommy needed help. He set up Tommy's appointment with the counselor and even went with him the first time. Tommy's dad also got more involved in his life. I have to tell you, it was a real surprise seeing these two men who normally don't get along pulling it together through Tommy's crisis. What a relief for me. Tommy was mad at me for months for breaking up the family, but we have started to talk again.

At first Jennifer started losing a lot of weight and really scared us. It helped to talk to our doctor and nutritionist. She also had a good relationship with a school counselor.

> It is one of the most beautiful compensations of life that no man can sincerely try to help another without helping himself.
> —Ralph Waldo Emerson

I guess I thought separating would be good for all of us, but it was even stressful for me. I've started going to a women's support group. It feels good to talk about me for a change, and it helped me realize that I needed to save *me* and not everyone else. At a very early age I learned to take care of everybody; I was like a little mother. It's really hard—and really good—to stop all that. Tim and I have started to talk a lot, probably more than ever before. I actually like him more now, but I feel it is way too soon to even think about getting back together. It feels like years since we separated, but it's only been a few months. I know our entire family needs to continue to work on ourselves . . . but the urgency is gone, and I'm happier. I'm in no rush.

One Year Later

Almost a year since Tim and Margie first separated, they remain apart. Margie has begun dating but still thinks about the possibility of reconnecting with Tim. They actually have a closer relationship now, and the communication has improved a great deal. Their communication is focused on their individual growth, development, and lives and not as much on their relationship. Both are doing a good job of co-parenting.

Tim has a new, full-time job in a lumberyard. He rents an apartment, is still sober, and attends AA twice a week. There appears to be no pressure from either Tim or Margie to change their situation.

DISCUSSION

Tim and Margie are an example of a couple whose relationship was very stuck in a destructive, noncommunicative pattern for a long time. Because they did not fight openly and their conflict was hidden from others outside the family, many people were surprised that they had separated. Their conflict was internalized within each of them. Tim drank away his feelings, and Margie took care of everyone to the point of burnout.

This relationship was not helping either one of them develop individually. Meaningful, intimate communication about their inner selves had become nonexistent.

Although their separation started as a predivorce separation, it turned out to be a trial separation, with the possibility that they would reconnect. Tim and Margie both needed to focus their energy on themselves, which they now do.

Tim and Margie's Goals

Tim's goals were sobriety and dealing with his depression. When he gave up drinking, he had to deal with the lifelong accumulation of feelings of shame, guilt, and poor self-esteem. His suicidal thoughts illustrate perfectly what can happen when one spouse is too dependent on the other and borrows his identity from his partner.

Tim has finally begun to get in touch with, express, and learn how to deal with the volume of shameful feelings he has carried with him most of his life. Tim's depression, anxiety, alcohol abuse, and withdrawal were very much involved with the beliefs and bad feelings he has had about himself. Remember the words *bad* and *good* are parental words. They usually are programmed into children at a young age, and have much to do with family and society's socialization process and moral development. Guilt and shame are often the result of your own inner critical Parent. Nonconstructive or self-destructive behaviors are often sought to avoid these shameful feelings, but usually reinforce the belief that we are in fact bad! It is important to reflect on those deeper inner feelings that we attempt to avoid and deny, and understand how we keep them operating within ourselves. We can begin to challenge ourselves to believe and feel differently and actually lessen the intensity and duration of these feelings.

Margie's goals were to refocus on herself. Her parts in keeping the relationship so stuck and unsatisfying were taking care of Tim and neglecting her own educational and social needs and desires. She had to learn how to enjoy all those things she had put off while taking care of others. Her decision to separate, and the work she then did on her own, improved the quality of her life a great deal. Although relationships are bigger than either partner, each partner forms and nourishes the foundation for their relationship. It's interesting to note that as each of their selves improved, Tim and Margie's capacity to communicate and relate to each other at a more intimate level also improved.

As a result of their separation, both partners also involved others in their lives more, which helped break their isolation. Taking space allowed them to reconnect with themselves, which paved the way to increased intimacy and connection with others.

As you've seen throughout the chapter, terms of separation can be simple, brief, and informal, or complex, lengthy, formal, and written. Terms can be any issues or areas that are important to the individuals and couples or that come up during a separation. No matter how things resolve, the process of negotiating terms is very useful for a relationship. It requires couples to provide at least some structure to their separation, clarifies their expectations, and provides the blueprint for later reconciliation or divorce agreements.

Terms of separation helped put structure into Tim and Margie's separation. Margie initiated the separation, and Tim reluctantly agreed. As usual, Margie, with the help of a counselor, planned most of it. If she had not pushed counseling and moving forward on working the terms, a separation might not have happened or would have been filled with more crisis and upheaval to all.

Terms of separation establish the specifics of how a separation will be carried out and in what order. Also, terms of separation further clarify the expectations and responsibilities for all concerned. The terms of separation take a vision for change and make it into a real, working, problem-solving process by deciding who, what, when, and how a separation will happen. Separating without terms often creates more conflict, power struggle, and confusion.

In Step 6, you'll look at examples of how parents in various types of separations have helped children cope with the effects of a separation. These examples highlight special issues to consider if you have children.

Step 5 Exercise: Decide on What Terms Are Necessary for Your Separation

This exercise can be done alone or with a partner.

1. If you are considering or are currently involved in a separation of any kind, are there terms for your separation and are they clearly stated?

2. Would you have used an agreement to decide terms of your separation if you had one?

3. How can getting clear on terms guide the process of changes you want in your life and your relationship's life?

4. If you have already separated with terms, how are they working? Have they helped you and your family? Which terms were more difficult to carry out? If there are no terms or they are not working, how has this affected you and your family?

STEP 6

Talking and Dealing with Children During Separation

You may strive to be like them, but seek not to make them like you.
For life goes not backward nor tarries with yesterday.
You are the bows from which your children as living arrows are sent forth.
—Kahlil Gibran

Often the issue most important to parents experiencing conflict or considering separation or divorce is the effect on their children. Parents often want to know how a separation will affect their children, both now and in the future, and usually want to protect them as best they can. Whether the separation was forced on them or they initiated it, most parents feel a tremendous sense of responsibility, concern, and guilt over causing damage to their children. In a sense, this takes us back to Step 1. Research literature and my own clinical experience make it clear that ongoing and unresolved conflict between parents, whether living together or separated, can have the most destructive impact on children. That's another reason why managing the conflict is so important.

Parents must agree to keep a boundary between their adult issues and their children and not expose their children to or involve them in the active conflict. This boundary also proscribes what can be said or inferred about the other parent. Of course, by virtue of living in the same environment and household as their parents, children will observe and feel the tension and conflict in the home. But parents can mitigate the effects by actively deciding to control and manage what children hear and what they are told during conflict and fights.

You may be wondering if it is too late if your children have already been exposed to too much fighting and information. My response is it's *never* too late to stop and change the pattern. Yes, some harm may already have been done, but anything you can do to reduce the stress will ultimately be for the good. Even only one parent working to reduce the conflict can have a positive impact on the children. The starting point is to take charge of yourself. Now!

How Parental Conflict Affects Children

When relationship problems and conflict become severe enough and continue for long enough, the whole family and household environment becomes increasingly stressful. Adults begin to worry more. They may become more anxious, depressed, and short-tempered. Even if parents have been very good about keeping boundaries between their conflicts and their children, children can often sense the tension. Infants and very small children usually *feel* these changes. Older children will have a better cognitive grasp of what's happening by observing changes in their parents' attitudes, moods, feelings, and behavior.

Just when the children need the most support, parents are often least able to give it. As parents struggle with their own difficulties, children will sometimes not receive the attention and comfort they may need. As parents worry and become depressed over the threat of a marriage ending, their patience for listening and dealing with children's issues may suffer. What parents can begin to do other than limit and stop the conflict is to get the support they need from other adults. Do everything you can to continue taking the children out of the center of your conflict!

Ground Rules

Parents considering separation need ground rules. The more difficult it is for a parent to maintain self-control, the tighter and more effective the ground rules must be. It must be emphasized, too, that ground rules and other methods will not, of themselves, stop the conflict between two angry, frightened, hurt, and disappointed people. Only the parents can make this happen. Behaviors that will help form a boundary between parents' conflict and their children include the following:

1. No Fighting and Arguing in Front of or Within Hearing Distance of Children If partners need to express anger and other negative feelings with each other, they must find ways to do this away from the children. The satisfaction of knowing that the damaging effect of your conflict is not being played out in front of the children will bring dividends for a long time to come. This will also set the stage and establish a model of how two parents can still be co-parents whether separated or even divorced.

If partners cannot agree not to fight in front of the children, then contact between partners should be limited until more control can be established. To establish a boundary regarding open conflict around children, I have had parents make agreements such as the one found in the Co-Parenting/No Conflict Sample Agreement.

CO-PARENTING/NO CONFLICT SAMPLE AGREEMENT

We agree not to fight or argue openly in front of or within hearing distance of our children. If an argument begins, each of us has the right to call time-out when either of us believes it has gone or is going too far and/or has become nonconstructive or destructive. Time-out means all talking and arguing stops immediately even if one parent believes it was unnecessary. One or both of us can leave the room or area without the other following, or continuing to talk or yell. We will attempt to communicate within twenty-four hours to decide if the issues around the existing conflict need to be discussed. Either partner may call a time-out. The partner who calls a time-out (a T sign with your hands) has the responsibility to contact the other partner. Contact can be made in person, by telephone, voice mail, e-mail, letter, etc.

---

2. No Negative Talk About the Other Partner in Front of the Kids When people are hurt and wounded by their partner's actions and decisions, it is a natural reaction to lash back and want to get even. One of these ways is to get the children to take sides. Things are said like "Your father has abandoned us for his girlfriend"; "Your mother doesn't love us anymore!"; "I don't understand how your father could do this to you!"; "That bastard/bitch doesn't care about anybody but him/herself!"

SAMPLE AGREEMENT TO SUPPORT THE OTHER PARENT

Regardless of what either of us believes to be the truth, circumstances or causes regarding who is responsible for our relationship problems and separation, we have a mutual responsibility to continue to protect our children and be the best possible parents that we can be. We recognize that although we may be hurt, angry, disappointed, feel violated, etc., by unfair behavior on our partner's part, we will strive to support and not do anything to negatively affect the relationship between our children and the other parent. We recognize that children need both parents and even though the future of our relationship is uncertain, a relationship with the children should continue. We will not share negative information about the other parent that could damage the existing relationship between the children and that parent. If there are questions about what children should and should not be told, or the best way to tell them, we will educate ourselves through reading, parenting courses, and counselors. We will make every effort possible to separate our personal feelings and beliefs about our partner and support the relationship between the children and the other parent.

Although it is perfectly natural to feel angry and hurt, it is not appropriate to tell or share these feelings with children. I recognize that this is easy to say and difficult to do, especially for the partner who feels wounded, betrayed, or blindsided and believes separation is totally unfair. Restraint can be especially difficult for a wounded parent in the early stages of separation when emotions run high and there is chaos and crisis in the family system. At this early stage it can even be too soon to consider boundaries, because parents are struggling with their own emotional survival. However, parents have an obligation to their children to do their best to gain control of the situation.

No matter what the issue, the purpose of establishing a boundary is to leave the children out of it. I sometimes hear parents say that children should know the truth. The only problem I see with this is that the "truth" is never completely unbiased, and children often have limited perspective. Parents must make every attempt not to put the other parent down or to share negative information about that parent with or in front of children. This does not mean you should keep children in the dark, but rather you should not overwhelm them with information and worry that they are not ready to handle.

Over time, children—especially older children and teenagers—will often find out more about their parents' conflict, such as the existence of an affair, and they may need help in understanding their discoveries. This can be very challenging for a parent. I believe that the parent who is responsible—for example, for the affair—should be the one to help the children process it.

It is, of course, up to you to decide how to apply these principles to your family situations and how to adjust them to your children's maturity levels.

An agreement to support the other parent can be verbal or written. It can also be tailored and modified to deal with your specific circumstances. Of course there are some family circumstances and situations that are beyond the scope of this chapter and book, such as an already-strained relationship with one's kids, families with special-needs kids, the existence of abuse or violence in the home, dealing with stepparents, or a parent who has a substance addiction. If your family is experiencing these or other challenging circumstances, I would encourage you to seek professional help or a support group, or at least read about your situation for support and help.

Safeguarding and protecting your children from the harmful effects of separation may be the most important and fulfilling thing you can do in these difficult times.

The Impact of Physical Separation on Children

In my experience, parents working on psychological separations, in-house separations, and even brief physical separations can usually continue to parent without disruption. It is the physical separations in which a parent moves out of the home that can often create the real challenges with and for your children.

Helping Children with Their Fears

Anyone who is separating from a valued relationship or has lost a loved one experiences some fear, and that includes children. Children often fear most that one or both of you will leave them, too. Even if children do not communicate their fears, parents should expect their children to have them.

Children express their fears in many ways. Younger children may regress in their behavior and start bed-wetting, thumb sucking, being afraid of the dark, having nightmares, and becoming more clingy to parents and caretakers. Daily partings for school, day care, or a baby-sitter, may become more difficult. Older children and adolescents will tend to act out more, withdraw, or isolate. Grades may drop, and kids may have more difficulty or begin having troubles at school. Chances are you already know what is normal for your child or children; this is a time to stay especially tuned into them to see how your separation may be affecting them.

What children need above all is extra reassurance that your relationship with them is for life. This is especially so during and after an actual physical separation. The nonresident parent should do everything possible to maintain regular visitation and regular telephone contact (even voice and e-mail contact). It is said that parents may separate and divorce each other, but they should not divorce their children.

Of course we want this to be true, but there are circumstances in which a parent who has left the home does reduce contact with children—most often dads, but moms do it, too. Whichever parent is living with the children must do the best he or she can to spend time with them and reassure them. This can be hard if that parent is also working and taking on more overall responsibility for the family *and* struggling with his or her own emotional turmoil over the separation. It's easy to see how tempting it would be to blame and attack the other parent for neglecting the children and abandoning the family.

You are entitled to feel how you feel, but remember to form that boundary with the children. If you need to express and work through your feelings, find others to do this with, not the children. Instead of just feeling guilty about what your separation may be doing to the children, do what you can to comfort, reassure, and build a better relationship with them during this stressful time.

Talking to Your Kids About the Separation

Under the best circumstances, both parents should tell their children about an upcoming separation, and only after there is a plan as to how it will happen. In preparation, parents must evaluate how each feels about telling. If the very idea of it brings up exceptionally strong emotions for either parent, more time may be needed before talking with the children.

If at all possible, children should be told sometime within the month prior to separation, and certainly more than a week before. It is ideal to tell children together, but I have found that older children often ask more and different questions that are beyond what younger children need to know, so telling them separately may be appropriate. That's going to have to be your call.

What children need to know most of all is where the leaving parent is going and what kind of contact they will have with that parent. I strongly encourage the noncustodial parent to maintain some daily contact with children after physical separation.

Some separating parents believe that they will best protect their children by not telling them what is happening. I strongly advise against this. Just imagine the feelings that might come up if your kid came home from school one day to discover that Dad or Mom had moved out! It's simply not fair. It is critical that you give your children accurate information about any events that will affect them, especially advance warning that a parent will be moving out of the home.

Of course there is no exact formula, but it is important that you offer reassurance, comfort, and information about what is happening. Children will then be reassured that you are in control during this unpredictable time.

I have seen parents and children cry together during these talks. Sometimes parents look sad, scared, or angry while telling children. Children may have the same feelings, which is perfectly normal. Communicate with your children as much as possible, offering them comfort and helping them handle their questions and fears.

Here's a sample of what you might tell your children with both parents present (of course, you will want to use your own words and tailor what you say to the age of your children):

Mom and Dad have decided to physically separate and live apart for now. As you may know, we have had a hard time getting along lately (or we have not been happy together, or Mom needs some time on her own, etc.) so we decided to try to get some space and distance from each other. Dad/Mom will be leaving on (date and time) *and will be in his/her own apartment* (or living with whomever). (In the case of separation but not divorce:) *We will be doing this for x months and then deciding what to do next.* (Reassurance that you are not abandoning them:) *We both love you very much and (parting parent) will see you regularly.* (Share the schedule.) *You can call (parting parent) anytime. You may feel sad, angry, or scared about this right now. We feel those feelings also. It is not your fault(s) that we are separating. This is our decision and responsibility and has nothing to do with anything you have or haven't done. We are separating from each other, not from you.*

Children may or may not have questions during this explanation time, and their questions can be difficult or even impossible (or inappropriate) to answer. Saying that these are complicated and adult matters that Mom and Dad are continuing to talk about and don't have all the answers to yet will let children know that the grown-ups are in charge. When in doubt, contact a counselor or family educator or do some reading on the matter.

When the Ideal Isn't Possible

Sometimes it is simply not possible for both parents to be there to tell the children. That's OK. It can certainly be handled well by just one parent. You can follow the same format. If your children have lots of questions, you can direct those back to the parent who left or agree to tell that parent that his or her child has questions.

Each and every situation is different. The main thing to remember is that it is better for children to be informed about what is going to happen than to be left in the dark.

Handling Children's Questions

Children will often ask whether their parents are going to get divorced. It is best to use simple statements about the truth and reality: "Mom and Dad will be separating for (weeks/months)"; "We are going to see if we can get along better during this time and not fight as much"; "We are going to work on our relationship while we are apart [with or without counseling]"; "We are going to get divorced" (if in fact this has definitely been decided); or "We know this may be hard for you to hear and understand, but we don't know right now whether or not we'll divorce."

Helping Them Cope

I have found that children tend to use one or both parents as their model for coping. They will watch and experience how parents cope and follow their leads. Sometimes children will not show any signs of distress until their parents are coping better. They don't want to add to their parents' burden.

Of course children are often frightened and scared or even angry about separations, just like their parents. Parents need to address, accept, and acknowledge these feelings. If you are having difficulty getting in touch with or expressing your own feelings, you may not be aware of your children's feelings, or their attempts to deny or discourage them.

As you work on allowing your own feelings, you will often start to recognize and allow them in your children as well.

We cannot insulate our children from the real and unpleasant experiences of life, but we can help them learn and build coping skills that they will have the rest of their lives.

The Role of Other Adults

Sometimes parents are simply unable to tend to their children's emotional needs. In such cases a grandparent or family friend can step in and become the supportive adult for the kids. You might involve a counselor or a minister, priest, or rabbi. The important thing is that children have continual involvement with a trusted adult. That's why it's so important to share information about a separation with our children's caretakers, teachers, coaches, other family members, and with friends and their parents. These people can be supportive as well as monitor children in a variety of settings over time to see how well they are coping.

Moving Day

Moving day is often very stressful for everyone. Some people choose to involve their children in the move, others choose to move when the children are not around. Some parents have found it helpful to have both parents visit the new living quarters with the children. What you decide to do will depend on the level of conflict management and communication (Steps 1 and 2), how well each parent has coped and accepted the separation thus far, and the type of separation and whether it offers any hope for reconciliation.

What to Tell Others

After a parent moves out, children often have more questions. They may need help deciding and practicing what to tell others who may know or find out about the separation and ask questions. Responses should always be tailored to what the child needs and feels comfortable with. A simple yes may work, as may "I don't know"; "It's none of your business"; or "Ask my parents." Some kids will want to give a brief and truthful explanation. These responses can be practiced at home in preparation for school or social events.

Before providing your child with pat responses, it is important to find out what he or she fears about being asked. The child may, for instance, feel helpless about what to say, or afraid he or she will cry in front of friends. Try to find out as much as you can about these fears as you help him or her prepare.

Helping Them After the Move

Consistency is often kids' number one concern. Some children do best with a posted weekly schedule so they can get a concrete idea or picture of what will take place from Monday through Sunday of each week. Others will be fine with just a basic schedule, for example, "You'll be with your dad Wednesday nights and weekends for the next three months."

Dealing with Children's Fantasies

Many children have fantasies about reuniting their parents. This is perfectly normal. They may even try to manipulate the situation to bring you back together. Sometimes, especially in struggling relationships, children have already had far too much power in dividing parents or manipulating closeness. If this is the case in your family, you can expect it to get worse during a separation. Again, think of the inappropriate power a child might feel knowing she can split up her parents or bring her parents closer.

This can also be an issue for the parent who resists the separation and wants reunification. This parent may be tempted to encourage the child to urge the other parent to return home. I have seen this play out in many ways, for example: "Call your father and tell him how much you (we) miss him at bedtime"; "Ask your father to join us for dinner tonight"; or "I become real sad when Mom won't stay over after dropping you off." I would like to emphasize that children are never responsible for their parents' separation or divorce, and should never be put in the middle like this.

Children are self-focused; they tend to believe they are the center of the universe. Therefore, many children blame themselves for their parents separating. Even though a child may never say this, he or she may think and believe it. When asked, "Why do you think your parents separated?" many children, especially young children, will respond, "Because I was bad or did something wrong." If a child actually wished one of his parents would leave or was angry with a parent, it makes sense that he or she might feel responsible for the problem.

It is important to attempt to get children to express their true deeper feelings of blame and guilt over their parents breaking up. Their distorted feelings and thinking should be corrected so as to minimize the chance of them carrying their baggage into their adulthood and relationships.

Parents who intentionally make a child feel responsible in any way for the separation or divorce should be aware that this can be severely damaging to a child's development. If one parent expects the other parent's behavior and actions to be detrimental or abusive to children, I recommend that that parent consider contacting a child or family therapist or counselor to gain insight and help with the situation.

Creating a Safe Space for Feelings

Creating a climate in which your children will feel open and free to express their feelings is most important of all. Just as you can ask, "What do you think caused Mom and Dad to separate?" you can also ask, "What is the saddest, scariest, or angriest thing about Mom and Dad's separation?" If you have trouble hearing how sad, scared, or angry your child is, you may need help understanding and accepting these feelings in yourself.

Accepting and acknowledging feelings—your children's and your own—allows them to be worked through much more quickly. Bottom line: the best way to help your children through the feelings and experiences of a separation is to help your self.

Now let's return to John and Mary to see how they dealt with their children regarding their physical separation.

Couple Situation 1: John and Mary: "He's Like a Third Child!"

As you will recall, John and Mary have been married for five years and have two children, three-and-a-half-year-old Denise and six-month-old Dan. Mary feels that John doesn't and won't share the responsibilities of parenting and caring for a home. John has reluctantly agreed to Mary's request for a separation. John is hurt, scared, and angry. In spite of these strong feelings and John's resistance to separation, he is cooperative.

John and Mary both realize that their children, being so very young, would not be able to understand the meaning of "Mommy and Daddy are going to separate." They also realize that their children could and would feel the tension and stress generated from the ongoing conflict.

When they would openly quarrel and yell, Denise would become very upset and tell them to stop or they would get a time-out, a method obviously used with her when she acted out and misbehaved. As they learned to control their conflict (Step 1), John and Mary both noticed that Denise seemed to relax more and become less demanding of their time. They knew that she would have a hard time with her daddy leaving. Their son, Dan, being just a baby, had no concept of what it meant to have his daddy leave the home. He simply needed to be dry, warm, fed, loved, and played with.

About a week before John was going to leave, he and Mary sat down with Denise and told her that Daddy was going to be staying at Uncle Jim's house for a while. John explained that he and Mary were going to take a time-out from each other for a while so they could learn to get along better. John and Mary were surprised that Denise seemed to accept this just fine, which actually helped them feel less guilty about separating.

The weekend of the move, they had Denise help out. She got to see where Daddy would stay and sleep. She continued to do well until bedtime the first night John was gone. With all the preparation, what was real for her was that Daddy was not there when she went to sleep. No matter what Mary did, Denise cried and cried and would not stay in her bed. Mary tried to call John so he could talk to Denise and calm her down, but John was not available.

In hindsight, John and Mary realized it would be helpful to have John there for a few days at bedtime. For about a week John showed up at bedtime each night, then one night he explained to Denise that he would not be able to come the next night but would call instead. When they talked at bedtime that next night, Denise fussed and cried some and tried to get John to come over, but after about a week or so of John alternately showing up and calling, Denise seemed to settle down. Denise also spent quite a bit of time with him at his new "home."

Dan spent much less time with John because of his age and attachment to Mary. But as John kept his time commitment to both of his children, he began to realize how much he missed them.

During the times John had the children alone, he began to appreciate how much work was involved in taking care of them. This actually gave him a new appreciation for Mary, but he was not quite ready to share this with her.

EXERCISE

1. What do you think and feel about how John and Mary handled their children regarding their separation?
2. What else would you have done in their situation?

DISCUSSION

Although they were not in agreement on whether to separate, John and Mary were able to be there for their children. They realized they had to work together as parents, and this was especially demonstrated when John made himself available at Denise's bedtime. Even though Mary wanted and needed space from John, she realized how important John's presence and relationship were to Denise and was more than cooperative as they adjusted their schedules to better meet their kids' needs. When John was at home, he and Mary made a point not to fight openly or quarrel in front of the children. They managed to maintain a good boundary to shield their kids from their marital problems.

Couple Situation 5: Dennis and Pat: "I Have Feelings for Somebody Else."

Dennis, thirty-six, and Pat, thirty-four, have been married for ten years. They have two boys, Matt, age eight, and Jerry, age six. Over the past year, Dennis has distanced himself more and more from Pat. Pat finally realized something was very wrong and got up the nerve to confront Dennis. Dennis admitted to having feelings for another woman. This plunged Pat into a crisis. She became depressed and anxious. She knew that they had grown apart and their communication was lacking, but another woman in his life was too much.

Dennis tried to protect Pat from the whole truth by not providing details about his involvement with Sue. The truth was, for over eight months he had been romantically involved with Sue and had become totally consumed by the relationship. Pat knew about Sue, but had been made to believe that Sue was Dennis's confidante and nothing more. Dennis refused to talk much about this and avoided any intimate conversations with Pat about his feelings. The bomb finally dropped when Dennis told Pat that he wanted a separation so he could figure out what he wanted to do.

Pat became consumed with thoughts of Dennis leaving her. She frequently expressed her anger at Dennis and attempted to even the score. The conflict had become so extreme that Dennis and Pat could not be in the same room for long without starting an intense argument.

Dennis and Pat contacted a counselor. Dennis was at Level 3, confused–ambivalent, or 4, wanting to end the relationship. But while his investment and commitment to Pat were minimal, he was very committed to his boys. Pat was at Level 1, still very invested and committed and hoping Dennis would change his mind. Dennis wanted a counselor to help them reduce conflict and manage a trial physical separation. Pat wanted a counselor to confront Dennis about how irresponsible he was being and to make him work on their relationship.

Because Dennis and Pat could not manage to work together to tell their boys about their impending separation, they decided to have a family session with their counselor to break the news. The boys did not do well with the information. Both cried and Matt ran out of the counseling room. While Matt was out of the room Pat blurted out to Dennis in front of Jerry, "See what you're doing to us!" Dennis looked sad and guilty but said nothing.

What Dennis didn't know was that Pat and the boys had been talking quite a bit about his decision to separate. She had secretly vowed to use the boys to get even, and even though down deep she knew this was not right, she justified her actions in the knowledge that the affair was not fair or right either.

Pat had a lot of difficulty maintaining a boundary between how she felt and what she told the boys. When she talked with friends about Dennis she was not at all good at checking to see if they were around. On several occasions the boys overheard her screaming that the "son of a bitch is probably out fucking his girlfriend right now." Matt was angry with his father, and Jerry was scared and sad.

Matt knew he could get attention from his mom by consoling her and joined with her in anger about his dad abandoning them, but down deep he really missed his dad and just wanted everything fixed. His grades dropped, and he seemed to be in more trouble at school than ever before. He looked more and more tense and angry. Pretty soon the only thing he and his mom talked about was how angry they were at his dad.

Although Matt initially honored the visitation schedule with his dad, he started to make excuses for not seeing him. Pat supported this. She would call Dennis and yell, "How could you blame Matt for not wanting to see you after abandoning us all. You better not have my kids anywhere near that bitch!" Dennis tried to get her to see the necessity of a boundary, but she insisted that it was all his fault.

Jerry continued to see his dad but felt really mixed feelings in regard to his loyalty to his mom. He could not tell his mom how much he loved and missed his dad, because he knew how angry she was at him. When he was with his dad, he felt confused and sad over the separation. He spent a lot of time alone and didn't seem to laugh anymore.

We'll pick up Dennis and Pat's story in Step 8 to see how Pat managed her grief.

EXERCISE

1. What are your thoughts and feelings about Pat and Dennis's story? Could you identify with either of them?

2. Is Pat justified in involving the children in their conflict? What would you do regarding the children if you were Pat, or if you were Dennis?

3. Any thoughts on how to repair this situation at this point?

DISCUSSION

Dennis and Pat's story illustrates what can happen when two parents can't manage their conflict and are not working together. Pat was so blinded by Dennis's actions that she could not maintain a boundary or a perspective about the children. She felt so crushed that she was willing to get even any way she could. Without any power over Dennis's decision, she resorted to the children to punish him. Her actions seemed to make an already stressful situation worse for the children.

Couple Situation 6: Amy and Fred: "I Think I've Outgrown My Relationship."

Amy, forty-one, and Fred, forty-five, have been married for fifteen years and have two children, Jane, thirteen, and Doug, eleven. Amy and Fred are also experiencing escalating conflict around an affair. In their case, it was Fred who was feeling very wounded by Amy's new relationship with Joe.

Amy is an artist and has long felt that Fred isn't interested in that part of her life. She has tried talking with him about it, but he doesn't seem to respect her for having other passions. Over the years, Amy has met many artists, who are a lot more like she is. Enter Joe, who is also an artist. Joe and Amy's intimacy grew as he validated Amy's work and her identity as an artist.

After struggling for many months, Amy knew she needed more space from Fred. With support from Joe, Amy told Fred she wanted to separate. Initially, Fred resisted, but Amy insisted it was their only choice. Their children were confused and caught in the middle. They had not seen their parents openly fighting that much and were suddenly aware of all the tension in the home. No one said anything about Amy's affair with Joe.

As Fred became more depressed, he considered telling the kids about Amy's affair, but Amy asked him to respect her right to tell the children on her own, if and when that became necessary.

After a couple of weeks of trying to change Amy's mind and feeling more depressed, angry, and desperate, Fred finally decided to go for counseling. Amy decided that she would talk with the children after she found another place to live. She invited Fred to speak with the children with her, and he reluctantly did. Amy started by saying, "You kids already know that Daddy and I have not been getting along. I'm sure you've heard us arguing with each other. Well, we've decided to separate and live apart for now. I've taken an apartment in town. I believe that taking space from each other will allow us to cool down and get along better. We both love you very much and do not want to hurt you by doing this. We know you kids are already upset and we are hoping that by getting space we can make things work more peacefully around here."

Fred, fighting back tears, said, "I'm going along with this for now but I want you to know that I feel very sad about it." When Doug saw his dad crying, he began to cry, too. Jane asked if this meant they were getting a divorce. Amy looked to Fred who said, "For now we are just separating to figure out what we will do. We have not decided on a divorce." Amy nodded.

Amy then reached over to hug and comfort Doug, who was still crying. Jane looked impatient and asked if this family meeting was over. Amy explained, "Things will feel sad, scary, and confusing for a while, but Dad and I will tell you what will be happening in the days and weeks ahead." She explained that this was an adult problem in Dad and Mom's relationship and that they (the children) had absolutely nothing to do with their decision to separate, and it was not their fault in any way. She reassured them that she would continue to be actively involved in their lives and invited them to see her new apartment that Saturday. Doug stopped crying.

Amy and Fred both seemed to do better after telling the kids about the separation. Fred held onto the thought that as long as there was any chance of Amy returning home, it was best to cooperate.

EXERCISE

How is Amy and Fred's separation story different from Dennis and Pat's? What do you think made a difference?

DISCUSSION

Fred was devastated and angered by Amy's decision to get more space. For a while he wallowed in his feelings and imagined getting revenge by telling the children about Joe. He even tried to contact and confront Joe. He continually hounded Amy to talk and reassure him that there was still hope. Amy did not feel or believe there was hope. After some initial nasty arguments with Fred, Amy learned to disengage. She refused to get into knockdown, drag-out fights with Fred. Whenever Fred would start an argument, she would up and leave (time-out but without an agreement to return to talk later). Amy, like Dennis in our last example, was confused and somewhat ambivalent (Level 3), while Fred, like Pat, was at Level 1 (invested, committed, and wanting to work). Fred struggled between feeling helpless and depressed and getting really angry and wanting revenge.

Fred was just starting a grieving process and had started working on his underlying feelings of sadness and fear in counseling. His counselor had discussed the benefits of medication as a safety net if Fred felt he was sliding backwards and needed a jump start to get out. Fred resisted since he was starting to have better days, but knew he could exercise that option if need be. Even though he was hurting a lot, he also realized that using the children would not bring Amy back. Cooperating with her need for space seemed like his best choice.

What Happened to Amy and Fred and Their Kids

Even though Amy and Fred had made an agreement to share both the children and the finances as they had always done, Fred, in anger, began to withhold money and make excuses for why the children couldn't see her. When they were with Amy alone, the children were able to be the kids they were. They would often do fun things together or start art projects. Secretly, both children enjoyed staying with their mother but felt guilty about it because Dad was home alone. When they were with their dad, they experienced his profound sadness and hurt. This would in turn trigger their feelings of sadness about the separation. They wanted so badly to have their family back together, but, like Fred, Jane and Doug didn't have any control over this. Doug seemed to identify more with his dad and cried a lot. He was beginning to experience depression and started to isolate himself more. He watched a lot more TV, played more video games, and began to gorge on junk food.

Jane coped by trying to act stronger and not focusing on her parents' problems. She started spending more time on the phone with her girlfriends and hanging out with boys. When she was with her dad, she took on the role of "little mother." Fred secretly liked being cared for by his daughter, although he was well aware that he still needed to be her parent and not the other way around.

In desperation he would tell Amy how she had ruined the family and screwed up the kids. Amy responded by threatening to file for a divorce. She told him she was really not ready to do this but that if he continued to bully her she would. This seemed to scare Fred into cooperating. He figured that as long as she didn't file for divorce, there might still be a chance at reconciliation.

Fred continued in counseling. The counselor could see that Amy wasn't going back to Fred, so his goal was to help Fred continue the grieving process and learn to take care of himself. The counselor explained that Fred might be having anticipatory grieving, the type of grieving one does in view of what *might* happen, which allows us to emotionally prepare for the inevitable. Fred agreed that at times he would grieve heavily, but he was also still in a great deal of denial about his marriage being over.

This kind of limbo period seems to serve the person leaving the relationship quite well, but not necessarily the one being left. It gave Amy time to be sure she was really ready to part, but for Fred it was slow torture. He was fearful of a final decision because it would mean their relationship was over. On the other hand, he wanted the pain to stop. He couldn't fully grieve without a firm decision from Amy.

Most people need a sense of finality before they move on. This was certainly the case for Fred. It took months before he accepted the fact that his relationship as he had known it was over. What seemed to help was a letter he received from Amy about three months into their physical separation.

In the letter, Amy reassured Fred that she would always love him and the family they'd created. She emphasized that they had simply grown apart over the years and that they were really different now. She insisted that she had not left him for another man, and that she intended to stay unattached for the time being. She reinforced their continuing roles as co-parents. Finally, Amy said that she was not coming home and had decided their separation was permanent.

While the letter dashed what little hope remained for Fred—he contemplated shooting himself—it was the finality of the letter, the closure to a long period of limbo, that allowed him to get on with grieving and putting his life back together.

After reading Amy's letter Fred sobbed and sobbed. He made a call to his counselor. It felt good to have this trusting relationship and someone to talk with. The counselor was able to acknowledge Fred's grief and to reassure him that the intensity of his pain would ease. He suggested gently that perhaps Fred didn't really want to die, just to end his hurting. Fred made an appointment with his doctor to discuss medication. His doctor prescribed an antidepressant and some sleep medication as well. Fred's doctor consulted with Fred's counselor regarding their patient's suicide risk. The doctor only gave Fred a very limited amount of sleep medication so Fred would have to return to obtain more. This was repeated until Fred felt more solid with himself and his risk of self-harm decreased. Fred also made a no self-harm/suicide agreement with his counselor. Fred had never reached out like this before to anyone. He had always thought of himself as very independent, and he never really focused on his inner self. But he simply had to learn to mend his broken heart. With a lot of counseling and the help of medication, his depression slowly lifted, and he found ways to move through his painful feelings by changing his hopeless beliefs into more hopeful ones. He also struggled through being bored and lonely, especially when the kids were with Amy.

Many people suffer from depression associated with grieving the ending of relationship. Taking medication is of course optional. It is totally up to the individual. I usually discuss the pros and cons of its use when people struggle with functioning—for example, not being able to sleep, get out of bed, work, cope with their children—or if they seriously consider self-harm as a way of coping. Some people feel medication interferes with the grieving process. But if you become overwhelmed with how much pain, depression, and anxiety you are experiencing, medication can be a useful jump start to help you regain hope so you can deal with your feelings. Also, chronic stress can affect the chemistry in your body and brain. If you feel overwhelmed with pain, depression, and anxiety, consider talking to your counselor and doctor or psychiatrist about the use of medications. Many people suffer needlessly when help is available.

As Fred felt better, he blamed Amy less and accepted more responsibility for himself. He even began to agree that they had grown apart as their life goals had taken different directions. About a year after she left, Amy finally decided to file for divorce. Although Fred was in a much better place by then, he still saw this as the final straw and once again slid into a depression with some fleeting thoughts of suicide. However, this time he did not stay with the feelings and saw them as old responses that he did not need to act on.

As Fred improved, he became increasingly concerned about Doug. Doug had been withdrawing from his friends, his energy was always very low, and he seemed to get sick more often. It was also a major chore to get Doug to do any schoolwork, and he missed many days at school. Finally Fred took Doug to see his counselor.

Doug took easily to the counselor since he knew his dad was already going and liked the guy. Doug worked with the counselor for a couple of months and gradually seemed to return to his old self, although he still wished his parents weren't divorced.

Jane seemed to avoid any painful feelings around her folks breaking up by continuing to act like a little mom. She didn't want counseling and seemed to identify more with her mother. Jane had the advantage of talking about the situation with her mom, but she still felt she had to take care of her dad and didn't want to burden him with any negative feelings.

As the active conflict between Fred and Amy stopped, the children seemed more at ease. As Fred improved emotionally and began to live life again, the children also responded positively.

Children will often cope with separation and divorce as well as, or as poorly as, their parents do. The trouble is, parents' perceptions of how well their children are doing can be unreliable. The partner who is leaving tends to minimize the kids' problems in order to avoid feelings of guilt, whereas the partner who is being left will sometimes overestimate how poorly the children are doing, projecting their own distressed feelings onto the children. Friends, family, and school personnel (guidance counselors and teachers) may be more objective, and this is another reason why it is important that they be informed about the separation.

Amy continued to have some contact with Joe throughout the year, but eventually the excitement started to fade. Amy had read about how the romance stage of a new relationship often ends and disillusionment sets in. She thought this was what was happening with Joe. She started to see more aspects of Joe's personality that she did not like. She knew she would always be grateful that being with Joe had allowed her to get up the courage to make a major change in her life, but she also realized that the relationship was transitional.

At this point Amy had no driving desire to be permanently involved with anyone. She just felt better than ever about her new life and her stronger sense of a free self. She loved her freedom. She knew that whomever she chose as a new partner would have to love this free self and not try to control it or find it threatening. She realized this might be a tall order. For the time being, Amy wanted to enjoy her freedom.

Over time Fred began to do better, too. He cooperated with all the conditions of the divorce and felt much stronger for having coped with his broken heart. Through his therapy he came to realize that although it may be normal to be hurt and wounded when a relationship ends, his suicidal thoughts pointed to a greater need to learn to love and strengthen his self.

> Pain makes man think. Thinking makes man wise. Wisdom makes life endurable.
> —John Patrick

What had started out as Fred's worst nightmare had become the very stuff to make him learn about his innermost self.

For Fred the ongoing task of learning to identify and deal with the many dark feelings he experienced as he learned to take care of and love himself shed a lot of important light. He can now see his controlling and jealous behavior as his own insecurity and has begun to think that maybe Amy was right to leave him. How could anyone be happy with the way he was? Fred now even thinks about getting more socially involved. He feels he has learned much about openness and intimacy in the last two years and has hope that he will meet a woman with similar values with whom he can share his new growth.

The separation between Amy and Fred had the potential for an all-out war. Luckily, Amy's move and refusal to engage in destructive fighting with Fred kept the children from the worst of the separation. There's no question that the children suffered through this separation—and the ever-sharper contrasts between an excited mother and a defeated father. If there was initially any hope for Fred and Amy, Fred's controlling behavior and his use of the children to lure or blackmail Amy back into the relationship served to push her further away. That's why my very best advice to people who are being threatened with a partner's decision to leave is to work on themselves and not try to coerce or manipulate their partner into staying, as tempting as this may seem at first.

> If your dependency on another person is strong enough that losing him or her would make you consider taking your life, take steps to work on your self now!

Attempting to understand what happened and letting go of the partner who wants to leave not only provides the best chance of salvaging whatever may be left of the relationship but gives you far more solid ground to stand on in the event of permanent separation.

How Fred and Amy Used the 10 Steps of Separation Management

1. Amy and Fred did not do well controlling the conflict between them until Amy moved out of the home. Although this was seen as a defeat for Fred and very difficult for the children, it did serve to end the daily battles.

2. Fred and Amy did not communicate well. Each partner had to turn to others (Joe for Amy, the counselor for Fred) for validation. It was only later, when Fred was able to cope better, that he was

able to at least talk to Amy about the children and the logistics of separation and divorce.

3. The purpose of their separation was to free Amy from the relationship. Needless to say, it was not decided upon mutually.

4. Their separation started as a trial and then moved quickly to a predivorce separation.

5. Although Fred initially began to manipulate things regarding sharing the children and finances, he eventually cooperated as he felt better and realized the manipulation would only hurt the children.

6. The children had a very difficult time with the separation and the distance between their parents. But as the conflict eased, and especially as they saw Fred coping better emotionally, they started to do better in all ways also.

7. Amy's self work, in her words, was to be true to herself. Fully aware that people might be harshly critical of her, she decided that she and only she could make this choice. She chose to turn to herself for validation and minimized the need for validation from others. It was validation from Joe that jump-started this process for her. She struggled with guilt, which is common, but she was determined to leave a relationship that she felt she had outgrown.

   Fred's core challenge was to learn to accept what had been forced upon him by Amy's decision to leave. Fred learned that Amy's leaving did not mean his life was over. It made him realize that he was too emotionally dependent on Amy. After getting through the lowest point in his life, he learned there was life after Amy and that he could make himself OK. Maybe he wasn't what she wanted any longer, but he was still OK. Fred learned he had the capacity to cope with a broken heart and find his self in the process.

8. Evaluation and final decisions were not difficult here. Amy knew what she wanted. Her time apart from Fred allowed her the direct experience of finding out what it was like to live on her own

and be free. And she liked it! If she had had a change of heart, she most likely would have approached Fred with a proposal for reconciliation; some partners do.

Fred had the bigger challenge. Like many people in his situation, he felt he had no options. There may be no options regarding reconciliation with a partner not willing to work through the relationship, but there are always options regarding how to cope.

Fred could have easily chosen to stay depressed or turned to alcohol or drugs; he could have isolated and turned bitter or quickly found a replacement for Amy. He could have decided to commit suicide. Instead, to his great credit, he discovered that he *could* cope. He could get through his pain and learn more about his self in the process. He learned coping skills that he would be able to use the rest of his life.

Fred is an example of someone who learned to let go of the anger, resentment, and grudge that he had with Amy over her leaving him. He could have held onto this anger and let it poison him well into the future. His letting go was not dependent on getting anything back from Amy. It was more of an acceptance and forgiveness of himself and his role in the breakup of his marriage. As he let go of his shameful feelings inside, they no longer consumed him, and he was able to get on with his life. Of course this takes work, but it is possible for everyone. Perhaps he will someday find a more compatible partner.

EXERCISE

See Ground Rules for Talking, page 17.

1. Can you identify with Amy? Can you identify with Fred?

2. Have you been in either situation with a partner?

3. Do you think Amy had good reason to leave Fred?

4. Should Amy have listened to others in making her decision, or was she justified listening to her self?

5. Should Amy have tried to work on the relationship with Fred before getting involved with Joe?

6. Do you believe that Fred would have ever worked on himself had he not been wounded by Amy?

7. Given the difficulty Fred had coping with the end of his relationship, how do you think he managed in dealing with his children through this experience? What advice would you have given him, and what would you have done differently in talking to and dealing with the children if you were Fred or Amy?

In sum, one of the key tasks of managing your separation is dealing well with your children. Step 6 emphasizes the things parents can do to help their children:

- Reduce or stop the destructive conflict that children are exposed to.
- Agree to set up or strengthen the boundary between parents' conflicts and their children.
- Agree to support the relationship between the children and your spouse regardless of how you feel about each other (this excludes abuse of any kind).
- Understand that children have fears and will blame themselves for their parents' separations.
- Be aware of and acknowledge children's fears of being abandoned and blamed.
- Reassure, comfort, and correct faulty assumptions and beliefs that children have about parental separations. Children are never at fault!
- Give children accurate information about what will happen to them and their parents during and after the separation process.
- Stay involved with and spend time with children throughout and after the separation. Maintaining and improving a relationship with a child during separation and dealing with questions and fears is the best insurance a parent can provide to help a child cope with this major life event.

Finally, if you have questions, concerns, or specific issues or challenges, get professional help! It is available.

Step 6 Exercise: Raise Your Awareness of How to Talk to and Take Care of Children During Difficult Times in Your Relationship

1. Have you and your partner made a plan about what to say and how and when to talk to your children about your separation?

2. If you are separated or thinking about separating, what have you learned that could help in talking and dealing with your children?

A Final Tip for Those Already Separated If you are unhappy with the way you worked with your children, stop now and begin to deal with them in a way you believe to be better. There's no point dwelling in the past!

STEP 7

Carrying Out
Your Decision to Separate

Change has a considerable psychological impact on the human mind.
To the fearful it is threatening because it means that things may get worse.
To the hopeful it is encouraging because things may get better.
To the confident it is inspiring because
the challenge exists to make things better.
—King Whitney Jr.

If you have turned to this step without reading the preceding ones, I would urge you to go back and think through the many factors introduced earlier in the book.

Many couples try to skip the planning and go right to this implementation step without much preparation. In my experience, however, considering each step of the process—being able to control conflict (Step 1), communicate enough (Step 2), focus on the purposes (Step 3) and types of separations (Step 4), and knowing your plan for the issues of separation (Step 5)—more often leads to a smoother transition for partners, parents, and children (Step 6).

Even if your partner refuses to cooperate and you are alone in this, taking *all* the steps will lead to a better ultimate result for everyone.

And even if you and your partner have already taken an initial physical separation to control your conflict, I encourage you to look at all the steps to ensure you have tools for dealing with the ongoing and painful emotions and sometimes complicated purposes and issues of separation.

Unless you are in a situation in which there is violence or abuse and immediate action is called for, it is almost always best to resist the impulse to separate without a plan.

By the same token, you don't want to simply do nothing in the face of long-term dissatisfactions that may have begun to affect your psychological and physical health. Sometimes separation *is* the best choice, and that's where Step 7 comes in. In this step you'll find out what's involved in carrying out the decision to separate and utilize the plans you have made with the help of the preceding chapters.

Carrying out a decision to separate, no matter what type of separation you choose or how well you communicate, can be very traumatic for one or all. Let's visit a few couples and see how they put their decision to separate into action.

Couple Situation 7: Ed and Beth: "When He Drinks Too Much, I Can't Stand Being Around Him."

Beth, thirty-eight, and Ed, forty, have been married for almost ten years. This is Beth's first marriage and Ed's second. Ed has one child, fifteen-year-old Jimmy, from his first marriage. Jimmy spends every other weekend with Ed and Beth. According to both Ed and Beth, they have had a reasonably satisfying marriage except when Ed drinks. For most of their marriage, Ed has been a weekend drinker. He tends to drink beer and, until recently at least, had only gotten seriously drunk a few times. But in the past year, since turning forty, Ed has begun to drink more often and has gotten drunk more frequently. A few of these times, Ed has been at home with Beth, drinking until he fell asleep, and Beth had to help him to bed. Sometimes Ed has slept the entire night on the couch.

When Beth started to see a pattern to Ed's drinking, she became quite disturbed. Her father was an alcoholic, and she can still remember waiting for him to come stumbling through the door late at night. She can still feel the fear from hearing her parents argue about his drinking well into the night.

For a while Beth tolerated Ed's drinking at home and felt OK enough about it; after all, he was not hanging out at the bars like her dad. But the turning point for Beth came when Ed started to drink too much when they were out with friends or at parties. Ed would drink then start flirting heavily with other women, and this embarrassed Beth. If she tried to speak to Ed about it, he would yell at her to get off his back.

Often he would say rude and inappropriate things about Beth in front of others, ranging from how she looked nude to how he felt about their scant sex life. It was as if drinking made Ed lose all judgment. And people noticed. At parties women friends would approach Beth to see if she was OK or ask whether she needed a ride home.

Needless to say, Beth became more and more upset and angry about Ed's drinking. When she would attempt to bring it up, Ed would tell her she was blowing things way out of proportion. His advice was that *she* start drinking more and "join the party!" This enraged Beth even more. Not only did she have to endure embarrassing drinking episodes, but she had to suffer the humiliation of being totally discounted, too.

After several incidents and no sign of stopping, Beth told Ed she'd had enough. She explained that she had been swallowing her feelings for a long time and couldn't do it any more. Ed needed to control his drinking or he would lose her! She told him how much she had begun to dislike him and said she could no longer live with someone who didn't listen to or respect her feelings. She further explained that the fact that her father was alcoholic made Ed's behavior even harder to tolerate. Beth announced that she had decided to move in with her mother for a while and would be leaving soon.

Ed was in shock. Beth had never done anything like this before, and Ed questioned whether she would actually carry it out. He spoke to a couple of friends, and one of them said, "Tell her to not let the door hit her in the ass on the way out!" Another friend, however, urged him to think of how important Beth was to him before "closing the door on her." Ed was confused and did not know what to do.

In the two weeks that followed, he withdrew from Beth and tried to punish her for her ultimatum. This made Beth even more upset. She began to wonder whether leaving would be the right thing to do. She talked to a close friend who was familiar with Ed's drinking behavior. All her friend had to do was remind her of how things had been and how humiliated Beth had felt, and Beth renewed her resolve to leave.

She felt so lonely in the relationship and couldn't stand it that Ed seemed to choose beer over her. But she also hated it that Ed wouldn't even talk to her. When one friend remarked that Ed was basically a good guy who once in a while drank too much, Beth again became filled with doubts and questioned if she really wanted to break up her marriage when all she wanted was for Ed to control his drinking behavior.

About three days before she had planned to leave, she decided to try and have one last conversation with Ed.

BETH: Ed, I'd like to talk to you about this whole thing before Saturday (leaving day). I feel like you don't understand why I'm leaving or what this is about. I really don't want to break up our marriage, but I do need some things to change.

ED: (*looking stern and angry*) I don't think I have anything to say. I think you're saying it all by leaving. What do we have to talk about anyway?

BETH: Maybe if I felt you were listening to me, it wouldn't have to go this far. I know you think this is just about how you behave when you're drinking. Yes, that is a problem we must resolve, but how can we resolve anything when you won't even talk about it?

ED: See what I mean? (*becoming more angry and defensive as he talks*) It's all my fault! All I'm trying to do is have some fun and that seems to really bother you. You need to be with somebody who just drinks tea. Why don't you get the hell outta here now? Why wait until Saturday!

BETH: Ed, please don't do this! Let's talk. Just try to see my side.

Ed got up and left. He thought to himself: *Good, she looks hurt and scared. If she actually leaves, it won't be for long.* What Ed was doing was taking a defensive, I'm OK, Beth is Not OK position. He was not going to budge on this one. He actually felt superior for a brief moment as he let his anger cover up his fear and guilt over how his behavior was affecting Beth.

The conversation solidified Beth's decision. With Ed still not listening, she knew she had to stick to her plan. She moved out that Saturday. Ed was not around. Ironically, he had gone out drinking with a buddy. When Ed came home, he found this note:

Dear Ed,

I left for my mother's. You know the number. If you decide that you want to talk, call me. I'll check in next week, and I'll also leave a list on how I/we could handle things while we're apart.
Love,
Beth

Ed ripped up the note and went out to have another beer.

How Ed and Beth Have Moved Through Separation Management so Far

Ed and Beth are engaged in an ongoing conflict. Although their fighting is not open and chronic, they are locked in battle nonetheless. Efforts to resolve their conflict as a couple have not worked, so Beth has resorted to working on her self. Beth also believes that unless and until Ed experiences some consequences for his behavior, he will neither listen nor work on any changes.

The "purpose" of the separation, as far as Beth is concerned, is to send a message to Ed that she will not accept his drinking behavior or his not wanting to talk about its effect on her and on their marriage. She intends to get space from Ed and let him know that there must be change. On the Relationship Investment–Commitment Scale Beth was initially at Level 2, willing to work on issues "There must be a change," but when Ed refused to cooperate she moved to Level 3, and was confused-ambivalent about remaining in the relationship. She knows she needs to take a stand for herself, but still has a lot of fear and many mixed feelings about what she is doing.

Ed is at Level 1, not wanting to separate at all, but not willing to spend the time and energy necessary to fix what's wrong (he has a commitment but no investment to work on improvement).

No one has told Ed's son Jimmy about the separation. He knows Beth has moved out but doesn't know why. Beth wants to write a letter to Jimmy to explain why she left. She has decided not to disclose information about Ed's drinking or behavior and only to refer to problems between his dad and her. But when she tried to talk with Ed about what to say to Jimmy, Ed said, "This is your thing, and I don't want to have anything to do with it."

Beth has not suggested a time frame for the separation because she's not sure it would accomplish much. On the practical side, because she is living with her mother, their additional costs are minimal. Ed and Beth both have good jobs and are doing well financially. They have not yet constructed ground rules on sharing finances or household responsibilities, but Beth is drawing up a proposal for Ed. She does not know whether he will respond and is worried that this will create more stress and problems between them.

This whole scenario amply illustrates the difficulty of a one-sided decision to separate. Ed is obviously affected but stuck in his anger. Beth is full of feelings but believes her decision is the right one for her.

EXERCISE

See Ground Rules for Talking, page 17.

1. What do you think about Beth's decision to separate from Ed?

2. In your judgment, does Ed's behavior warrant a separation or should Beth "lighten up"? What would you do if you were Beth?

3. Do you believe that Beth attempted to get Ed to work with her on their relationship before she left? Should she have done more before her exit to her mother's?

4. Do you think Ed needs help? What would you do if you were
    Ed?

What Happened to Beth and Ed

During the first two weeks of their separation, there was little contact between Beth and Ed. Although Beth took a strong stance on the issue, she still felt very sad and depressed about their situation. She confided in her mother and a close friend, who have both supported her. Beth felt she had done enough to attempt to fix their relationship and believed it was Ed's turn.

As Ed got increasingly depressed over the separation, he started drinking even more heavily and drank himself to sleep several nights in a row. Although Ed tried to ignore and minimize Beth's complaints about his behavior when he drank, he started to think about them. He began to see how he had slowly started to rely on alcohol to escape the stress of daily life. This started to frighten him, but he became too sad and angry at the thought of giving up alcohol.

Ed decided to talk to several of their friends to get some feedback on his so-called "embarrassing behavior." Some of his male friends were reluctant to take a stance and said that they didn't think he had done anything wrong. But others confessed that their wives were very concerned about Beth after seeing how out-of-control Ed's flirting got when he was drunk. Several of the wives made it very clear that they would not put up with such behavior. One of Ed's male friends went so far as to tell him, "Ed, you pretty much make an asshole out of yourself every time you get drunk, and in the past year that's been every time we've been together."

Ed felt devastated. He knew that Beth had a point, but all he could think about was how much he didn't want to stop drinking. He figured maybe he could just cut down. Ed decided to talk with a counselor. He picked a name out of the phone book and told no one about the appointment. Although he was feeling depressed and scared, he decided to be open and honest with the counselor about his drinking, as well as his wife's and friends' reactions and feedback. The counselor was very accepting. Ed was quite relieved to have someone to open up to about this.

When Ed talked about Beth and the possibility of losing her, he started to cry. He realized how much she meant to him. He also shared how fearful he was to give up his drinking. Ed explained that he had drunk ever since he was a teenager. He didn't think he really had a big problem with it, but he did realize that he was becoming more dependent on alcohol as he got older.

As the counselor tried to get Ed in touch with the underlying feelings associated with stress from work and life, Ed began to realize just how little he understood himself and that drinking had allowed him to further avoid what he might be feeling. The counselor helped Ed understand his drinking patterns. Most of the time Ed's drinking was confined to weekends, but when stressed he drank on weekdays also. Ed admitted that he did remember flirting and telling dirty jokes and even making fun of Beth when out with their friends. He acknowledged that he was often so hungover the next day that he couldn't do anything productive.

The counselor confronted him about denying the role Ed played in Beth's marital unhappiness. Ed confided that he was terrified that he would never be able to drink again. The counselor agreed that that was a possibility, but reminded Ed that it was his choice, and no one could force him to quit.

The counselor shared a number of experiences he had had with people who drank. Some of his clients had refused to change, refused to look at their drinking, and stayed with the same patterns. Some developed health problems or problems with their relationships, employment, and even the law. Some even had to go to inpatient alcohol treatment programs.

Others stopped drinking completely. Some found this easy to do, some with and some without support from programs such as Alcoholics Anonymous. Still others tried to learn to drink more responsibly. This meant learning more about how to monitor and manage how much they drank and when they had had enough.

Ed joked about learning "when to say when," as the beer commercials encouraged, but he honestly did not know whether he could control the amount he drank. He did read about drinking in moderation but wasn't sure he could do it. The counselor agreed to work with Ed on this during a trial period. Ed was starting to feel a bit more encouraged and optimistic.

The counselor talked with Ed about the importance of understanding himself better, of discovering how to get at his own feelings and know his own stress triggers. The counselor encouraged Ed to find other ways to reduce his stress levels besides drinking.

Ed was skeptical but willing to experiment. He realized that he could no longer reach for the beer without thinking first about drinking in moderation. He also tried to be aware of how much alcohol he had to consume before his behavior started getting out of hand.

By the sixth week of their separation, except for small talk, Ed and Beth had talked very little. Ed knew he should share his decision to work on his drinking with Beth, but he hesitated because he didn't want to encourage expectations that he couldn't live up to. He finally decided to call Beth and ask to get together so they could talk. Beth had been waiting for such a call and agreed to meet with Ed.

ED: Beth, it's been a long month and a half without you. I've done some soul-searching during this time. I have been seeing a counselor about my drinking. I now realize that maybe I drink too much, and I admit I sometimes lose control over my behavior. I have not been able to listen to you about how much my drinking and behavior has affected you. I'm sorry.

BETH: (*starting to cry*) Ed, you have no idea how much this means to me. I tried so hard for you to see how embarrassing you were not only to others and me but to yourself as well. I felt so frustrated. Have you decided to stop?

ED: Not yet. But I have decided to try and drink more responsibly. I don't know whether I can do this or not. My counselor and I are going to work together during a trial period. He doesn't believe I can be spontaneous about my drinking. I can't come home from a hard day or week and just start pounding beers. I have to think about how I feel and the amount of stress I'm carrying. I'm beginning to learn ways to deal with my stress better, but I realize that the first step is to develop awareness of myself.

I realized through this that I don't think about me much at all. It isn't until after four or five beers that I slow up enough to think about me. But by then I'm pretty numb. I may need to monitor how fast I drink and set limits on how much I drink.

BETH: (*looking distrustful*) Ed, are you sure you can do this? What if you can't? (*beginning to become anxious and frustrated again*) I just don't think I can tolerate any more acting out when you drink!

ED: Beth, I want you to believe in me and support me, but I understand you might not be able to do this now. I have begun to accept that this is my responsibility. I guess I can't blame you if you don't like being around a drunken asshole. If I can't control myself, then I guess I'll have to quit altogether. I have to try to see if I can take control over this.

BETH: As long as you don't fool yourself again. Ed, I want to see if we can save our marriage, but I think you'd better work on this and you first. I guess I'm a skeptic and need time and proof that you can control your drinking. I think I'll continue to stay at my mother's until we can work things out.

ED: Do you think we can talk more often or even go on a date?

BETH: (*reluctantly*) I guess we could try.

Beth thought she might be giving in way too soon, but she also felt good that Ed was finally taking responsibility for his drinking and behavior. She felt especially good about finally being heard by Ed and having some power in the relationship. She wasn't at all sure he could control his drinking and was frightened that she would end up in the same situation with him again. She felt that by staying at her mother's she would keep the pressure on Ed to work on his problem.

With the help of his counselor, Ed spent the next month sober. He did struggle with wanting to drink, especially on the weekends, but found himself having fun in other ways. He became aware of the stress-related tension in his body and actually started to listen to himself. He learned better ways to breathe deeply and a good relaxation exercise. He found that taking walks after work, instead of heading straight for the beer, helped him feel better. He also started to see Beth again.

Beth felt happy to be with him when he was sober. She commented on how much fun they had, how well they talked about many things, and how emotionally present Ed was when he was sober. Ed began to see this as well, and he realized that being sober was beginning to feel good. He hadn't realized that his drinking had robbed him of those good, basic, natural feelings. He was reclaiming that fun-loving, relaxed little boy within himself. He even questioned whether he should ever start drinking again.

After a full month of sobriety, Ed decided to have a beer. He actually sipped it, and it felt good. After two drinks, he felt relaxed and loosened up a bit. He thought to himself that he liked the feeling he had right then and decided to stop at two. He was able to stop and that felt great. It didn't even feel like a struggle. Ed thought to himself, *Is this what it means to drink responsibly?* He discussed his experience with his counselor.

The counselor cautioned that it was very early in the experiment and that many people become overconfident and slip back into their old patterns without even realizing it. Ed vowed to stay on top of his drinking. With his counselor he figured out what times and under what circumstances he would drink. This gave Ed a guideline to follow. He also knew that he had to think and not just drink.

Ed continued to experiment and even decided to drink with Beth when they were out for dinner. Ed had two beers before dinner and stopped. He seemed to feel satisfied. The next morning he loved how good and hangover-free he felt.

After about two months of controlling his drinking without any episodes of acting inappropriately, Ed asked Beth to return home. Beth accepted. The real tests came when Beth and Ed were out with their friends. Ed continued to monitor his drinking and was very proud when he realized that he could. He described himself as someone who could easily have a problem with alcohol but decided to keep it under control. Ed and Beth's life returned to normal.

Although Beth was still a skeptic, she could not discount the fact that Ed seemed to be doing so much better. Ed would even ask Beth the day after a party whether he had been a jerk or done anything to embarrass her. Beth felt pleased that Ed had heard her and was turning into a responsible drinker. At forty years old, Ed was pleased that he had managed to control his drinking and save his marriage.

As time went on, Ed did have a few slips, mostly at home. Beth did not hesitate to say something about them. Ed knew that these were reminders of the old patterns. He realized that he was outgrowing the need to get really drunk. He liked the relaxed feeling and buzz a couple of drinks gave him, but no longer liked feeling out of control or hungover.

Beth appreciated that they seemed to agree on what was OK drinking and behavior, and what was not. Ed was open about this and was even able to talk about those high-risk times when he felt like escaping through alcohol. Ed knew he would have to work on it throughout his life, but he was confident that he could deal with his drinking problem. His Adult was very involved in how much he drank.

How the Steps of Separation Management Were Used in Ed and Beth's Situation and How Beth Put the Separation into Action

Beth started the process the moment she realized that Ed's drinking behavior was no longer acceptable to her. After many failed attempts to talk with him and too many embarrassing episodes in front of friends, Beth took a stand and moved out.

Ed resisted taking responsibility at first, but eventually felt pressured enough to do something about his situation. The consequence, Beth's moving out, forced him to do something about his drinking. For Ed this separation became therapeutic. Ed needed to work on himself, and Beth's leaving created the opportunity to do this. But Ed didn't just stop or learn to control his drinking for Beth. To have done so would have only had his overcompliant Child doing something for Beth's Parent, and in my experience this doesn't work very well.

Ed needed to change for himself, too. He decided not only to become more knowledgeable about his alcohol use but his overall stress levels as well. And so he worked to become more aware of his feelings and to just listen to himself in general. Ed learned to take better care of his inner Child and not escape through drinking.

By controlling his drinking, Ed also acknowledged Beth's complaints about him. Beth felt heard and that she had some influence with Ed, which I believe is a major issue in relationships, regardless of the problem. Many times blame, defensiveness, avoidance, and denial prevent partners from communicating and working on their issues.

Please bear in mind that not all people who discover they have slipped into problematic drinking will ever be able to become responsible drinkers like Ed did. Many people find that they are not able to drink at all, and may need help from a 12-step recovery program like Alcoholics Anonymous.

Beth obviously had enough of her own inner strength to take a stand and leave Ed, and it was this decision that set up the changes that took place. Even though Ed and Beth have reunited, Ed is still at risk of slipping into problematic drinking. The difference is that he seems to have built insight, techniques, and guidelines to help him. He has reached out to others as well.

To date, Beth and Ed are still together after almost a year since their separation. Ed has done well, despite a couple of slips at home. But the bottom line is that *he* was the one to decide that he no longer liked being drunk and obnoxious, and he was the one to take control of his drinking. This seems to have been enough for Beth to feel more at ease in social settings as well as at home.

They were able to make the decision to stay together only after their separation goals—to get Ed to look at and change his drinking behavior—were clear and after Ed took responsibility to work on those goals. It was fortunate that Beth's goals for their relationship lined up with Ed's goals for himself.

EXERCISE

See Ground Rules for Talking, page 17.

1. Can you identify with Beth or Ed? What factors do you think made this situation change?

2. What do you think changed within Ed to create a change in his behavior?

3. Would you have gone back if you were Beth? Can you trust the changes Ed made?

4. Have you, a partner, or someone you know been in Ed or Beth's shoes? What did they or you do?

5. How well did Beth plan and carry out her separation from Ed?

6. Are you ready to take action on a separation?

People have a way of becoming what you encourage them to be, not what you nag them to be.
—Phillip Larkin

Couple Situation 8: Jill and Stan: "If You Love Me So Much, Why Are You Always Trying to Change Me?"

Jill is in her late thirties, and Stan is in his early forties. They have been married for six years and have two children, four-year-old Katy and two-year-old Kim. Jill is an elementary school teacher and Stan works for a large brokerage firm as an accounts manager. Jill and Stan are good parents and felt they had a loving, close relationship for the first five years of their marriage. But ever since Kim came along, things have felt strained between them. Jill has become increasingly irritated with Stan for not doing enough to help her around the house or with the children. Stan feels he is and always has been an active father and family man. He knows he values his family a great deal and is not married to his work like other men he knows, but this isn't the way Jill sees it.

Over the past year, Jill has become more critical of Stan. Whenever Stan helps with the children, it seems like he doesn't do it well enough. Stan feels like Jill is always correcting him, always telling him the right way to do things. Jill keeps telling Stan how much she loves him, but in the next sentence she reminds him how he needs to improve. As Jill has become busier at work and as Kim has become more demanding, Stan says that Jill is less fun to be around. Although Stan believes he loves Jill, he thinks that perhaps he is beginning to not like her very much anymore.

Jill says she still loves Stan but over the past few months he has been heard mumbling, "If you love me so much, why is everything I do so wrong?" To which Jill responds, "There's a right way and wrong way to do things."

This has even crept into the bedroom, where Stan has been criticized for how he makes love. Not that they make love much anymore. The way he sees it, who would want to get close to someone so critical and controlling as Jill? He's never said this to her, but instead finds ways to avoid her.

These days this same attitude carries over to Stan's responsibilities around the house and with the girls. Stan has begun to come home later from work, watches more TV, and goes out with his friends more often. In the past two months Jill has become increasingly angry with him and now criticizes him nonstop.

Stan has threatened to move out. Jill continues to say she loves him but seems to be unable to stop finding fault with what he does. She doesn't seem to realize that the amount of criticism she directs at Stan is causing his withdrawal from her. They're on a hamster wheel, and they can't seem to get off.

The last few weeks have gotten so bad that Stan has begun to spend some nights with a friend. Stan feels terrible about this but feels he has no choice. When he looks at Jill, all he sees is an angry Parent who feels she has to correct everything he does.

Jill is outraged that Stan is not sleeping at home. She's stuck with all the work around the house. They have not done anything together in months, and their sex life is nonexistent. Jill is afraid the marriage is over. Stan stops at the house every evening after work to see Kim and Katy. He tries to avoid Jill as much as possible.

Jill and Stan are at Step 1 of the ten-step process. They haven't yet learned to manage their conflict. And yet they have fast-forwarded to Step 7 by separating. Neither knows why they are at this point or, more importantly, how to stop it. They are unable to communicate in any meaningful or productive way. Each is confused and in crisis. Both are having trouble concentrating at work, sleeping, and managing day-to-day. The children have become more clingy and demanding, making Jill's home life much more trying and exhausting than it was before Stan left. Her anger and blame at Stan have only risen, increasing the threat of escalating conflict.

Many couples enter my office at this point. They are unclear on why they have separated except that life has become a daily crisis and it appears there is nowhere to turn. They wonder how they will move from continual conflict to resolution. Although Jill and Stan's separation seemed impulsive, it has served to stop the immediate conflict. It has also created a bigger crisis regarding their future as a couple. Will this separation and crisis serve to get them to address the problems in their relationship or simply be the first move toward a divorce?

Work at It or Break Up?

Jill and Stan have been separated nearly a month. When Stan visits, Jill always seems angry. About half the time an argument breaks out. Stan realizes the fights and arguments go nowhere. He has even stopped fighting back or defending himself. This seems to make Jill even angrier, and she often refers to him as a "passive–aggressive wimp." After about six weeks of separation and no break in the conflict, Stan suggested that they try counseling. Surprisingly, Jill agreed. Stan obtained the name of a local marriage counselor whom some friends had seen and called to set up an appointment.

Jill and Stan's First Counseling Session

COUNSELOR: I'd like to hear what each of you has to say about what is not working. Remember that you each have a perspective, and each will get a chance to express what you think and feel as well as respond to your partner's side. Who wants to go first?

JILL: (*pointing at Stan*) You suggested counseling, so why don't you go first?

STAN: We have been separated for about six weeks now. We have not been able to communicate with each other at all. Our talks always turn into arguments. I decided to leave our home because I had had it with Jill's continual criticism of me—

JILL: Why don't you tell the counselor the truth instead of that baloney!

COUNSELOR: One guideline I teach couples right away is to share the floor. Each will get a chance to respond to the other. Communication works best if there are no interruptions unless you want something repeated.

STAN: I feel really sad about staying away from our girls. I know they miss me terribly, especially Katy. But I can't take the criticism any longer. Jill makes me feel so bad about myself. I try so hard to carry my end of the family, and all I get is "it's not good enough!" (*looking at Jill*) I don't think anybody could please you.

JILL: (*has been shaking her head no and looking very disapproving and angry*) Why don't you tell the truth? I hate liars! Stan, you have never been able to hold up your end of the responsibility for this family. You talk a good game but never do! I have to tell you everything and then you do a half-assed job at it. I always have to finish your work or do it over. Boy, if a job is to be done right, I have to do it myself! (*looking at the counselor for validation*) Most of our arguments occur because I do most everything around the house and with the kids. I get up, get breakfast, get the kids to day care. Then I go to work and work my butt off, then pick up the kids, go home, get dinner, baths, bedtime stories, and fall down exhausted. Yes, once in a while he does take them to day care, but this lazy good-for-nothing could never keep up with what I do.

COUNSELOR: (*addressing Jill*) It sounds as if you are on overload, Jill.

JILL: I am! I feel I am in this alone and get no help from him at all.

STAN: It's not because I don't want to help, it's because when I do, it's never right. I can't remember when I last got a compliment.

JILL: Who compliments me? Nobody!

The counselor made an effort to get them to see that they each have a side to this, and even though they may be angry and disappointed with each other, resolution usually means trying to control the fights and begin to hear each other's side.

JILL: (*Looking annoyed and impatient with the entire process, gets up and starts to pace. She turns to Stan.*) You've never been there for me or the girls. All you ever think about is yourself. It's easy to sit here in front of a stranger and tell more lies. Maybe you can try to fool him too, but you can't fool me. (*Jill left the counseling session angrily before it was over. She banged the door shut behind her.*)

STAN: (*looking sad and rejected*) See what I mean? She won't listen to anybody. It's hopeless.

The counselor then shared the observation that sometimes people are so stressed that it's hard for them to see anybody else's side. Stan shared some about his family and Jill's. Stan came from a "good" family, he said. He was the youngest, with two older siblings, a sister and a brother. His parents are still together and seem to still care about each other after many years of marriage. Jill's parents are divorced. Jill is the oldest of two. She has one younger brother. Her dad left when she was eleven, and she had to assume full responsibility for her little brother. Jill's mom struggled with depression for many years, so in a way Jill lost both her mother and father at the same time.

Jill was not all that close to her dad before he left. When he left she saw him even less. By the time she was fifteen she stopped visiting him, and he saw her briefly twice a year. Stan wondered out loud whether Jill might not be dumping all her anger at her dad on him.

The counselor helped Stan see that underneath anger is often hurt, sadness, disappointment, unmet wants, stress reactions, etc. Unless one begins to address these feelings, the anger works to protect and defend oneself.

Stan began to feel some compassion for Jill. He saw how hard she pushed herself, how high her expectations seemed to be, and how these were applied to everyone else as well. Stan then became very sad as he realized that he could not live with her pressure. He talked with the counselor about what to do. Stan felt that Jill would not return to counseling and probably felt the counselor was not on her side.

The counselor suggested that Stan continue to take care of himself. He assured Stan that excessive criticism is very difficult to be around. He suggested that Stan continue to tell Jill when he felt criticized but also learn to protect himself and disengage if she wouldn't stop.

Stan left the counseling session feeling OK about himself but very discouraged about the future of his marriage.

Stan and Jill's physical separation continued for the next several months.

Several times over the months Stan tried to talk with Jill. He even sent e-mails and a letter. But she kept insisting that he was the one with the problems. Jill even suggested that Stan go to counseling alone until he could learn to take more responsibility for himself and his family. Stan felt he had no alternative but to stay physically separated. No matter how hard he tried to understand her, she would not give an inch. The only thing Stan knew for sure was that Jill wanted an apology from him—a full apology where he admitted to being a real screwup. During this time there were numerous breakdowns between them, especially when Stan picked up or dropped off the girls. No matter what Stan did or how he approached Jill, it seemed that her perspective of him was frozen. She saw him as incapable of taking the kind of responsibility she wanted him to take and unwilling to look at how that affected him, her, or their relationship.

With no change, after almost eight months of separation and after talking with friends, Jill sought out legal advice. After talking with an attorney, Jill decided to file for a divorce. She felt more determined than ever that she was right and that the reason Stan was not returning home was that he wouldn't admit it. She felt that Stan and she were not compatible or able to work out their differences. Stan was hurt and saddened. He was still hanging onto hope that Jill would come around and see his side.

Applying Separation Management to Jill and Stan's Situation

First off, even after months of physical separation, Jill and Stan were not able to manage a cease-fire. As a result, communication between them did not work toward a better understanding or resolution, but continued to fuel the battle and power struggle.

The physical separation was initiated by Stan to protect himself from Jill's put-downs and criticisms. He still had enough of a self to realize he was unwilling to be a victim to Jill any longer.

But no matter how hard Stan tried, Jill would not acknowledge his side. Stan would often become very sad when he thought about Jill and how hard she worked and pushed herself. He had to fight with himself not to run and see her or call her, because he knew she would refuse his efforts to connect.

Stan also had to battle his own guilt and feelings of failure over being helpless in this situation. Even though he was doing what he thought was right (Stan's Adult), he often doubted himself (Stan's scared, compliant, and Not OK Child) and felt maybe Jill was right. Stan realized that over the years he had given Jill way too much power over him. Now he was attempting to take that power back. He realized that, as he worked on his own internal critical and controlling Parent, being around Jill was too hard. He couldn't be around her and remain OK with himself. He began to realize that in many ways he was stronger and more able to empower his self after separating from Jill. Stan even found himself thinking, *If being in this relationship is making me feel worse about myself, then maybe it's a good time to evaluate whether this relationship is any good.*

Stan still loved Jill and wished that she could learn to be more aware of where she was with herself. But that was not happening.

What About Jill?

The part of Jill that no one saw was that she sometimes felt so driven she thought she was having a nervous breakdown. At night she would sometimes cry herself to sleep, because she was desperate for help. This is when Jill would become so angry with Stan for not living up to her expectations. She would often resort to thinking, *This is how men are.*

Even though Jill was well aware that she had been made to grow up fast, with her dad leaving and her mom battling depression, she had to fight hard not to see herself as "weak" like she viewed her mom. Ever since she was eleven years old, Jill had prided herself on being the one who could take care of everything, alone. No one else could be counted on. It was true that Stan couldn't do anything right, she thought; only she could.

Jill did not see her part in sabotaging the very thing she said she wanted. By expecting Stan to help but always putting him down for not doing anything right, she was only making things worse and undermining his efforts. In turn, this justified her continuing to see Stan as Not OK. (Jill's situation is a classic example of a self-fulfilling prophecy.)

For things to work with Stan, Jill would have to accept that it is okay if he wanted to do things differently than she does. She would have to learn to give up some control. Sometimes this happens naturally when one gets so overwhelmed by doing it all. She would have to be willing to open the door and see that Stan simply wanted to be treated like a respected human being.

Unfortunately Jill and Stan never got there. Jill never reached Step 8; she never got to the place where more responsibility for one's self and one's own issues can be addressed. Instead, Jill and Stan got divorced. To date they still have a strained relationship, although the active arguing seems to have let up. Stan gets to be with the children about a third of the time. He has begun to date a woman who thinks he is really special.

Jill has not dated and struggles with ongoing stress and pressure from work and the great amount of responsibility she continues to take on. Her life continues to feel hard and she actually feels she gets no support from Stan and is "in it alone." Her view of Stan is that he is still irresponsible and incapable and always will be.

EXERCISE

See Ground Rules for Talking, page 17

1. Can you identify with Jill or Stan?

2. Do you think Stan was justified in deciding to leave Jill?

3. Do you think Stan thought out his decision to separate?

4. Is the *way* they first seek space from each other indicative of their inability to communicate and hear each other?

5. Why do you think it was so difficult for Jill to understand Stan's side of this situation?

6. What do you think was the primary reason for Jill and Stan's breakup?

7. What would you have done if you were Jill? If you were Stan?

As you can see from these stories, individuals and couples often struggle to cooperate on making a transition from living together to separation. By having a process to work with, couples and individuals can map out where they might be in the process and see what's ahead.

Step 7, as you have seen, assumes that some progress has been made in the first six steps and that couples are ready to put their separation into action and move deeper into the change process, be these separations in-house and psychological or out of the home and physical, or both.

Of course the first few steps must continue to be priorities throughout the process. If conflict is not controlled and communication is not at least stabilized, ongoing stress and pain often use up the available energy. As I have seen separations work in people's lives, I have gained great respect for conflict and crisis as a predecessor of change. Because relationship separations affect us at the core of our selves as human beings, separations often provide us with an opportunity for growth. Steps 1 through 7 allow you to create a structure to help you manage the direct fallout and shock of separation. Provided the conflict and other aspects of separation continue to be managed—a major goal in itself—Step 8 allows you now to focus and deepen your work on your self and your relationship, if you have the chance or choose to.

Step 8 will begin to address some of the underlying reasons for separation, reasons that could not be seen or understood earlier on. I often find that individuals and couples do the most work on their selves once they've separated. Whether learning to grieve a loss, be alone, accept differences, mend a broken heart, communicate more openly, experiment with new behavior or a new lifestyle, or anything else, this is the step that gets you past the initial crisis and into those underlying issues that may have followed you around your entire life, issues which, I believe, the separation may be intended to stimulate and uncover in the first place.

Step 8 should be a time to reflect on how well you are doing so far. Steps that have not been worked through may need to be attended to. It is up to individuals and couples to decide if and when they are ready for change. Each of us is unique and we should not be judged or compared. You are where you are. Start there!

Step 7 Exercise: Decide on a Specific Plan for the Day You Separate

See Ground Rules for Talking, page 17.

You can do these exercises alone or with a partner.

If you are planning a separation or already are separated:

1. Have you planned for separation day?

2. If you already separated, how well do you think it was planned?

3. Do you believe you have enough of a structure in place to handle the stress of a physical separation?

4. Was it (or will it be) cooperative?

5. What do you think separation day will be like for you? What might you feel? If it already happened, how did it feel?

6. How are you talking and dealing with your children about separation day? If it has already happened, how do you think the children are doing? Evaluate how well you think you and/or your partner are doing in dealing with the children.

7. Have any of the situations and information presented helped you decide how and what to do? What else do you think you need?

STEP 8

Developing, Clarifying, and Changing Goals for Yourself and Your Relationship

Life is just a mirror, and what you see out there,
you must first see inside of you.
—Wally "Famous" Amos

Until now, the steps have been focused largely on controlling conflict and setting up a structure so that some type of separation could take place, if necessary. In fact, many couples remain stuck in those earlier steps and never make it to Step 8. Separations are often an emotional roller coaster of hurt, anger, disbelief, conflict, chaos, acting out, etc., but if you have reached this step, chances are that at least one, if not both of you, has begun to see that you have played a part in your relationship crisis and are now ready to take a deeper look at your own issues.

Step 8 is about what happens after the dust has settled and one has begun to cope with the realities of a decision to separate. The main tasks of Step 8 have to do with working on the self. You will be identifying and taking responsibility for your own contributions to your relationship situation and then beginning some crucial self work.

As we've seen, separation often triggers basic feelings and insecurities from childhood. Current relationship problems often make us reenact and amplify those lifelong issues as well as reexperience old feelings of hurt and despair. One of my clients, facing a fourth breakup, reported that he finally realized that his overcontrolling and jealous behavior had cost him three relationships, and he was finally ready to confront this issue before he lost his fourth. If he had stayed stuck in his feelings of anger and resentment at being left again and if he had not found a way to let go of the conflict, he would not have allowed himself the opportunity to look at his own role in his relationship experience and get on with his life.

There are many theories and models on how people cope with the trials of life, but through my work I am always amazed at people's ability to bounce back from difficulty, to be resilient. Many people find the strength to cope through their religious or spiritual beliefs. Until people get in touch with and address their inner dialogue, they continue believing the same things about themselves or their situation, and they often remain stuck. (This is an example of a self-fulfilling prophecy.) Many of my clients laugh when I suggest they have an affair with themselves, but a renewed love relationship with one's self is often the best and most important outcome of a separation

As you get to know your *self* better through the work of this step, your goals for yourself and your relationship will naturally change.

We'll be looking at your feelings, perceptions, and expectations for yourself and others, since your core beliefs shape your behavior with yourself and your partner. We'll look back at the early programming you received in your family of origin to see if some of these old childhood feelings and reactions may still be running your life. Work on understanding and altering your outdated beliefs and behaviors can help open up new choices and options, whether you stay in your marriage or separate permanently. In the process of looking more deeply at your own beliefs and behaviors, you may well discover issues that you will want to work on long-term, in therapy if necessary. Understanding ourselves and how we became who we are is the work of a lifetime, but it's especially important to undertake this work when your relationship hits a crisis. In fact, it's your opportunity to do so.

Step 8 is all about recognizing that you are responsible for how you respond to life. You may well be in a relationship in which you are being controlled, for example, but what you do about that (stand up to it, learn new skills for meeting your partner on equal footing, leave, etc.) is up to you.

As always we'll be looking at building your positive Parent, strengthening your Adult, and reclaiming or (re)discovering your inner Child.

With a stronger grasp of your self and your own wants, you will be better able to evaluate how compatible you and your mate are and how healthy your relationship is. You will also be able to see how your partner's behavior is affected by his inner beliefs and how and whether this does or does not support you as you are changing and growing.

Let's revisit Dennis and Pat, to see whether they developed goals for themselves or their relationship (Step 8).

Couple Situation 5: Dennis and Pat: "I Have Feelings for Somebody Else."

Remember that Dennis had been having an affair with Sue from work. He had withheld information about his affair from Pat, and they were having a difficult time managing conflict, communicating, and talking with and preparing the children.

Two weeks after Dennis left, Pat sank to a new low. She had already felt that her world was falling apart and Dennis's leaving only made her worst fear come true. She felt she had no power over him at all and spent every waking minute fantasizing about him and his new girlfriend. Pat was horribly depressed and started having anxiety attacks. She often wondered how she would ever make it through one of the most stressful periods of her life. She began to think about hurting herself, alternating between feeling that she couldn't go on and the rather perverse thought that if she were hospitalized, maybe Dennis would come back. Pat was a nurse and was familiar with medications that could end her life. She really started to scare herself when she thought about taking an overdose of one of those pills. She struggled daily just to get up and go to work.

Her boss, a physician, was very concerned about her. But Pat was proud and didn't reveal to him how dark her thoughts had become. It was easier to talk about what a bastard Dennis was for leaving her and the boys. The only people she spoke to about her depression were a close friend and her mother. However, the only person who *really* mattered was Dennis.

Initially Dennis and Pat attempted to manage and control the open and destructive conflict. However, there was still no productive communication between them. After Dennis moved out their contact was even less frequent, but they still had to interact around sharing time with their boys and taking care of household responsibilities. The tension between them was greater than ever. Of course even the unspoken conflict was felt acutely by both of their boys (see Step 6). Both children continued to struggle. Matt became more oppositional and tested all the limits, especially with Pat as well as some teachers at school. Jerry continued to feel more stressed, with inner turmoil about loving both his mom and dad. He felt he had to take sides, and this caused him worry and confusion.

When we left them, Pat and Dennis were in a trial separation. Dennis was at Level 4 and had decided to leave the relationship whereas Pat was at Level 1 and remained invested and committed. She still hoped that Dennis would come to his senses and return home.

Given these circumstances, how could Dennis and Pat move into Step 8 of their separation process? Now that the separation was a reality, what could Pat do for herself, and how could Dennis develop his own goals?

Pat continued to struggle, and it showed. Her boss noticed how tired and stressed she looked and said so. He was concerned that her attention was not on her work and suggested that she continue to see the family counselor even though Dennis would not go.

Pat saw little value in counseling if it wasn't going to help her marriage, but she made an appointment anyway just to say she did. At her first session, Pat was scared to begin talking about herself. What she managed to communicate was her profound anger at Dennis for leaving and for what his leaving had done to the boys. Grieving partners often remain angry or stay busy to avoid thinking and feeling about their own pain and hurt.

As the counselor attempted to refocus Pat on her own feelings, she began to cry and shake. It was as if a dam had broken. She sobbed and sobbed and could hardly get out a word. She managed to tell the counselor that her heart was broken and she never thought it could be mended. She believed that Dennis was the only person who could ever make her feel better. Pat shared with the counselor that she managed to get through the days by keeping very busy, but the nights were horrible. She barely slept and she felt she was sinking into a deeper depression. She often cried herself to sleep.

Through talking with the counselor, Pat became acutely aware of how dependent she was on Dennis for her well-being. She explained that she felt OK when her children were with her, but when she knew she was going to spend a weekend or evening alone, her anxiety would skyrocket.

They discussed antidepressants. At first she resisted, but after another week of poor sleep, no appetite, and further weight loss, she gave in. Pat was at the beginning of a grieving process.

Pat had not heard a final verdict from Dennis. In fact, Dennis had still not been totally truthful about the extent of his relationship with Sue. This lack of honesty had allowed Pat to have false hope. This in turn had delayed her feeling the painful emotions of grieving. She had anticipated that the relationship was over but still hung onto any tiny bit of hope.

After about a month of taking an antidepressant and continuing counseling alone, Pat managed to feel a little more stable. She was still very unhappy, moderately depressed and lonely, cried often, and experienced every day as a chore. She was not gaining any weight but was not losing any either. As the weeks moved on, she began to feel real dislike and anger for Dennis, not the kind that covered her deep desire to reconcile. She thought, *If he still loved me, he would not ignore the pain and agony that I am going through.* She noticed that slowly, over time, her sadness was lifting and her anger and rage at Dennis, which had been keeping her so stuck, were beginning to ease as well.

> The difference between loneliness and solitude is your perception
> of who you are alone with and who made the difference.
> —Anonymous

Through the help of her counselor, Pat started to see herself progress through her grief, but at times it was so slow and seemed to take so
long. There were some weeks when there were more good days than bad,
but then something would trigger a backslide. She was impatient and
wanted to feel like her old self again. She had a very hard time accepting
that she would have to stay in touch with her feelings and thoughts and
learn to express them with little idea as to when this agony would stop.
Pat did recognize that it was getting easier to be alone. At times she even
started to like being by herself. This made her feel a little guilty and she
couldn't help remembering how terrified she had been when Dennis
first left. Facing this fear allowed her not only to tolerate her anxiety better, but also to cope better all around. She learned to practice relaxation
and began to enjoy reading. She played a lot of music. She even started
to get into some of the self-help books her counselor suggested.

Pat and Dennis saw very little of each other, mostly by Dennis's
choice. Although Dennis actually did want to see Pat more often, he
knew that doing so would only encourage false hope. Pat's goal for
Step 8 was to grieve the ending of her relationship with Dennis and
accept the reality that she would have to go on without him. If Dennis
so much as smiled at Pat during their exchanges of the children, Pat
would fantasize that Dennis had had a change of heart. When this
would not happen, Pat would take a downward turn and find it more
difficult to get back to where she had been. This all made her realize
that she had more work to do to really let go of Dennis.

How long does this grieving process usually take? I'm afraid
that's a question without answer. Although there are many common
phases or stages to a grieving process, each individual must do it his
or her way and in his or her time frame. Elisabeth Kübler-Ross's
five stages of grieving from her book *On Death and Dying* can be

extremely useful here. Although she identified these as stages of the process of grieving a death, I find that they apply equally well to grieving the end of a relationship.

Stages of Grieving

1. Shock and Denial This is the "I can't believe this is happening to me!" stage. You may know that your partner's feelings have changed, that he or she is having an affair or wants out of the relationship, but you have not allowed yourself to feel the many emotions around this experience. You may have trouble accepting the reality because your partner has not yet left or is still giving mixed messages about the future of the relationship.

2. Anger The "How could you do this to me?" stage. Once you come out of denial, anger often follows. This anger may be expressed at your mate and/or at the person with whom your mate is involved. Sometimes this anger turns to violence. If the anger is not expressed outwardly, it will often turn inward in the form of self-blame or self-destructive thoughts, or as depression. Other people become ashamed or guilty about the anger they feel (the inner critical Parent at work).

3. Bargaining "Maybe I, you, or we could have or should have done something different that would have made our relationship work." What often comes next is the feeling that you have not been given an adequate chance to make things better. You may entertain thoughts such as, "We should have gone for help"; "He should have told me he was attracted to someone else"; or "I should have lost those ten pounds."

4. Grief and Depression "It's really over." Although still part of a grieving process, the first three stages seem to keep the pain away and hope of reconciliation alive. You enter this fourth stage when you finally get it that it's over and start to feel the loss. It is at this stage that old feelings and fears from childhood often surface. Some people begin to grieve a current loss only to get in touch with a major past loss such as a parent, another relationship, or a pet.

This is the stage in which people often find themselves in low-grade depression. Depression is a natural and sometimes necessary part of a relationship loss and grieving process, but you want to watch out for a deeper clinical depression and seek help if you feel that you are not coping well. Signs of a deepening depression are ongoing problems of loss of concentration, energy levels, or productivity, or self-destructive or otherwise violent feelings and thoughts that begin to move into the action phase. Negative "black hole" thinking can produce helplessness, discouragement, and a perception of having no options. There can be symptoms of weight loss or gain, insomnia, excessive sleeping, reliance on drugs, alcohol or other medications to help you cope. Some people become very sad and lose their ability to find joy or fun in life. Some people withdraw from others. Productivity and concentration are often affected. These are all signs of depression. Talk to your doctor, minister, counselor, or a trusted friend. Sharing with others can really help. Grief passes! Sometimes medications can be useful.

5. Acceptance "I can handle this." Acceptance, the knowledge that you will be all right and that life can go on, seems to slowly weave in over time. Acceptance, like grieving, can roll in and out like waves. There are days when it can seem as if one has not left the starting gate of grief and others when one might feel back to normal.

The Coping–Grieving Graph illustrates how one's mood and emotions may vacillate over time. Notice it does not go in a straight line from beginning to end. And sometimes even bigger drops can occur after much time has passed. I have found it helpful to know this pattern so that backslides can be seen as normal and necessary and not permanent failures. Backslides make you focus again on what is continuing to trigger your grief. As you work with this each and every time, renewed confidence and inner emotional strength can develop.

I have seen hundreds of individuals grieve the loss of a partner, and I am convinced that we are made to grieve and to recover. Experience tells me that the pain will pass, even though when you're going through it, it may not feel that way.

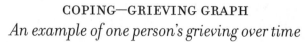

COPING—GRIEVING GRAPH
An example of one person's grieving over time

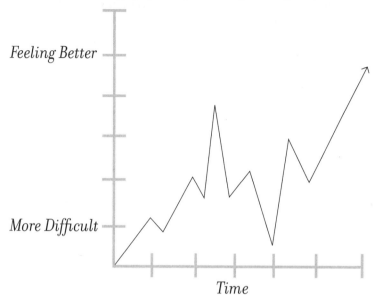

It is important to recognize that the stages of grieving aren't always sequential. You might go through them in any order and any time frame. You might feel denial, anger, and grief all in a day, or within minutes for that matter. You can also become stuck, remaining angry, for instance, and never letting yourself express and feel the pain of grief. We've all known people who have become chronically angry, bitter, and cynical. This is often a result of not moving through the stages of grief and addressing those feelings.

Many societal and family messages work against the grieving process, such as "Oh, don't feel bad"; "Look on the bright side"; "Don't worry, you'll find somebody new"; and "Just give it time." Sometimes the people in our lives can become overwhelmed—or themselves triggered—by our strong feelings and try to cheer us up to avoid their own painful feelings. In our culture, sadness and pain are probably the most widely avoided feelings, yet often the only way out is to feel them. In the grieving process, sometimes people's feelings are intense and all over the map. They think they are going crazy. This is often a quite normal reaction for many in this situation. Let's revisit Pat and Dennis and see whether Pat works through her own stages of grieving through this crisis in her relationship so she can move forward.

Pat's grief started with denial and shock. When Dennis first disclosed his feelings for someone else, she heard what he said but felt numb. She then started to feel very angry as she tried to punish and guilt him into returning home and even used the children as her weapons. She tried to bargain with him to work on the relationship in counseling together and finally got in touch with her broken and wounded heart.

Pat stayed depressed for several months. She realized that she did much better if she did not see Dennis, but like an addict, yearned for contact with him. Early on, she did not believe she could survive without the hope of reconciliation. But when she finally decided to accept her situation, she was able to make some progress in letting him go.

What's Happening Now

After relying on her mother and best friend for support for nearly a year, Pat has slowly begun to seek out other social experiences. She managed to increase contact with friends and thought about going to a divorce-recovery group but decided not to. Joining a group can be an excellent way to face grief and obtain support, but Pat wasn't quite ready for it.

During this year, she learned to nurture, support, and soothe her self. She realized how much she had relied on Dennis for her self-esteem. In fact she began to wonder whether she had borrowed her self-esteem from him rather than producing it herself. Pat realized that she often took an I'm Not OK position, while seeing others as more OK than she, even though she gave the appearance of being really OK and in charge.

In short, Pat relearned to parent herself. She stopped blaming herself for Dennis's actions and tried to accept his relationship with Sue.

She became clearer about the patterns in her marriage and what she now wanted from a partner. She knew that she would expect more communication, openness, and intimacy with a new partner and not accept such a long period of disengagement. With the benefit of hindsight, she could see that she and Dennis had drifted apart a long time ago.

Pat was even beginning to think about opening the door to a new relationship. That was a huge step. She started to feel her energy return and even occasionally felt really happy. The first time she had a really good belly laugh in the company of friends, she realized that she was recovering that fun-filled little girl within herself and it felt good! Having come through the experience of losing Dennis, she developed inner strength, realizing she had the courage to know and tolerate her feelings and not run from them, deny them, avoid them, or abuse substances to cope.

As a result of dealing with her fears, sadness, and grief, Pat felt she developed a greater capacity for emotional and verbal intimacy with herself and others. She had begun to bring her new self forth with an increased assertiveness and confidence.

As Pat moves through Steps 8, 9 (evaluating goals), and 10 (making decisions), she is coming to the end of her grieving process and beginning to grow. Even though the little girl in her sometimes hopes and wishes it could have been different, she knows as a grown-up Adult that her marriage has ended, and she is now considering a divorce.

She even feels confident that if Dennis were to want to reconcile, she would not consider it because too much has happened, and she seems to have truly let him go. She knows she must work on building healthy trust and intimacy and on bringing her new sense of self to a new relationship. Some people can do this self-development within their present relationship, but for others like Pat, there is no turning back. Neither way is right or wrong. The decision has to be a personal one. Pat is yet another example of someone letting go and learning to forgive and accept what has happened to her. By doing this she drained the poison out of her heart that kept her angry, bitter, and depressed. This acceptance was very much tied to her going through her grieving process. Pat was able to let go without any help or assistance from Dennis.

Although Dennis has stayed with Sue, over the past year, they have moved out of the romance period and into the disillusionment/compromise stage of their relationship. At first Dennis really thought the excitement and passion with Sue would never end, but it has, and now it is dawning on him that perhaps every relationship gets to this point. At times Dennis even wonders whether he left Pat and the boys too quickly. He occasionally has doubts about his decision to leave but gets terrified by the thought, especially since Pat seems to have accepted the end of their relationship and is talking about divorce.

It is often the case that the one who is left behind is forced to do the most growing. Dennis has not yet processed the experience of his separation. Although he had mixed feelings about leaving Pat and the children, they were overridden by all those new, exciting, and romantic feelings for Sue. Now that these feelings for Sue have cooled some, Dennis is experiencing some delayed grieving. He would do well to talk with a professional.

It is almost a part of our cultural paradigm that when the going gets really rough, one partner makes a break and starts a new relationship. The trouble is, we've become almost addicted to the rush of the new.

What About Pat and Dennis's Children?

Matt and Jerry both had a difficult year. Matt acted out initially, and Jerry struggled to be loyal to both his mom and his dad. As Pat began to work on herself and to see her grief and sadness, her anger eased. She became aware that it was unfair to put her children in the middle. This realization took time to surface, but once it did, Pat began to see her children's feelings as theirs and not extensions of her own. She also realized how much she had wanted to use the children to fight with Dennis.

As Pat got in touch with the pain in the little girl in herself, she was able to see the pain in her kids. She was able to listen to them and give them permission to feel their feelings and not just hers. Pat and Dennis both felt that the children could be helped through counseling. Matt saw a school counselor and joined a group at school for children whose parents were going through a divorce. Jerry started counseling with a woman who specialized in working with children coping with their parents' divorce. Both started to do better, though it took some time.

> A mind that is stretched by a new experience can never go back
> to its old dimension.
> —Oliver Wendell Holmes

How Learning to Manage Their Separation Has Affected Dennis, Pat, and Their Children

1. Although a separation was forced on Pat, and was very difficult for her, she did learn to cope and now realizes that not only could she endure a major life change but that there were actually some benefits in it for her. She realized how dependent she had been on Dennis and set about developing an inner awareness and strength. Going forward, Pat will need to continue to try to understand what happened to her marriage. Fortunately she is in a good position to look at that now. All that she has learned will benefit her as a person and in a new relationship, should that occur. Over time, Pat turned a life crisis into a growth experience.

2. Dennis got a surprise opportunity to work on himself. An affair often serves as a transition out of a primary relationship. Sometimes the affair grows into a permanent relationship, but more often it does not. Some people learn much from it. For others, it is a costly detour.

   Dennis now has an opportunity to learn about himself and take what he has learned into his future relationships. If he declines this opportunity, he runs the very strong risk of reproducing similar patterns with Sue as he had with Pat.

3. Regrettably, Dennis and Pat, like many couples who split without counseling, will never have the opportunity to look, together, at each

of their contributions to the dynamics of their relationship. This, too, would have been a great learning opportunity for both of them.

4. Their children, Matt and Jerry, both struggled for about the same time period that Pat was in her deep depression. During this time it was very helpful and supportive to talk to counselors and other kids going through similar experiences. But as Pat became more stable as her depression lifted, Matt and Jerry seemed to relax more as well. As Pat and Dennis were able to be civil with each other, the kids took notice as well. They even joked that maybe Dad would move back home. Like many children of divorce, they needed help accepting the finality of their parents' parting. Even though they were wounded by this experience, watching their parents cope and learn to co-parent has helped these two young boys cope as best as possible with a major life experience.

EXERCISE

See Ground Rules for Talking, page 17.
You can do this exercise alone or with a partner.

1. Can you identify with Pat?

2. Can you identify with Dennis?

Without self-discovery, a person may still have self-confidence, but it is a self-confidence built on ignorance and it melts in the face of a heavy burden. Self-discovery is the end product of a great challenge mastered, when the mind commands the body to do the seemingly impossible, when strength and courage are summoned to extraordinary limits for the sake of something outside the self—a principle, an onerous task, another human life.
—Kurt Hahn

3. Are you or someone you know grieving the end of a relationship? What was the experience like? How long did it last? What helped? Did you pass through any of the discussed stages?

4. What do you think Pat discovered for herself through her grief over her relationship ending?

5. Do you know of anyone who remains stuck in her grief and has not moved on?

Relationship problems and separations are powerful experiences that offer much opportunity for your self to become more aware and learn. Separations offer us this opportunity—to work or rework our beliefs (our truths) on how lovable we are and with whom we choose to share that love.

In the spirit of the development of the self, I challenge you to take the responsibility to learn more about you, for it is our capacity to understand, accept, and love ourselves that allows us to do the same in our relationships with others.

EXERCISE

1. Think about how you would describe your self.

2. Who are you? What is your true or natural self or nature? Are there many different parts and subparts to you that come out at different times or with different people?

3. What are your unique beliefs, values, and ways to experience life? How do you think you are different from others? How are you the same?

4. What do you like most about you? What do you like least?

5. What are you aware of that has changed in you since you were a child, teenager, young adult? What has remained the same?

6. How are you similar to your parents or siblings? How are you different?

> Listen to the mustn'ts, child, listen to the don'ts. Listen to the
> shouldn'ts, the impossibilities, the won'ts. Listen to the never
> haves then listen close to me—anything can happen, child,
> ANYTHING can be.
> —Shel Silverstein

7. With whom or where do you feel your most free and natural self?
   Perhaps you are totally and unconditionally accepted for who you
   are in this place or by them or your self.

More Tips from the TA Front

Once again the terms *Parent, Adult,* and *Child* from TA can be useful as you decide which parts of you to develop and which parts to let
go of. You'll want to think about developing your positive nurturing
and protective Parent, while shrinking your critical or overcontrolling
Parent; to strengthen your Adult (your thinking and problem-solving capacities); and to allow your freer and more relaxed and feeling
Child to have fun and experiences in the here and now. In addition, by
developing our inner positive rebel Child, we find ways to stand up for
ourselves as necessary.

Awareness/Survival Exercise

The following exercise can be a useful tool to develop awareness to
maximize the allies or supportive and positive parts of your personality
and minimize the Not OK parts. I often use this exercise with people
who want to become more aware of what they are feeling and how
their inner thoughts and beliefs help create those feelings. It can help
you change feeling states in the moment as well as direct you to ongoing goals you may choose to work on.

You can do this exercise alone or with a person with whom you
feel free to express and be yourself. Lie down (or if with a friend, sit

comfortably face-to-face), breathe deeply for a few moments to relax your mind and your body, and focus on the following:

1. **Your Inner Child** What are you feeling and where in your body are those feelings? As you take a run through your body become aware of bodily sensations and tensions such as hurt, sadness, fear, excitement, happiness, contentment, relaxation, anger, guilt, and shame. Remember the Child speaks in short words: "I'm scared!"; "I feel bad!"; "I'm lonely!"; "I feel great!"

2. **Focus on Your Inner Parent** Often when you are feeling Not OK, your inner critical Parent is active and working you over. Become aware of this voice within.

As you sit quietly, think of what your inner Parent may be saying to you about your current situation. This might be something you heard as a child or something that is new to this situation, such as "You always did have trouble with relationships"; "What did you expect? You've always been difficult to live with"; and "If you only made more money, you wouldn't be in this mess."

3. **Discover Your Inner Allies** Your inner allies are your nurturing Parent, your Adult, and your free Child and positive rebellious Child.

Nurturing Parent Your nurturing Parent, you'll recall, is the one who supports and validates you. Many people have a lot more loving Parent in them than they realize. Is there anyone in your life who accepts and loves you unconditionally? Or can you think of someone from your past who gave you empowering strokes? Perhaps your nurturing Parent is what you call God, Jesus, Buddha, or some other religious figure.

See if your nurturing Parent messages can override negative critical messages. This may take practice, especially if your critical Parent has been active for some time. Imagine your critical Parent blaming and criticizing your scared, hurting Child. Then imagine a nurturing, loving Parent intervening and telling your critical Parent to get lost and assuring you that you are an OK kid and don't deserve what you are getting. You may want to write down what your ideal nurturing Parent might say to you, such as "I love you!"; "It's OK to feel your feelings";

"It's OK to cry"; "You can learn to take care of you"; " I accept you no matter what"; "It's OK to ask for help"; and "You will make it." Whose nurturing Parent would you want to borrow if you could?

Adult A strong Adult may be the greatest strength of your personality. Your Adult provides the power to think of choices and develop options.

When people are feeling Not OK or having intense Not OK feelings, their Adult can often think and problem-solve for them. Remember that feelings and especially Not OK feelings can drain energy from your capacity to think. Learning to activate and use your Adult to think of options and make other decisions can bring you unexpected power. Through the use of your Adult, you can redecide an old outdated decision. Your Adult can make plans to deal with the worst scenario, should it happen. It can help you do a reality check. Your Adult can help you replace fear and anger with understanding and a renewed perspective about you and your role in your relationship.

Free Child and Positive Rebellious Child Your free or natural Child has energy that can stimulate and empower your Not OK and overcompliant Child to move out of a stuck place. The free Child can help you find humor in a difficult situation. It can help you see adventure where your scared Child sees disaster. Your free Child can be a source of much joy and satisfaction for you.

We also have an inner positive rebellious Child. This part of us can help us enormously by disobeying those critical Parent messages. The positive rebellious Child is the part of us that comes out in wonderfully assertive bursts like the following:

"Fuck him, I'm not going to let his reality become mine!"
"I'm taking my power back!"
"Go to hell, I'm not listening to that crap about me anymore!"
"I'm done being afraid, it's time for a change!"
"He's not worth ending my life for!"

I have found that the energetic free Child or positive rebellious Child and the thoughtful and resourceful Adult make a great team for making new decisions about you and your life.

> Remember: We do not always have control over what happens to us in life, but we can take charge of our reaction to those experiences. We and only we can decide how long to hang on to the negative feelings that are triggered during these stressful life experiences.

Psychological separations involve letting go of how we have learned to perceive our partners and opening up to the possibility that we will discover new and different aspects of ourselves and each other. I often ask couples whether they really see each other or simply see what each has created the other to be. If I perceive you as selfish and nongiving, this is what I will then expect to get.

Think of a disruptive child who is disliked by his teacher. If that child leaves his or her seat, he will be perceived by the teacher as unruly. When that child talks to another student, he is thought rude and disrespectful. If that child asks a question or interrupts the teacher, he may be considered belligerent.

If the child is moved to another classroom with a teacher who likes him, his behavior may be perceived as curious and confident. When the child leaves his or her seat, his teacher may view him as taking initiative. If the child talks to another student, his teacher may think he is trying to be social. When the child talks out of turn, it may be thought that he is being assertive.

Which perception of this child is accurate? It's impossible to say! Perceptions are not facts; they are judgments based on perspective.

A central belief of Separation Management is that until you stop to reflect on your self, you most likely will continue to operate from your old familiar belief system and keep getting the same results. Remaining in the crisis and turbulence of a relationship separation often prevents you from this deeper study into your self. But by managing Steps 1 through 7 as necessary, you make the time to do the self-learning that will allow you to grow and develop and make healthy and truly informed decisions about your future. In fact, steps 1 through 7 were developed to allow the process to slow up enough so you could begin this work on your self and to gain awareness, clarity, and direction on goals (Steps 8 through 10), be they relationship goals or more inwardly oriented goals.

Couple Situation 9: Steve and Jan: "I Married My Father."

Steve, forty-five, and Jan, thirty-six, have been married for over ten years. Jan had just graduated from college and was starting a new job in a computer company when she met Steve. Steve was recently divorced with a young son, Jeremy, and worked in the same company as Jan as a computer programmer. Early in their marriage, Jan and Steve had a child, Ginny, who is now eight.

Because Steve is older than Jan, he has always been the one more "in charge" in their relationship. Jan's parents broke up when she was three years old. Her dad moved out of state and her mom raised her and her older brother. Jan's mom never remarried. Steve was the first guy to ever really get involved in Jan's life. Jan had had difficulty settling down and she felt that Steve had provided the grounding that she needed to grow up.

Steve loved it when Jan decided to stay home with Ginny instead of returning to her career. He was the oldest of three boys and had always been a take-charge kind of guy. Steve would often say how perfect Jan was for him, since she needed someone to show her the way, and he liked being the one. This arrangement seemed to work well for the first eight or nine years of their marriage. But when the child rearing became less demanding for Jan, she found herself becoming more frustrated with Steve's controlling behavior. As Jan rediscovered her friends and new hobbies, Steve seemed to be overly concerned with how Jan spent her time. He would often confront her about how much time she spent out of the home when she was not working and reminded her that her first job was taking care of Ginny and him, and Jeremy when Steve had visitation.

Jan does not like confrontation, and she began to resent Steve and found herself sharing less and less about her life with him. For the past year, the emotional distance between them has grown wide. Steve has noticed that they hardly talk anymore and their once-good sex life has diminished to an occasional quickie. According to Jan, many of their talks seem to end up being Steve's lectures to her about keeping up with her responsibilities. Steve has begun to scold her when she doesn't keep up with the housework and other weekly chores. When Jan is out with friends, she often worries about getting home on time to avoid Steve's anger.

Even though they both work, Steve, who has always managed their money, tells her when and on what she can spend money. Jan is conflicted over how much control Steve should have over her life. She knows it would be good for her to be a little less of a "good girl," but she also feels really guilty when she thinks too much about her own selfish wants.

As things have heated up, Jan has begun to share her unhappiness with her close friend, Diane, who keeps telling Jan that Steve sounds more like a father than a partner. Jan thinks she's right but feels guilty just for talking to Diane about her problems with Steve.

After several months of this silent power struggle, the tension between Jan and Steve has reached an all-time high. Jan hardly speaks to Steve, and all Steve does is lecture her about her shortcomings and responsibilities. He even comments on how she dresses and has made her change her clothing when he felt that what she was wearing was inappropriate for a mother. She stays away from home more often and secretly worries about her future with Steve. If it's this bad now, she wonders, what will it be like in ten years?

Ginny has even begun to notice the tension and often asks whether her mom is angry with her dad. Jan always says no. She even denies her anger to herself sometimes; she can hardly bring herself to think that she does not love Steve any longer and may want out of her marriage.

Things reached a crisis point recently when Jan came home after her "curfew." She had been out dancing with Diane and some other friends and had had a few too many drinks. Jan seldom drank and was not driving so she thought it was no big deal. But it was for Steve! When she walked in the door, he immediately started lecturing her about not living up to her responsibilities.

STEVE: (*with a stern, disapproving parental look and tone of voice*) Just where have you been?! I've been worried sick about you all night and was about to call 911 thinking that you were lying in a ditch someplace. Obviously you've been drinking and partying and not giving much of a shit about me and Ginny. (*Steve is careful to keep his voice low enough so that he won't wake Ginny.*) You look drunk and awful. I'm sure you had fun and probably danced your ass off, right?! (*Steve begins pacing and looking more and more frustrated with Jan while pointing his finger at her like a scolding parent.*)

JAN: (*Listening to him rant and rave. Deep inside she reflects on how much fun she had and how she now has to face the music for what she did.*) Steve, I did nothing wrong and am beginning to really resent the way you control me. I'm not your teenager. I'm a grown woman.

STEVE: You're sure not acting like one!

JAN: (*beginning to raise her voice and become angry, helped, she's sure, by the alcohol*) Steve, I think I've had it with you. Everybody I talk to thinks you sound like my father, not my husband.

STEVE: Sure, tell all your friends what a controlling prick I am. I'm sure you'll get support from them.

JAN: Just be quiet and let me talk. (*Steve looks shocked that Jan takes a stand with him.*) Maybe there was a time when I appreciated you running my life, but I no longer do. You have no idea how resentful I am of you. I have begun to question whether I want to stay married. I don't even like being around you anymore. All you do is tell me what I'm doing wrong. You comment on how I spend my free time and even how I look and what I wear. I can't take it anymore. (*Jan begins to cry really hard and leaves the room.*)

Steve was in shock. He had no idea that Jan felt so strongly about these things. He was just trying to be a good partner. Steve started to get scared. Was he losing control over Jan? Was his marriage falling apart? For the first time in a long time, Steve did not know what to do.

In my experiences with couples, I have found that as new, natural changes occur in one or both partners, old patterns in a relationship can become problematic.

Until now, Jan had accepted Steve being more in charge of her life. In fact, she rather liked it. Being safe with Steve had helped her grow up and learn to be an adult and mother. Maybe he was the father she never had! But after ten years and more life experience, she wants a change.

With increasing conflict and time, Jan seems to have reached her boiling point. She has finally told Steve how she feels. Because Jan and Steve don't fight openly, their conflict pattern is more of a passive power struggle. Jan has learned to be passive and quiet during their heated discussions because arguing with Steve often results in his pulling a power play and her ending up being lectured into submission (Steve's overcontrolling, judgmental Parent).

Jan and Steve had built an ice wall between them, and they needed to learn how to talk and listen to each other. They had become stuck in their Parent–Child relationship, with Steve in the I'm OK–You're Not OK position and Jan in the I'm Not OK–You're OK position.

Many people choose partners to work through developmental issues that started in their families of origin. Such was certainly the case for Jan and Steve. Initially Jan seemed to thrive on having Steve be more of a parent figure, but as Jan grew and developed into a more self-sufficient and independent person, she no longer needed nor wanted the kind of Parent–Child relationship they had.

Some people in Jan's position might decide to leave and find someone more equal. But if they don't come to recognize their pattern (attracted to a substitute dad or mom) they will often just repeat it in future relationships. Steve and Jan are at a crossroads. Jan has spoken her piece and knows that she needs a change. Steve has a choice: to begin to listen to her and treat her as an equal partner, or to try to talk her out of her position once again. In short, they must learn to manage their conflict. As always, this is the first step. Even with a passive conflict like theirs, unexpressed feelings of anger and resentment must be allowed to surface or they will destroy any positive feelings that remain.

Over the next few weeks Jan and Steve tried to talk about what Jan had shared the night she drank too much, but the one time they actually tried, Jan found herself clamming up and Steve ended by lecturing her for over an hour. Jan was more frustrated than ever and felt she had nowhere to turn.

After talking things through with her friend Diane, Jan decided to offer Steve an option. She asked him if he would go to couples counseling with her so they could learn to talk. Steve's first response was just to become bossier. He told Jan he didn't believe in counseling, but after several days and one more effort to talk, Steve agreed to go.

Steve and Jan's pattern became obvious to the counselor after a few sessions. The counselor realized that Jan needed to learn to express herself more openly, and Steve had to learn to make room for Jan in the relationship. He had to learn to listen to her and not just bully her with his beliefs, opinions, and controlling behavior. Steve had to start talking about his own feelings, too. He did not really talk about himself much, but focused on Jan's behavior most of the time. It took Steve and Jan many weeks to learn how to just talk and listen. Jan realized that by not expressing herself she had had a part in letting Steve make all the decisions. She knew that she'd have to start speaking up. Steve found it easy to make decisions, but as time went on, he actually found himself overwhelmed with responsibilities and wanted a partner to help out.

Steve and Jan learned to use time-outs whenever they slipped into the pattern of Steve controlling or Jan becoming quiet. This was very hard to do; despite their best efforts they often found themselves back in the same rut. This is perfectly natural. It had taken them years to develop this pattern, and they needed patience, awareness, and work to change it.

Steve and Jan had begun to tackle the first two steps of managing their separation. Now they had to decide what to do next. They wanted to stay together. They each had begun a psychological separation, as well as a therapeutic separation for their relationship, the purpose of which was to see if they could change the stuck, limited, and lopsided Parent–Child pattern they had created and learn to develop and grow as individuals and a couple.

Their couples counselor helped Jan and Steve come up with language to help them develop goals for themselves. It is important to have goals so progress can be measured. Sometimes goals can be seen outwardly; for example, Jan has really begun to speak up and is less fearful of conflict. Sometimes goals can only be evaluated by you and how you feel and experience differently inside.

Jan's Goals During This Three-Month Period

1. Learn to express herself as fully as possible to Steve, which meant she could no longer have hidden agendas. This was frightening to her since it could create the possibility of Steve becoming angry with her. With an emerging stronger sense of her self, Jan wanted to handle Steve's disapproval and disappointment with her. For this to happen, she needed to learn to self-validate (to believe and support her ideas and actions by herself without Steve's approval or permission).

2. Learn to call a time-out whenever she felt Steve was acting like her parent. This would give Steve and her a chance to break the stuck communication pattern. Whenever Jan called a time-out, she was signaling Steve that she was not comfortable continuing in the pattern they were in.

3. Decide what she wanted to change to make things equal in their relationship. Jan no longer wanted to ask Steve's permission to do things, like go out with her friends or spend money, but instead wanted to negotiate these kinds of issues like an adult. Jan was working on trading in her overcompliant Child for a more powerful, grown-up Adult.

Steve's Goals During This Three-Month Period

1. Learn to listen to Jan. Steve practiced being quiet and letting Jan express herself. He used to finish her sentences and butt in whenever he felt that she was taking too much time. Steve had

to learn to relax and calm himself down while he learned to acknowledge and validate what Jan was saying. He also knew that he did not have to agree with what she was saying, and he would have a chance to discuss his point.

2. Learn to express his feelings through "I" messages. This was extremely hard for him to do, since most of his communication started with "You need to . . ."

3. Learn to give up some of the control over Jan and the family functions. Although Steve complained that Jan did not take responsibility well, he managed not to give her much, then criticized what she did as he did it over his way. This would be hard for him to give up. Steve would have to learn to relax, express more inner feelings, and have more kid fun in his relationship. He would have to learn to lighten up. He had been so responsible for so long that he forgot how to have fun. When Steve started to realize this, he knew he was just as unhappy as Jan in their stuck pattern.

Steve and Jan's New Communication Patterns

JAN: Steve, I'm scared even trying to use our new communication skills. I'm afraid that I'll say something you won't like, and we'll have an argument.

STEVE: Let's just try talking and see where we go. All I know is the therapist told me I had to listen more and not interrupt or finish your sentences. This will be hard for me to do.

JAN: Steve, maybe it's too soon, but I think I need to talk about my free time away from the family. I have enjoyed doing things with my friends, but feel guilty when I know you're not happy with my being gone. How could we talk about this in a reasonable way?

STEVE: I'm OK with you having friends, but I do need to know that you have finished all of the work around here first.

JAN: (*becoming anxious and concerned*) Steve, this is where I feel I have to call a time-out, because I just felt frustrated with your deciding when I could see my friends. You said I had to be sure all my work was done. I think I should be able to decide this and not have to wait for a clearance from you.

STEVE: (*finding himself getting angry*) Jan, does this mean anytime you want to go out, the hell with me and Ginny? Tough luck, you guys are on your own? Whatever happened to the idea of family?

JAN: Steve, I hate to be so pushy, but I believe in our family, too. It's just that I feel you are so controlling that unless I fight for what I want, I won't get it. It's like you're not on my side, and I feel like a little kid asking Daddy if I can go out to play. You have no idea how frustrating this is and how much I have disliked even being around you at these times. Our couples counselor told me that I would have to stop the communication process whenever I felt parented, controlled, or overpowered by you. I know this will be hard for you to hear, Steve, but it happens a lot.

STEVE: (*looking sad and disturbed*) Yes, I know I am one controlling bastard in your eyes.

Steve was trying to lighten the climate between them with some humor. Jan responded with a laugh. Both were able to talk about how controlling Steve was, and it did help them both move on in the conversation.

What was positive for Steve and Jan in this brief demonstration is that they started to talk about how they communicate and how they relate to each other.

Jan wanted to be free and was now working on acting free. She was trying to take her new freedom and not wait for Steve to grant it to her. She was just learning to use her Adult more. Her separation involved firing Steve as her father and hiring him back as her partner. This new OK–OK place was where a more fulfilling adult relationship could grow.

Steve, for his part, often had a difficult time knowing when he was being a parent to Jan. He was not always aware of his body language, his raised voice, pointed finger, judgmental statements, and stern looks. He was learning quickly but realized it would take a while to become equals. It was very hard for Steve to realize that his control over Jan was an illusion and that the more control he tried to exert, the less he had. By learning to confront and work with his old ways of being and to accept and listen to Jan, Steve was becoming privy to what she was really thinking, feeling, and wanting. As Steve showed his willingness to listen to Jan and recognize her wants and changes, she allowed him in more and more. Over time this type of change in their relationship would allow Steve and Jan more emotional verbal intimacy as well physical and sexual closeness.

Steve realized that by learning to identify and express his feelings, he stood a better chance of having Jan hear *him* as well. Until now his feelings of being fearful or overwhelmed with too much responsibility would trigger attempts to control and guilt-trip Jan into doing more for him. Even though it was Jan who started to become fed up with this pattern of theirs, Steve slowly realized that he was not very happy either. So what started out as a crisis actually offered both Steve and Jan an opportunity not only to save their marriage but to learn ways to grow and develop into more satisfied and fulfilled individuals within their relationship.

Steve and Jan's therapeutic separation was successful because each of them worked both on themselves and on the relationship. By agreeing to enter counseling, Steve showed Jan that he was willing to go along with her first major request, and this was very important too. It often doesn't work out this way. Some men (and women as well) are too threatened by the idea of counseling and by saying no may often actually put a final nail in the coffin of their relationship without even realizing it.

Slowly Steve was learning to give up some control (critical Parent) and listen to Jan (Adult) instead. Of course at times this was difficult to do. When he was tired, stressed, overworked, and overwhelmed, he would revert to control, but as this stopped working for him, and as he realized that he had an insecure little boy in him who hardly ever saw the light of day, he started dealing with the feelings of frustration and using them to learn new things about himself. Steve was developing methods to help him relax and have fun and experience life more in the present. He was learning to let go of having to control everything.

Meanwhile Jan was learning that she had her own personal power. She would at times backslide to her old ways of being, but through her own awareness and help from Steve, she was able to stay on track with her new, more assertive self. She began to like herself more and was able to rearrange her responsibilities in the family to include more outside activities.

But she was most pleased with Steve for working with her. Now, when he would slip into what he termed his "controlling bastard" role, Jan could simply look at him with a smile and say, "C'mon, Dad, give me a break." This would usually break the ice. They would both laugh and then proceed to talk.

Occasionally Steve would get mad and withdraw, but he learned to use this cool-down period for a little self-examination. Many couples can lighten up their fights by turning to humor; it is an excellent way to defuse conflict. Just be sure it works for both of you, because poorly timed or too much humor can also feel disrespectful and minimizing, and work against repair and change. Jan no longer needed to depend on Steve to stop controlling her. She discovered that she had the ability to not accept and not get hooked by his power plays.

After about six months, Jan felt ready to commit to staying in the relationship, but first she needed to hear Steve say that these changes would last and grow. Steve reassured her that he would do his best and that if they got really stuck he would return to counseling. Along with better communication tools, and with both partners feeling positive about their changes, Steve and Jan realized that they each had far more control over their relationship than they had thought. At this point, both could see that they could manage themselves better than they could control each other, and that changing their own behavior could greatly benefit the relationship.

As they approached Steps 9 and 10, evaluation and final decisions, they were no longer afraid. They had learned to repair their process and this allowed them to meet more wants and feel more satisfied with each other. They had actually created what they each wanted in a relationship. There is little that is more satisfying than that.

EXERCISE

See Ground Rules for Talking, page 17.

1. Are you or someone you know locked into what seems to be a Parent–Child relationship?

2. What did Jan do to start a change process?

3. What did Steve discover that controlled his overcontrolling, critical behavior?

4. Can you relate to either Steve or Jan? In what areas?

Step 8 Exercise: Questions and Thoughts to Consider

The goals that you develop and decide to work with in Step 8 should be unique and specific to you and your relationship. As far as it is possible, they should be things you can work on about your self that have become problematic for you or are affecting your part of your relationship pattern. You can often see the results of a good goal. For example, a vague goal could be something like wanting to be happy, while a better goal would be to determine what specifically would make you happy. Examples of a specific goal might be telling your partner when you want more affection and hugs or giving yourself three positive strokes a day.

If a separation has been forced on you, if your partner has decided to separate from you physically, psychologically, or emotionally, some goals to work on might include the following:

- Mending your broken heart and grieving your loss
- Learning to soothe and reduce fears that arise from worrying about how you will cope and survive
- Deciding to no longer be a victim to anyone or to yourself; to stop feeling sorry for yourself, groveling, or begging for your wants to be met by an unwilling partner; not acting out your pain in harmful or destructive ways
- Deciding that you *will* live through this, grow, and move on, and that you are worth it even though you may not feel it now
- Shrinking and disobeying your overcontrolling and self-critical inner Parent
- Learning to let go of that which you cannot change
- Developing your nurturing and loving inner Parent
- Developing or reconnecting to your spiritual self and life. People have adopted God, Jesus, Buddha, Muhammad, etc. as their true, unconditionally loving inner Parent.
- Strengthening your thinking ability (Adult) so you will be able to help your Child think and solve problems in the here and now
- Learning to reach out and ask others for help
- Learning to get close and trust others over time. This can increase as you strengthen and take care of your self and develop realistic expectations of others. Learn to protect yourself and reject negative and destructive strokes from yourself and others.

If you are the one leaving, you might also decide to take this time to work on and develop your self. Be aware of what you are experiencing as a result of getting the space you wanted. What are your feelings towards the partner from which you are taking space? Relief, guilt, grief, increased empathy for their pain, other mixed feelings? Be honest with yourself. What are your feelings regarding your new relationship if you are in one? Are you surprised by how you feel? What are your feelings about your new space and relationship to your children?

Other Goals for All Partners

1. Self Work

- Beginning to work with your diet, breathing, exercise, yoga, relaxation, recreational activities, stress management, self-esteem building, spiritual practices, meditation, etc.
- If you are dissatisfied in your relationship, thinking about whether you are expecting too much or too little. How realistic are your expectations?
- Understanding how your own upbringing in your family of origin helped you form your assumptions, beliefs, expectations, and relationship patterns
- Treating your self better. Learn to relax and experience more free Child contentment, fun, joy, feelings, and pleasure. Learn to live in the present. Give yourself more strokes; accept strokes from others.

2. Relationship Skills

- Managing anger and conflict
- Learning to fight fairly; controlling anger if it is harmful or destructive
- Working on expressing feelings, thoughts, opinions, and wants directly without criticisms, defensive games, manipulations, over-control, withdrawal, and underlying ulterior motives. Learn to talk "straight," openly, and honestly.
- Equalizing the power in your relationship without one partner having to be a bully or the other a victim. Learn to stop abusing, projecting, or expressing your Not OK feelings, negative thinking, and beliefs (your critical Parent) onto your partner, children, or others. Take responsibility for your self (feelings, opinions, beliefs, thoughts, and behavior).
- Learning to say, "I'm sorry," and to work on changes when you have discounted or hurt others' feelings either intentionally or unintentionally

- Deciding to address addictions, past traumas, shame or guilt associated with acting out and problem behaviors
- Being aware of your part of your relationship process. Knowing the difference between process and issues. Learning to create a safe OK–OK climate in which you and a partner can express your selves more openly and intimately.
- Learning to repair your relationship process when necessary and normal breakdowns occur
- Learning to listen better and develop more empathy for your partner. Deciding to give your partner strokes that he wants.

3. Family Relationships

- Creating a better relationship with your children
- Creating boundaries between your relationship conflicts and your children
- Learning to work better with your partner to parent children cooperatively

Remember you don't need your partner's cooperation to work on your relationship with yourself. From a different position and perspective, you are in a much better place to evaluate and make decisions on how and whether your relationship can improve and whether you want to remain in it.

How to Work on Identified Goals

The goals above are only a sampling of things to work on. Be realistic and remember that you can only work on your self. Your partner must decide the same for him or her self.

1. First, identify what you believe is and is not working for you or what you are and are not getting. Focus on you. What is your perception of the problem?

2. Focus on an image or vision of what you, your partner, or your relationship would be like if changes were made. If you went to bed tonight and woke up and your problems were resolved, what would be different? How would you be different, and what would you (and your partner) be doing differently? Remember to stay with your part of this process even if your partner does not cooperate. Remember a change in you can effect a change in your relationship.

3. Create and develop small steps and a plan to accomplish how to get you to where you want to go. What's the first step?

4. What and who will help you get there? Friends, family, self-help courses, support groups, recovery groups, 12-step programs, ministers, counselors, coaches, physicians?

5. What is stopping you from working on your goals or objectives? Your old self-limiting beliefs, thoughts, feelings, patterns, and behavior? Fear of change?

6. While backslides are predictable and necessary, how you cope and react to backslides in your inner process as well as your relationship process is a very important part of this work. Achievable goals are realistic and flexible. It works best to have a time frame to review and evaluate how you are doing and decide whether you want to adjust goals to your experience and new information.

The work of Dr. John Gottman, Dr. Phil McGraw, Dr. Janice Abrams Spring, Terrence Real, and the other authors listed in the Bibliography can add to your knowledge and skills on how to work on specific aspects of your self and your relationship.

Evaluating Your Goals

The key to realizing a dream is to focus not on success but significance—
and then even the small steps and little victories along your path
will take on greater meaning.
—Oprah Winfrey

As we saw in Step 8, it is crucial to get to know your self and to understand your part of the patterns you bring to your relationship before making any decisions about the future. Even if a separation is forced on you, you can seize the opportunity to do a lot of good work on your self, to get to know yourself and your beliefs, behaviors, and expectations about relationships, and to clarify your own desires for your next relationship.

Ultimately, some decisions will have to be made about whether to separate permanently or come back together. With the couples we have discussed so far you could see where and how various people made such a decision. Sometimes the decision is obvious: a couple decides to reinvest in their relationship and learns to listen and communicate with each other in more meaningful ways; a frustrated partner adjusts her expectations of her mate's behavior and ends up more satisfied; someone else simply chooses to leave and stop working on the relationship or won't end an affair. Other times the decisions are much more difficult. One partner desperately wants to work things out but the other isn't sure; the status of an affair remains unclear; etc.

Ending a relationship is, for many people, the most difficult thing they will ever do, and even more difficult when it involves children. There is certainly no one-size-fits-all resolution. But the bottom line is that deciding whether to stay or go and how to cope with your unique situation is ultimately your responsibility.

That said, we can certainly learn from looking at couples who have already gone through the decision-making process. As we look at some familiar couples in this chapter, think about what type of learning, new information, and self-understanding helped them decide how to move forward as individuals and as couples.

Couple Situation 1: John and Mary: "He's Like a Third Child!"

We have followed John and Mary throughout this book to show how they have navigated through their separation. Remember that Mary was very depressed and unhappy with her relationship with John. She was fed up and critical of John for not sharing more family responsibility. She was tired of taking on so much of the work herself and realized that this had much to do with her feeling so unfulfilled. So instead of waiting for John to meet her expectations, she decided to detach from him, take some space, and figure out how to take care of herself. She then told John she wanted a trial separation. John reluctantly cooperated.

What Happened to John and Mary

John and Mary initially agreed to separate for three months and review where they might be after this period of time. They have been physically separated for about two months.

Remember that John did not want a physical separation and was initially quite angry and scared. He thought that Mary was a real bitch for forcing him out of the house and breaking up the family. Although John did not initially state any personal goals for the separation, after his initial anger started to subside, he began to miss his kids terribly and to understand what Mary had been trying to tell him.

Before the separation, John spent very little time with the kids, mostly playtime when he came home from work. Now he had to feed, bathe, and change the baby, and entertain them as well. After John had had one or both of his children overnight, or even for the day, he would try hard to give Mary the impression that he had everything under control. But the truth was, he was exhausted. He began to appreciate how hard a job parenting is.

Because John would visit the kids at the house, Mary would also give him a list of chores to do. John struggled to get them done. He realized that raising kids, taking care of household chores, and working left little time for much fun. He began to look forward to time alone. But most importantly, he developed an appreciation for Mary and how well she handled all of the work.

Perhaps for the first time in five years, John began to really think about Mary's feelings and efforts. He began to realize that her requests were not all that unreasonable. At times he even became frightened, wondering if Mary was right about him not doing his share around the house. This was a major breakthrough, and he came to it on his own, without Mary's nagging and complaining.

Living the life of a single parent, even for a short amount of time, and getting some distance from Mary helped John develop a greater awareness of himself and his role in the family pattern. It increased his capacity for understanding and his empathy for Mary. His new dilemma was whether to tell Mary what he'd realized. Would she laugh and say, "I told you so!" or would she respect him for coming around? Did he have enough courage to admit that he'd been wrong? Would she see him as weak? Was it too late for them? Would Mary even take him back? John was scared.

Meanwhile Mary was continuing to do fairly well. She felt proud that she had taken such a big step to help herself. She was no longer angry with John and was beginning to feel much better about herself. She found herself less stressed. She was beginning to learn how to balance her work, parenting, and household chores with some fun. She discovered that her whole life was not work, which was not an easy lesson for Mary, given that she was raised to think of others first.

She worried that she was neglecting her kids and blowing off work. It took time and continual permission from her counselor and friends and finally her self to begin to realize that all work and no play was her prescription for depression. She also realized that what had attracted her to John in the first place was that he could relax and play. Because she did not have permission from her inner Parent to do likewise, her work during the separation period was to develop this sense of permission.

It's difficult to undo old childhood patterns, but it can also be the key to taking better care of one's self. Mary had to develop a more accepting and self-nurturing inner Parent, and she did so. Had she remained a victim to John, she would have continued living in her prison of anger and depression while waiting for someone to rescue her. By developing her Adult, Mary could also take pride in having made the decision to change.

Mary did not need to change any of her initial goals. She seemed to be doing a fairly good job of taking care of herself, which was getting easier. She was not depressed and burnt out like she had been, and she was not obsessed with John any longer. She was secretly pleased about how he was parenting and sharing the children as well as keeping up the chores. Their communication regarding the children, finances, and household was good.

What was not happening was any talk about them and their relationship and what was going to happen next. Who would make the first move to address this?

After about two months of separation, John asked Mary to have dinner with him without the children. Mary was surprised, but she agreed. Until now, their separation had been conflict free largely because they didn't interact much. They did a fairly good job of dealing with children, but nothing more. She had no idea what to expect at dinner.

Dinner turned out to be very pleasant. It wasn't until after the meal, on a walk, that John began to share what he had been thinking about during the past two months.

JOHN: Mary, this is really hard for me to do, but I have been thinking more about you and us, especially in the last month or so. Having to take care of the kids and do chores and go to work every day, I now realize how much you do in our family and for me as well. I guess that until now, I haven't really seen it from your side.

(*Mary's eyes well up with tears, and she can't speak. She begins to cry and drops her head in her hands.*)

JOHN: (*John is startled. He doesn't expect this reaction. Mary always seems so in charge and so distant, especially lately. What had he done? He puts his hand on her shoulder.*) I'm sorry if I said the wrong thing!

MARY: (*softly, fighting back her tears*) John, you've finally said the right thing. All I've ever wanted to hear from you is that you appreciate me. I've never gotten that from anyone. (*Mary begins to cry harder, and John holds her.*)

Needless to say this brief interaction between John and Mary sparked some new and different energy between them. Through all the work of marriage, family, jobs, and life, John and Mary had neglected one of the most important things in their relationship: each other. Each did what came naturally from what each had learned in their families of origin, until it became unbearable—at least for Mary. The separation process allowed them to stop what was happening and change the pattern. Mary was beginning to learn how to take responsibility for her own happiness. John realized that he had to learn more about his role as a parent and partner, how to nurture and express empathy for Mary, and how to assume more responsibility in their working partnership.

It felt so good to Mary to have John hold her. She had spent so much time feeling angry, hurt, and deprived, but all she had wanted all along was a partner to share the workload. As she spoke to John that night she admitted that she was afraid the situation would fall back to the way it was. John said he was scared, too. Both were feeling good about this new dimension of openness and honesty in their communication. Although they were still young, they both felt that they had aged and grown during their brief period of separation. Both expressed how much they missed the closeness they had felt before they had children. A much-needed bond was redeveloping.

Of course, many couples make the mistake of thinking this is all they need, and quickly move back in together. John and Mary were cautious. Although they did decide to make love and were genuinely high on each other, each realized that this was not enough. They knew they needed to figure out how to maintain the changes they had just started. They knew that this might only be a kind of honeymoon period after things had been so bad for so long.

John and Mary decided to stay separated for the last month of their three-month separation. They did begin to spend more time together and enjoyed each other's company. Their communication seemed to flow more easily. And most importantly, they did not forget their new goals. Moving on to Steps 9 and 10, John and Mary began to evaluate their decision to remain a couple. But how would they know?

Each of them now had had an experience of how awful, conflict-filled, and unsatisfying their relationship could become. During their separation, each took distance from the relationship and that pattern. Mary started by working on her side of the pattern, and John eventually followed. As they started to get closer again, they rekindled positive feelings for each other by exchanging appreciation and strokes. They realized that these feelings were still there, but needed to be stimulated.

The ongoing conflict as well as their difficulty in meeting their individual wants while living under the same roof had seemed to bury any positive feelings between them. As John's changed thinking became more evident, Mary slowly allowed him back in. They knew that getting back together was a risk—a risk they could keep in check through improved communication, a stronger and better sense of themselves, and some new mutual respect. Mary knew that she would never again let things get as bad as they had been, and that if she did, she now had ways to take care of herself. She no longer felt a victim to John. For his part, John began listening to Mary, which was a huge help in reducing conflict and getting Mary's wants met.

They agreed that John would come home after the three-month period was over. He had been staying at the house more and more during this time (trial union). The real test would be time and whether or not the changes would become a permanent part of their relationship.

John agreed to go to counseling if they became stuck again. Mary remained in counseling and continued to focus on taking care of herself and communicating her wants and complaints to John. Their relationship is not perfect—no relationship is—but what they have is much better and fulfilling than what they had before. And the changes were realistic. Neither was expecting the other to be something he or she couldn't be, but they were able to rekindle something that had been neglected for too long.

One year after their separation, John and Mary are still together. Although both have admitted that their separation was one of the most difficult and emotional experiences they have ever gone through, it also allowed them to grow and change like nothing else ever has.

Mary and John's Accomplishments

During their separation Mary and John worked on themselves, which allowed them to change the way they perceived and related to each other. The following is a list of what Mary and John accomplished during their three-month separation.

1. After realizing that she was unhappy and stressed, Mary made a decision to help herself and to learn to relax and have some fun.

    She began by seeking the help of a counselor and some close friends. With the support of someone out of her immediate situation, she began to teach herself how to feel better. This was difficult, because she had learned early in life to take care of other people and not her self. She started to practice detaching from her expectations of John and refusing to allow herself to be a victim any longer.

    This is what propelled her psychological separation from her pattern and from John, to whom she had given the power to make her feel so bad. She learned over time that she and only she had the power to make herself feel better.

    Mary began to develop a loving, caring, nurturing inner Parent, who gave her permission to become more aware of her wants and learn to care for herself better. With this decision, the family conflict eased, which was not only good for Mary, but for the children as well.

2. As Mary learned to ease her own anger and feel better, her next step was to tell John that she was unhappy, that she wanted a working partnership and not a Parent–Child relationship. She said if he was unwilling to work with her, she wanted a physical separation. She decided on a trial separation in which neither of them would be expected to work on the relationship. Mary committed to working on her self, and John resentfully went along with her decision.

3. Over time John began to get in touch with how much he missed Mary and his children. He began to realize and appreciate how much Mary did for the family. John also had to confront and separate from childhood programming that told him that his wife would do all the household work, and take care of the children and him. Without realizing it, he had expected Mary to be the same kind of parent his mother was. This may have worked for his parents, but as he came to realize, he had to update to a new era.

    He also recognized that he felt lonely without Mary and the kids, and that maybe he could learn to be a better partner. John realized that he had to learn to listen to Mary and not just get defensive. He was learning to express nurturing and care for her. He took a big risk by approaching Mary to tell her how he felt and with a request to work on their relationship.

4. Because the separation had allowed Mary to grow and feel better, she was in a better position to respond. She respected John for being truthful and felt closer to him.

5. John and Mary stayed physically separated for another month, although John began to spend more time at the house. Their trial separation turned into a therapeutic separation. His more frequent visits were a kind of trial-union period during which they could see how well they got along with each other and if the changes they talked about would be maintained.

6. John eventually moved home. Both John and Mary felt that they had learned much through their separation experience. They both realized that they each had a responsibility not only to meet their own wants better but to communicate those wants and dissatisfactions to each other. They worked on learning to listen to each other better. They decided to make time every week and sometimes more often to talk. By doing this regularly, they allowed each other in at a deeper level and were able to monitor each other's stress levels. They felt they were beginning to learn emotional caretaking, one of the most important aspects of a relationship and family. Mary had to learn to be aware of controlling her anger at John when it flared up. She had to continually practice asking for help and planning family responsibilities with him.

Their weekly talks were about specific wants and responsibilities for the children and how they would divide up the work. Sometimes this had to be talked out and negotiated. Mary also had to learn how to give up some of the control over the family. Remember, her training was as Super Mom, a fast track to burnout.

She also had to learn to tolerate that John doing things *his* way was OK, which was tough for her.

Mary also had a hard time giving herself permission to have more fun. Balancing work with relaxation was something she had to learn and to remind herself to do. She couldn't leave the household tasks to John, because he wouldn't necessarily see or think about what needed to be done around the house. Sometimes she would just have to tell him. This shift in perspective made all the difference. This sense of entitlement—the right to ask John for his help—was Mary's core issue and perhaps the biggest lesson of all for her.

John, for his part, had to remember to take responsibility to share the work of family life. The more he did so, the more loving and appreciative he felt toward Mary. They still had conflict, but they learned to resolve it more quickly and talk through what they wanted from themselves and each other. They knew that they would probably become stuck again, but now they had a way to work through any rut. Every time they worked through a stuck place, they gained confidence in themselves and each other.

Before the separation period and process, Mary saw John as the problem, and John viewed Mary as the nag. After the separation period, they appear to have a more realistic understanding of each other and have learned a valuable lesson on how to take responsibility for themselves and create satisfaction in their relationship and family life.

EXERCISE

See Ground Rules for Talking, page 17.

1. What do you believe are the important factors for Mary and John each getting their relationship back on track?

2. What changed for John?

3. What changed for Mary?

4. Can you see how the basic process of John and Mary's relationship improved? How did a change in John appear to affect a change in Mary and vice versa (circular)?

5. Can you see how John and Mary evaluated whether their separation was having any effect on improving their relationship? Was it the physical space alone that created a change, or what happened to each of them while they were apart? What were the core changes that resulted in their deciding to reconcile?

6. How are John and Mary's issues and process similar and different from yours? Are you at a point where you need to evaluate whether your relationship is making any progress or changes? Or do you need to work on other steps of Separation Management?

Couple Situation 10: Jane and Randy: "Romance Lost"

Jane and Randy have been a couple for a little over two years. Jane just turned thirty-eight and Randy forty. Although Randy had been in several short-term relationships, he was never married. Jane was married for ten years and has two girls, ages twelve and ten. The first six months of Jane and Randy's relationship was like a dream for both of them. They felt like soul mates. They did everything together and had so many similarities that both couldn't believe how great they each felt. They often joked about pinching each other to see if their relationship were real.

But somewhere between six months and their first-year anniversary, things started to change. Randy became more stressed at work and found himself withdrawing when he got home. During the day Jane took care of other children in her home and looked forward to Randy coming home so they could spend the evening talking and playing family games. But more and more often Randy couldn't find the energy, and when he did, he would not stop complaining about his poor work situation and supervisor.

Jane found herself getting bored and angry. She had been supportive of Randy and his job situation for months, but she was beginning to see him as selfish and self-consumed. She felt a lack of connection with him and was angry that he had changed the rules on her. Early in their second year together, Jane started to become more vocal in her criticisms of Randy's moods, attitude, and behavior. Randy became defensive and protective of himself.

For several months, Randy would respond to Jane's criticisms with promises to do better, but he found himself shutting down to her. He felt that he could no longer talk about what bothered him the most. What had been such a wonderful, warm, supportive connection with Jane was now becoming emotionally unsafe and troublesome.

Their communication process was clearly not working. Whenever they sat down to talk about their relationship, Jane almost immediately became angry and went on the attack. Randy was already so stressed from work and lack of sleep that he would often start to doze off. At first Jane became very angry and even more critical and then began to withdraw from Randy to teach him a lesson.

Many couples enter marital or relationship counseling when one or both believe the romance is gone. This was certainly the case with Jane and Randy. Neither of them expected the glitter of their relationship to slowly fade—a normal part of a developing relationship—and both truly believed they had fallen out of love.

Being able to successfully negotiate the shift from the romance stage to the disillusionment/compromise stage often determines how the rest of the relationship will go. Couples who work to keep a healthy degree of love, affection, and sex (as defined by each partner) through the transition are more likely to be able to create a satisfying relationship beyond the romance stage. People hooked on romance, however, may struggle with the reality of a good enough relationship and a mutually positive working partnership.

Goals Jane and Randy Set for Themselves

1. Getting Some Good Information About What They Might Reasonably Expect from a Relationship at This Stage They might seek out other couples who have made it successfully through this stage or find a couples group, course, seminar, workshop, or counselor.

2. To Acknowledge Their Grief and Disillusionment and Begin to Grapple with Compromise As you begin to see the humanness of your partner, you often grieve the fantasy of what you wanted or thought he or she would be. Expectations must now be adjusted to a real person. We must challenge the fantasy and unrealistic expectations of our illusion that the "madly in love" phase will last, that our partner will always make us happy or know just what we want. We sometimes react to these differences as if they are rejections, betrayals, and punishments. Jane and Randy must learn to adjust their expectations. They might look at what they were taught about relationships as children. They might look at their favorite childhood fairy tales and think about what those stories taught them about what to expect from marriage.

3. Attempt to Redefine Their Wants and Expectations and Learn to Communicate Those to Each Other The more one knows oneself and can verbalize this, the better he or she can communicate with a partner.

Jane and Randy must learn to talk and listen to each other, as well as to stop conflict when it arises; in other words, they would take on Steps 1 and 2. They would also work Step 3, Goals and Purposes of Separation, which would include gaining insight into what they can reasonably expect from their relationship.

By the time a couple reaches the disillusionment/compromise stage, they have begun to see their partner's limitations. If I were working with Jane and Randy, I would ask them to remember what attracted them to each other initially. I would also help them focus on how they can again meet each other's new wants and expectations in the present. Jane and Randy might actually benefit from some type of separation to get some distance and learn to meet their own individual wants. The type of separation they might choose would depend on how much damage has already been done.

EXERCISE

See Ground Rules for Talking, page 17.

You can do this exercise alone or with a partner.

1. Reflect on your childhood fantasies of what you expected in a relationship. Can you remember what you thought about a love relationship or marriage growing up through grade school and high school?

2. Can you remember what your favorite fairy tales or childhood stories were? How did men and women behave? Did couples live happily ever after?

3. Think about the romance periods of relationships in which you are currently involved or have been involved. What were they like and how was it when they ended?

Jane and Randy Change Their Relationship

Jane and Randy were both in shock over how they were feeling about each other. Remember, they had felt like soul mates for their first year together. Now they were questioning whether they were even friends.

They decided that they needed to talk with a third person about their changing relationship. Jane had already been in a ten-year relationship and felt that Randy was a different type of man from her ex-spouse. Randy had never really been in a long-term relationship and had little idea of what to expect from a relationship over time. They thought that perhaps a counselor could help.

The counselor started their session by having Jane and Randy each talk about their perspectives on how their relationship had been in the beginning and how it had changed.

JANE: I remember how great things were with Randy when we first dated. He was so thoughtful and kind. We would spend hours at a time just hanging out with each other, laughing, talking, and sharing the little things in our lives. We never wanted to part. We were so affectionate that we couldn't keep our hands off each other. We would only get together on those times the girls were with their father. But those times were so special. Our lovemaking was passionate, new, exciting, and frequent, wow!

(*Jane bursts into tears.*) I just don't know what went wrong. But over the past year things slowly started to decline. After about a year of dating, Randy moved in with the girls and me. I was so thrilled about having him with us full-time. No more sad endings on those days the girls returned from their father's and Randy had to leave.

The girls had a hard time initially, but they saw how well Randy and I got along, and they seemed happy that we had a man in our house once again. But slowly I started seeing parts of Randy that I hadn't seen before. I noticed that he seemed moodier than I thought he was. He would come home from work and just want to sit around or withdraw into his hobbies. He no longer wanted to sit and talk or play games. He said that he needed time to relax and be with himself.

I felt so abandoned by him. We were spending less time together now than we had in our first year. At times the girls and I would be hanging out after homework, just talking or doing a project or even watching a TV program, but Randy was off by himself and not around. I had always hoped that a new partner would be fully involved with the girls and me. I started to think, *What's the point of his even being here?*

Whenever I approached him with my unhappiness, he seemed to get defensive. He would give me all the excuses he had to explain his need for time alone. I know I started to become angry and attacking, but he really changed the rules. We just don't communicate anymore!

RANDY: (*shaking his head while Jane told her side of the story, at times looking really sad and hopeless*) I'm confused about what happened. All I know is that we had something great, and now all we do is argue. I feel that Jane doesn't like me very much. This is so upsetting because I wanted so much to please her and make our relationship work. I try to listen, but often I am so tired from work that I just want to withdraw into my hobbies.

COUNSELOR: Randy, what type of hobbies do you have?

RANDY: Well, I like to work out sometime in the evening, which means a trip to the gym. I also like woodworking. I've set up my tools and equipment in our garage, and I just go out to putter around. It's a way to clear my head after a long day.

COUNSELOR: Jane, how have Randy's retreats to the gym or garage affected you?

JANE: Well, I think he's avoiding the girls and me. I want him to join us in our talks and games and even to watch a TV show, but he hardly does that anymore. I remember when I couldn't keep Randy off of me.

Jane again starts to sob and says she is so disappointed and unhappy. Randy puts his head down and mumbles that he is trying very hard to be a good partner but feels criticized for not living up to Jane's expectations.

The counselor explains how all relationships go from the romance stage to the disillusionment/compromise stage. She explains that even people who are aware of these stages still have a difficult time accepting the slow shift out of the initial honeymoon. Randy and Jane are a good example. They had dated for almost a year before moving in with each other. During that first year, Randy spent a lot of time with Jane at her place and she at his. Their time together was limited but great, with each of them feeling total involvement and intimacy without the weight of responsibility.

But after Randy moved in, a slow separation started to take place. This was experienced as a cooling period in their relationship.

For one thing, they began to see each other daily. Before this, Randy usually had Jane all to himself. But now he had to share her with the girls. Of course he knew before moving in how much Jane loved her girls and that they came as a package deal. What Randy didn't realize was how much he might start to have negative feelings about the girls always being around. It was so much easier with just Jane and him.

It helped Randy and Jane to hear that the change of feelings and disappointments they were experiencing was normal. But this information was not enough to make either of them feel OK. They just didn't know if they could salvage what they still had.

The counselor helped them see that their communication pattern was not working, that talking always seemed to break down into blaming and defensiveness. Adjusting from Stage 1 (romance/fantasy) to Stage 2 (disillusionment/compromise) or 3 (reality), was difficult enough for most couples, but it would be impossible for Randy and Jane unless they learned how to stop their conflict and really talk and listen. So, with the help of a counselor, Randy and Jane learned how to listen to one another once again. At first this was hard to do. They had become used to interrupting the other or using body language or facial expressions that indicated that they weren't listening.

Randy had a way of looking down when Jane was talking. When Jane shook her head no as Randy talked, he would shut down. With the counselor's vigilant guidance and coaching, Jane and Randy learned the first major lesson in communication: Each partner will have his or her own reality (consisting of his or her own truth, beliefs, feelings, opinions, and thoughts) and both are right. There is not a right or wrong reality, just different. You may not like everything about your partner's reality, but it belongs to your partner. The best you can do is learn to listen to it and understand it. You may not always agree with it, but at least you will know where your partner is coming from.

In order to survive long-term, the individuals in a couple must allow room for two realities in their relationship. Otherwise they will find themselves fighting, arguing, or having passive struggles over who is right.

Jane's Expectations

Jane came from a single-parent family made up of just her mother and younger brother. She remembers how lonely her mother felt at times and how she would often say, "We sure could use a man around here!" Jane's father divorced her mother when Jane was five years old. Her relationship with her father was OK but not great.

Jane had hoped her first husband would provide so much. But according to her, he was a poor communicator and never really was a family person. Jane's unmet expectations from her dad and ex-spouse resurfaced and were now placed on Randy's shoulders. During the first year, Jane felt that she had finally met her dream partner, but the second year was a real disappointment.

Randy's Expectations

Randy is a third child, after an older brother and sister. His parents are still together, but he doesn't remember them talking, fighting, or even loving much. They seem to just coexist. Randy feels he didn't have much of a role model for how to *be* in a relationship. It felt so good to be so connected to Jane during their courtship. But he was so used to living alone that it was hard to find the boundaries between alone time and family time. It was even harder to find time alone with Jane.

Getting Unstuck

The counseling stayed focused on helping Jane and Randy get unstuck. With time and practice, each was able to call time-out whenever feelings became too heated. With time-out came the responsibility for the person who called it to come back and talk again after a cooling-down period. This could be ten minutes or an hour, but not more than twenty-four hours. Randy and Jane also learned to share the talking time. Each took between three and five minutes to talk while the other listened. They understood that listening was about understanding and not necessarily agreeing.

Jane and Randy learned that they became defensive and reactive to each other when they did not like what they heard or when what they heard was different from what they may have wanted. In other words, fighting and arguing came second to feeling hurt, disappointed, fearful, or threatened. They learned that they would have to start examining their relationship by talking and listening, and that they had to work at understanding and accepting the other's perspective. They learned to speak using "I" messages, such as, "In *my* opinion . . ."; "I believe . . ."; and "I think and feel . . ."

What each learned in counseling and couples courses was that they were both responsible for the breakdown in their communication pattern, and each of them had to understand his or her part in that breakdown. Jane and Randy learned that it was not necessarily specific subjects that created such problems for them, but the way they talked. Neither had anticipated that they would have such a major adjustment to make.

As Jane and Randy learned to talk, listen, and control conflict better, they began to talk more about what each wanted and expected from the other. Each acknowledged how good it felt to be heard again. They had been so worried and tired from all the conflict, but now the counselor helped them focus on their strengths, and they had some hopes for their future.

With the help of a counselor, Jane and Randy were able to negotiate compromises and to ensure Randy some alone time. Jane came to realize that Randy's need for time for himself did not mean he wasn't willing to spend time with her and the girls.

Slowly, these two recovered from the stuck "black hole" they had slowly sunk into in the past year. They realized that each of them could influence the other if they approached the other with respect. They realized that when each took responsibility for him- or herself, this would open the door for the other to take responsibility as well.

Much to their surprise, Jane and Randy started to feel closer and even began to like each other again. They learned that when their communication process broke down, they had a way to come back and repair it. They were beginning to regain trust and confidence in each other. And as things improved and each of them felt better, they became more relaxed and accepting in their relationship.

Randy learned to use his voice and tell Jane when he felt judged and attacked, and much to his surprise, she heard him. As their communication process improved, Jane and Randy began to talk about their vision of what they wanted their relationship to be. They discussed values and what things were really important. They rediscovered the many things they had in common and were even a little baffled at how they had become so stuck. They hadn't fallen out of love with each other, but were learning to go from romance to a deeper love and friendship with each other.

They also realized that although the romance stage was great, in many ways it lacked reality. They could see that life had, in a way, stood still while they were consumed and even addicted to each other. In a couples communication course they learned that most couples have similar experiences in their relationships. Randy and Jane came to dearly appreciate commitment and how it helps when things are not going well. They realized that commitment can be the glue that holds partners together during difficult periods of time.

What Happened to Jane and Randy?

Jane and Randy are now in year three of their relationship and the good and loving feelings they had in year one are alive and well. They are now better able to negotiate time alone and time together, and they have learned to accept their differences and how to stop "go nowhere" arguments. They have learned to take care of each other and themselves.

Each has learned to probe beneath their anger and frustration to find the real underlying disappointment, hurt, sadness, fears, and wants. Before this, both partners felt they could not cope or go on unless they got what they wanted from the other. Now they realize that they will not always get what they want, but what they do get is becoming "good enough."

Each has accepted his or her part in making things work and the importance of give and take. Each has taken some risks to joke more and have more fun in the relationship. More importantly, they have learned how to be friends. Sex is still good, which has definitely helped things outside the bedroom as well. Jane and Randy have been successfully making the transition from romance to acceptance, stability, and reality. They realize, as many couples do, that leaving the romance stage may be one of the most difficult periods of adjustment for any couple, but that it may also be the start of a real relationship.

How Jane and Randy Used Separation Management

1. Jane and Randy learned to reduce and stop their conflict and communicate with each other again. They did this with help from a counselor and a couples course.

2. With improved communication and reduced conflict, Jane and Randy were able to replace defensiveness and blame with listening and understanding and thereby develop empathy for one another. Each was able to accept his and her part to their communication breakdown. Although Jane felt justified and angry over Randy's abandoning her, she came to realize that her blaming and attacking kept him from reconnecting to her. Randy learned to balance time with Jane and the girls and time alone. They had to separate from their fantasies of what they felt a relationship should be, and modify their expectations to fit their real partner's wants. Their psychological separation turned therapeutic for their relationship, and helped them to sort out their expectations and behavior and to balance self-care with reasonable expectations of the other.

Initially both Jane and Randy would have best fit Level 2 ("There must be a change") on the Relationship Investment–Commitment Scale. They were committed to trying to change before breaking up, and they were willing to take responsibility for their parts in the problem.

Their renewed investment and commitment served to get them through some very difficult times. And the renewal of empathy gave them important protection against future problems.

3. Because they were able to manage their conflict and improve communication, their evaluation, Step 9, was relatively easy. If they had tried to evaluate and decide during their bleakest period and before all of their learning, chances are good that they would have ended their relationship. But because they gave themselves the time and space to learn and grow, they felt closer and more connected and knew they wanted to stay together.

EXERCISE

See Ground Rules for Talking, page 17.

1. Identify and discuss what you think were the key points that allowed Jane and Randy to adjust from romance through conflict to a more real and fulfilling relationship.

2. Discuss and think about how your relationship(s) has changed since you left the romance stage.

3. How did you and your partner adjust and cope with the transition?

4. How did expectations change as you became more familiar with each other?

5. What do you think about the purpose or goals of Jane and Randy's separation? What are they separating from? Do you think a separation would accomplish this?

6. As we discuss more and more couples, can you see the qualities that go into making a relationship work? Identifying those qualities can be useful during evaluation and decision-making time.

Couple Situation 11: Judy and Tina: "Mommies"

Judy and Tina are both in their early forties and have been living together for the past five years. Judy had been attracted to females since she was a teenager, and declared herself a lesbian at an early age. She had many intimate male friends, but has only been romantically involved with women. Judy met Tina at a party and they felt attracted to each other immediately. Tina had been married for ten years to a very controlling man somewhat older than she, and finally ended the relationship. After a few years of short-term lesbian relationships, Tina seemed more than ready to settle down. Tina and Judy dated for about a month and then became more serious. After six months they began living together, and they have now been together for five years.

Both women knew they wanted children, and this bonded them even more. They decided that Judy would be the one to become pregnant and carry their child. The pregnancy went very well and both women felt a great deal of love for each other and their unborn child. Jennifer was born healthy, and Judy and Tina celebrated the new addition to their family. Judy bonded instantly with the baby and was relieved that breast-feeding came fairly easily. Tina shared in the care of the baby in all ways possible. Both women continued to work.

Things went fairly smoothly until Jennifer started to become a more active little person with a mind of her own. After about six months Tina began to notice how much Judy's attention was focused on Jennifer. Tina tried to do some of her own bonding with Jennifer, only to have Jennifer cling to Judy, demanding that Judy be the one who put her to bed, feed her, change her, etc. Even though Judy continuously attempted to involve Tina, Jennifer would demand Judy and Judy would comply with those demands.

It was obvious that Judy loved being the much-needed mother. Tina had difficulty putting her feelings about this aside. Tina felt guilty about feeling jealous and competitive over all the attention being given to Jennifer. After all, Jennifer was a baby, whom she should love unconditionally as her child. But along with beginning to feel somewhat rejected by Jennifer, Tina also began to resent that she had so little time with Judy. After work, Judy was involved with Jennifer. They played, ate dinner, had bath time and story time, and Judy had little left over for Tina.

Judy was aware of her strong bond with Jennifer and would often ask Tina if she felt left out. Tina could not admit that she did. It seemed such a primal response. As Jennifer grew, the problem only became worse, and she began to throw temper tantrums and demand all of Judy's time.

Finally, after several months of really struggling, Tina started to become depressed and to lose hope that anything would ever change. She also noticed that her anger was showing more, which only made matters worse. Jennifer would run to Judy and say, "Tina's being mean to me," which only made Tina feel worse.

Jennifer was a very bright and verbal two-year-old, and learned quickly how to play Judy and Tina against each other. To complicate matters, Jennifer had always slept between her mommies. Even though this made for a cozy and warm threesome initially, Tina was now keenly aware of the symbolism. Jennifer *was* between them all the time.

Over time, Tina found herself withdrawing more and more and fighting with Judy about everything, including her parenting of Jennifer. Tina still could not openly tell Judy how left out, hurt, and disappointed she felt. Tina missed their warm connection, and sex didn't seem an option. It just didn't happen anymore. One night, after a little too much wine, Tina's feelings surfaced.

TINA: (*looking sad and worried*) Judy, I'm not sure I can continue with the way things are.

JUDY: (*puzzled*) Why, what's wrong?

TINA: You mean you don't know?

JUDY: No, I don't.

TINA: Well then, you obviously don't care much about me or us anymore.

JUDY: (*getting frustrated*) What are you saying?

TINA: (*with a raised voice that is beginning to crack*) Because all you do in your nonworking time is care for Jennifer, and our relationship is at the bottom of the list.

JUDY: (*more irritated, with raised voice*) C'mon, Tina, for God's sake, she's a baby! I don't believe you're jealous of her!

TINA: (*beginning to openly cry, yelling*) You just don't get it, do you?

Tina left the room to spend the night in the spare bedroom.

Judy was confused. She had noticed Tina getting more short-tempered with Jennifer in the past few months, but she thought it was just the usual power struggles with a two-year-old. Now it was obvious that Tina was upset with Judy and expected something from her. But exactly what she wanted was unclear.

That night Tina thought long and hard about her problem. She felt so angry with Judy that she was having a hard time being around her. She felt the same with Jennifer, who obviously felt her tension and acted out even more. Tina did not know what to do. She decided she would leave the family bed for now and stay separated within the home. She told Judy that she was taking some space from her and Jennifer until she could figure things out for herself. Judy tried to get Tina to talk, but Tina refused, saying it would be best if she just stayed away for a while.

Tina contacted a good friend with whom she could talk about her situation. Tina's friend could see right away that Tina was really hurting and suggested that she talk to a professional. Tina took her friend's advice and sought out a family counselor she could see alone. Tina told no one about her situation.

First Counseling Session

Tina explained her family situation and talked a lot about how, for many months now, Judy had been preoccupied with Jennifer and had turned away from Tina. Tina was beginning to believe that her affection and love for Judy was dying fast.

COUNSELOR: Tina, tell me what your feelings are about Judy's relationship with Jennifer.

TINA: I guess I'm OK with that. After all, Jennifer is just a baby. I can't be upset with her.

COUNSELOR: Feelings are feelings, there is no right or wrong. I hear a very rational, grown-up reaction. What does that little kid in you feel?

TINA: (*becoming very serious and sad looking*) I'm so mad at both of them. (*She bursts into tears.*) What a horrible person I am to feel this way!

COUNSELOR: (*letting Tina cry, get angry, and criticize herself for a few minutes*) You're really beating up on yourself for feeling this way, aren't you?

TINA: Shouldn't I be? After all, I'm a grown-up. This is my . . . our child, and I should be filled with love and happiness over even having a family. Instead I want to run away and never see them again. Listen to me. I'm pathetic.

COUNSELOR: No one has ever told you that your feelings are quite normal?

TINA: No! I just always thought I'm one sick, selfish little girl inside this adult body.

The counselor went on to say how many families, both heterosexual and homosexual, have difficulty adjusting and balancing to a new family member. Having kids often puts a strain on intimacy within the couple. Dads often feel this very strongly as moms bond and turn their attention to infants and toddlers.

Because Tina and Judy both expected to be the "moms," Tina felt real disappointment when Jennifer seemed to bond more with Judy than with her. The counselor suggested that they were probably experiencing some natural competition. With Judy being the birth mother, it was more likely that an early bond would form with her, and they weren't prepared for what that would mean.

As Jennifer got older, the counselor suggested, Tina and Jennifer could certainly develop a better relationship. All was by no means lost. The counselor asked Tina if she was ready to talk more about this with Judy. Tina again started to cry and expressed shame for having jealous, angry feelings. She said she wanted to wait until she had more control over herself before talking with Judy. She was afraid that after suppressing her feelings for so long she would blow up and they would get into a bad argument, which could perhaps end the relationship. Tina really had doubts as to whether she could ever get over this.

What Tina Did

Tina continued to distance herself with an in-house separation as well as some brief time away from home to be with friends. Judy was becoming very concerned, and did not really know what had happened or what she had done. Judy felt that Tina was blaming her and punishing her by withdrawing and refusing to talk.

Finally, after almost a month of Judy and Tina not sleeping together, hardly talking, and building an icy cold wall, Judy had her meltdown.

JUDY: (*Busting into Tina's room after Jennifer was asleep, with a desperate and raised voice*) Tina, I have had it! I know you're angry with me for something, and I'm not sure why but I know I can't go on this way. The climate in this house is icy cold and we need to talk.

TINA: I'm not ready to talk.

JUDY: No, we have to talk now. I don't care how much it hurts to hear what you have to say about me; anything is better than what we're doing now.

Tina tried hard just to stay angry, but she was quickly in tears as she explained how resentful she had become of Judy and Jennifer. Tina shared that she had even gone to counseling to help her deal with her feelings and that she now understood her problems, but didn't know if she could change how she felt.

Tina even admitted that she had thought about breaking up. She went on to explain that the counselor had told her that her feelings were very normal, that lots of parents experience feelings of resentment at being outsiders in their own families, but that somehow her feelings were really being aggravated by her poor relationship with her own mother.

TINA: (*holding back tears*) You know, my mother always favored my older sister over me, and seeing you bond so tightly with Jennifer is just bringing back all those old feelings of emotional abandonment and not getting what I needed as a child.

She began crying hard. She explained that she felt ashamed about feeling so hurt, but just couldn't shake the feeling of rage. She felt she was entitled to Judy's love and was actually in competition both for Jennifer and with her, as both mom and child.

Tina also admitted that she had been waiting for Judy to fix the problem, but had realized through counseling that this was her issue, and she needed to resolve it on her own.

JUDY: This is *not* your issue alone. Real partners work on this kind of thing *together*.

Judy approached Tina tentatively to give her a hug. Tina cried and cried as she let herself be held and soothed by Judy.

Judy explained that she was not angry at the way Tina felt, especially after hearing about her family experiences, but she was angry with Tina for not trusting that they could work this out together. Judy explained that her own shame about not being able to handle things better and her fear that Tina would reject her had also been keeping her all bottled up. She told Tina how much she'd missed her and how sorry she was that things had gotten so strained between them. Tina rejoined the family bed that night.

Judy requested that she go to a counseling session with Tina and did. Together they worked on how to maintain their relationship and not let Jennifer get between them. The icy cold wall that had been slowly building had broken. Tina and Judy's communication immediately began to improve, and they once again started to feel attracted to each other. They realized that they really were on the same page about how to raise Jennifer, and began to feel close again.

DISCUSSION

How did the steps of Separation Management apply to Judy and Tina? What did they use to evaluate and decide what to do about their problems?

1. Judy and Tina were more at the passive–avoidant end of the Conflict Scale. They would mostly avoid conflict after feeling terrible about open fighting. This seemed to work well enough for a while, until finally the avoidance of underlying feelings and problems became destructive.

2. Communication was blocked. Tina felt bad about herself and about not sharing her feelings for fear that she would be viewed as another baby for Judy to take care of.

3. Tina initially blamed Judy for the problem. By acting out more with Jennifer and distancing herself from Judy, Tina only made the problem worse.

4. Tina found the courage to seek help, but also found out that she and her own history were playing a part in how she reacted to the family triangle. Even with more knowledge, though, Tina was frozen on how to work through her problems and feared that talking would end their relationship. So she unilaterally chose to withdraw into an in-house separation to reduce conflict. This may have temporarily reduced conflict and protected Tina from the threat of more shame, but did nothing to solve the problem.

5. By challenging Tina to talk, Judy not only opened the door to working on their relationship, but also signaled to Tina that she was willing to be a real partner to her. Judy apologized for missing the signals of Tina's desperation, but reminded Tina that she could not be expected to read her mind. The renewed bonding between Judy and Tina allowed them to work on not letting Jennifer get between them to the extent that she had, and avoiding a competition for Judy's love and attention.

It was only because Judy persisted in pushing Tina to talk that the underlying reasons for their separation could surface. Judy's investment and commitment to Tina and the relationship provided the basis for working on their problems.

A year later, Tina and Judy are still together and both very active in parenting Jennifer. They must continue to work through conflicts focused around Jennifer, but seem so much better off when they realize that the source of those conflicts come from how they are feeling and communicating about each other at the time.

This couple learned a new way to work through their problems, which restored their satisfaction in each other and family life. Tina learned to trust that she and Judy were truly in this relationship together (a major evaluation point for her) and that she had to work on new ways of dealing with Jennifer, too.

For this couple, the physical separation allowed space, which simply highlighted the severity of their problem. Their willingness to work together allowed them to psychologically and therapeutically separate from an unproductive pattern, and both learned to share responsibility to change this pattern.

EXERCISE

See Ground Rules for Talking, page 17.

1. Can you identify with either Tina or Judy's side of this problem?

2. Do you ever feel like you're the outsider in your family?

3. Have you had feelings that you could not admit having toward your child(ren) or partner?

4. How do you get unstuck? Have you talked with your partner about this? Would he or she listen?

This is a common and familiar problem in family life after a baby is born, or in blended families with children. There are ways to work on it. Talk about it, listen, and seek help if needed.

Step 9 Exercise: Evaluate Your Goals

Step 9 is about reflecting on and evaluating whether your goals for separation are working.

I encourage you to find some time to sit alone quietly and think about the difficult period (of weeks, months, or years) you have been going through that led you to this book.

What is different now from when you first started working on your current situation or separation?

If you have already begun a separation, how have things changed for you and in your relationship (regardless of what type of separation it is or was)?

Areas to Focus On:

1. Review the steps already covered so far to see if any need to be reconsidered or reworked.

2. Your process

   A. If you were left by your partner, how do you think you are handling it? How do you think and feel you are doing in your grief and recovery? What's OK? What's still Not OK? What and who has helped? Are you stuck in denial, anger, sadness, or feeling sorry for yourself? Is it OK to grieve? Have you moved on or do you need more time?

   B. If you are working on you, do you have a vision of what you want or how you want to be? Have you accepted responsibility for your side of the problem? What specifically do you want to change about you? Have you reached any of your goal(s)? Are you still stuck in the same place you started? Are you focused on your inner self and/or your relationship? Do you need to review goals from the Step 8 exercise? Learning to accept yourself as OK right now, while you are working on ways to accomplish your goals, is a goal in itself!

   C. If you are working on your relationship, what specifically is different in you, your behavior, perception, beliefs, feelings, and expectations about you and your partner? Do you have any observations or experiences of what may be different for your partner in these areas? Has this changed anything in the pattern or process (psychological separation) of your relationship? Is your partner invested in changes or not? How are you both doing on relationship skills such as controlling conflict, communication, repairing a broken process, intimacy, meeting each others' expectations and wants better, exchanging strokes, and asking for what you want? Are expectations and goals clear, realistic, and measurable? Are they too high or too low? Do any changes and goals relate to the original purpose of your separation, or are things different with time and more information? If your partner is not cooperating with the goals of separation, are you working on you or waiting on permission from your partner?

3.   What is your inner Child feeling and saying about you, your partner, and your relationship now? How have your feelings changed over time? Be aware of those feelings and intuitions that come from your free OK Child as different from those coming from your scared, angry, overdependent or overcompliant Not OK Child. The free OK Child may be able to see possibilities and healthy changes. The Not OK, scared, or overanxious Child may feel she needs to cling to the old patterns and old relationships and not discover the inner power to make new dreams and see positive changes. Get in touch with what you (and the Child in you) really want!

Is a more empowering, loving, nurturing Parent helping you cope, develop new messages and permissions, and become motivated to be who you are? Is a critical or overcontrolling and self-limiting Parent keeping you where you are with self-doubt and fear to be you and speak your mind? What should the Parent you (versus the Child you) do? What will *you* do? Attempt to be as honest as you can with your self (Adult).

What does your Adult think about your situation (or separation) from the beginning to now? What does the bigger picture look like to your Adult? Are your expectations reasonable and attainable? Are you and/or your partner invested in reaching goals? Do your goals need to be reviewed and reworked?

Sometimes you may feel something is Not OK, but you follow your Adult thinking instead. For example, you (scared Child) may feel you should stay with someone in an abusive relationship, even though you know (Adult) it is not good for you. I have found that even though changes may be scary, if your Adult decides it is right and good for you, your confidence in the change may increase. Of course, it is best if you continue to evaluate a change over time.

Sometimes trying on a change for a day or more can bring insight and feelings about how you might do with that change. For example, acting as if you were separated from your partner or acting as if you were reunited and feeling very close to a partner may give you a sense of what the situation would be like if it were a reality.

4. On a scale from 1 to 10, rate yourself on how you feel you're doing now as compared to when you first started working on your separation or situation, with 1 being the lowest and worst place you have ever been and 10 being the highest and the best place. You can also pick a range instead of a single number; for instance, "I used to be a 3 or 4 and now I'm a 6 or 7." You can also rate yourself on how you think you were before separation became an issue.

   Are you moving up or down? How changeable are you?

5. If you are working on a relationship, is it clear what is being worked on and who has responsibility for what changes? Do you need to review the areas of the relationship identified in the Step 8 Exercise?

   If you were to evaluate your relationship in terms of how positive and OK it is in all areas, what would you rate it? Maybe 50 percent positive–50 percent negative? Maybe 60 percent positive–40 percent negative? How has this changed over time?

6. How are you stopping yourself from reaching your goals? Is it time to stop avoiding and start working? Is it time to change goals because your current ones are not working? Maybe your goals need to be restated or rewritten to be more specific or action oriented. Perhaps you are not ready, have not made an investment or commitment, or you haven't taken responsibility to work on your goals. Are they your goals or someone else's? Is it time to ask for help?

   Talking with a trusted friend, family member, clergyperson, or counselor or therapist, joining a self-help or support group, taking a couples course or seminar, or reading some personal growth books can all be helpful as you think about, feel your way through, and evaluate your situation and goals.

   If you talk with a family member, friend, or clergyperson, just be sure this person knows the difference between what you want and are struggling with, and what he or she may want or fear for you. Choose a safe and trusted person who can listen and be concerned with *your* expectations, wants, and welfare. You don't need to be rescued or criticized for what you have or haven't done.

Too Good to Leave, Too Bad to Stay by Mira Kirshenbaum is a excellent resource for those still on the fence.

It is your life, relationship, and future, and only you can decide whether it is working for you!

Conclusions

In sum, every individual and couple will have to determine whether their goals are being reached in their separation. There's no standardized test here. As we've seen, some people decide to end their relationships, others are forced to end theirs, and still others decide to stay together. Remember that this is a circular process, with all the steps weaving in and out of each other. For example, if conflict is not satisfactorily controlled or the purpose of a separation is not clear, it will be difficult to evaluate whether you are meeting your goals. Not being able to adequately evaluate your goals may interfere with good decision making.

No one can tell you how to do this; the decisions you and your partner make will depend on your histories together and apart as well as each of your expectations, your willingness to do some work on your self, your degree of empathy for your partner, etc. Ultimately, however, it comes down to you and your relationship with your self.

As I have so often pointed out in these pages, the better you understand your self, beliefs, values, feelings, wants, behaviors, expectations, and patterns in your relationship, the better you will be able to evaluate how your relationship is working and meeting those wants.

Examining how reasonable and appropriate your expectations are allows you to further evaluate how well your relationship may or may not be meeting them. In Step 10, we'll be looking at where you go from here. If you have had any success in working through the nine previous steps of Separation Management, you will be far better able to decide whether to recommit, negotiate more time, or end your relationship.

STEP 10
Making Decisions

Your life changes the moment you make a new, congruent,
and committed decision.
—Anthony Robbins

My purpose in presenting so many couples' stories throughout this book has been to show you the range of ways to work things out in your relationship, to help you define and clarify your own expectations, behaviors, beliefs, and goals, and to help you evaluate the issues around separation choices as they exist in your relationship and for you as an individual.

By now you have read numerous tales of how individuals and couples have reached decisions about the future of their relationships. No story will mirror yours exactly, but some of the general dynamics should have seemed familiar. For example, if verbal communication is the most important aspect of your relationship, then improvements there will be a decisive factor. If what's important to you are nonverbal forms of communication like affection and sex, or feeling secure or holding similar values, or agreeing about how to raise the children, then improvements or changes in these areas will matter most. In some relationships having a lot of space and independence is a good thing, whereas in others it can feel like an absence of caring, a lack of intimacy, or a lost connection.

The reason one person decides to stay and work on himself may be the very reason another individual decides to leave. The balance between how well you meet your own wants and what you receive and let in from your partner is something only you can evaluate for yourself.

Step 10 is about movement. Realize that you have more than two options here. Making a decision doesn't necessarily just mean recommitment or breaking up. It means doing something different in your pattern. What's important is that the previous nine steps have prepared you well for making an informed, healthy decision. But even if a breakup is being forced on you, you can move forward in a way that best honors you and your needs.

Couple Situation 12: Frank and Peg: "It's Either Me or Your Mother!"

Frank and Peg are in their early thirties and have been married for four years. They dated for two years before that. They have one child, two-year-old Meg. Peg is a secretary for a private law firm, Frank has a good job in a construction company, and Meg is in day care full-time. Although Frank and Peg have been in other relationships before, this is a first marriage for both of them.

Frank and Peg live close to Frank's family, and early in their marriage, they spent much of their time with them. Peg's parents are both deceased, and she has a long-distance telephone relationship with her only brother. Initially Peg really appreciated the closeness of Frank's family; it seemed to provide the extended family security she had never had. This all changed after Meg was born.

For the first six months or so, Frank's mother was quite helpful and supportive with the new baby. But soon Peg began to feel smothered. Frank's mother was always quick to hand out advice on how to raise Meg. Whenever Peg would hesitate even slightly about what to do, Frank would say, "Call my mom, she knows everything!" Peg really started to resent Frank's strong attachment to his family and wanted things to change. She started asking if they could spend more time alone, just the three of them. But Frank bristled and refused to stop hanging out with his family. At first he would ask Peg if she wanted to join him, but stopped because Peg almost always said no. Soon she was finding herself home alone with Meg a lot and openly questioning Frank's loyalty to his new family. Frank would always laugh it off, and then Peg would feel guilty for taking such a hard stance against the people Frank loved. She was completely torn between feelings of abandonment, anger at Frank, and self-criticism for rejecting Frank's family.

Frank couldn't understand why Peg was upset. As far as he was concerned, his family had always been nothing but welcoming, loving, and helpful to her.

When Peg discovered from Frank's mother that Frank had been sharing intimate details of their relationship with her, it was the last straw. She decided to talk to Frank.

PEG: Frank, I really need to talk to you about how much time we, and especially you, spend with your family.

FRANK: Are you still worried about that? I've told you how much my family loves you. What's wrong now?

PEG: I have a really hard time bringing this up because this is exactly what happens when I do. But things have been getting worse, not better, and it has gone on long enough!

FRANK: (*raising his voice and becoming irritated*) Just what seems to be the problem?

PEG: Now that Meg is two, I want us to establish more of a family ourselves. Everything we do is with your family. When you are not working, you are at your mother's house. Last week she called you three times to do things for her, and each time you just picked up and ran. I'm not sure what I have to do to get that kind of attention. I come home from work, I'm tired, and I could use some help with Meg and dinner, but you're never here. Half the time you eat dinner with your family. That's not how it's supposed to be, Frank. You're married with a child now.

FRANK: (*more upset*) You knew how close I am to my family when you married me. Think of how much they have done for us. Don't make me choose between them and you. It would destroy me.

PEG: I don't mean that you have to give up your family. I'm just feeling kind of neglected by you, that's all.

FRANK: (*frustrated, raised voice*) That's it, now I really don't know what to do. You've put me between a rock and a hard place. I always thought we would all get along so well together. You know, Peg, you'd better think twice about forcing me to choose between my family and you. You might just *not* come out on top!

PEG: Well, Frank, you have just confirmed my feelings and fears exactly.

FRANK: This is bullshit! I have always been close to my family, and you just don't know how to do this since you're not close with yours.

PEG: You always choose them, Frank. I'm at the bottom of your list. Until now, I've been able to take it, but I can't anymore. If they are first on your list, why don't you go and live with them?

FRANK: (*angry, yelling*) I think I will.

Frank didn't realize Peg would push this issue so far. He proceeded to pack some things and left for his mother's house. Peg was a wreck. She had thought Frank might finally hear how upset she was, but here he was, doing exactly what she'd complained about, running to his mother's. She was terrified that Frank would tell them all about their argument and that his family would turn against her. But she had felt so left out of Frank's life for so long that she just wasn't going to roll over one more time.

Applying the Ten-Step Approach to Frank and Peg's Situation

Clearly, there is a conflict and neither is trying to control it. Whenever Peg tries to talk with Frank, he becomes defensive, communication breaks down, and conflict increases. She neither feels validated nor heard. She feels torn because she doesn't want Frank to give up his family, but she does expect him to increase the time he spends with her and Meg.

Frank's leaving seemed to serve the purpose of cooling things down. But the fact that he went to stay with his mother, the very person in the center of their marriage-threatening situation, could be very damaging.

This particular family issue can be very charged for couples because it involves a family of origin. Friends, work, sports, hobbies, and other things can come between partners, but families of origin often bring out the most intense conflicts. Does one partner have the right to question his partner about her investment and commitment to her family?

EXERCISE

See Ground Rules for Talking, page 17.

This exercise can be done alone or with a partner.

1. Do you think Peg has a right to ask Frank to limit his time with his family of origin so as to spend more time with her and Meg?

2. What do you think about how their decision to separate was decided and carried out?

3. What would you do now if you were Frank? What might you do if you were Peg?

4. Do you think there is a resolution? What do you think Peg is asking for? What do you think Frank is asking for?

5. What are your values, beliefs, opinions, thoughts, and feelings about this type of situation?

What Happened to Frank and Peg

Frank decided to move in with his family for a while to get space and to protest against Peg's complaints. He had always been close to his family, and it had never occurred to him that marriage and family life would mean he couldn't see them any longer. Frank was angry and frustrated with Peg and did not see a compromise solution.

Frank did tell his mother what was going on. She took Frank's side and actually called Peg a couple of days after Frank left. Peg was devastated. She couldn't believe Frank had again blabbed to his mother. *Boy, he just doesn't get it*, she thought. All she had wanted was for Frank to find a better balance between the time he spent with his family of origin and his new family, but now she felt like they were in a full-blown power struggle that was going nowhere fast.

When Frank's mother called, Peg tried to make light of the issues, but when she kept insisting that they were just one big family now, Peg got really steamed. She turned to one friend who had had some similar issues earlier in her marriage. Peg's friend told her to stand her ground on this one, or she'd be competing with Frank's mother the rest of her married life. That helped a bit but not enough. Her friend seemed to have forgotten just how painful and tangled this situation could be.

Frank stayed at his mom's for a couple of weeks. He would call Meg daily and come over to play with her after work. Meg missed her dad at bedtime and often had to call him to talk. But the stalemate continued. Peg did try to bring things up again but Frank cut her off, accusing her of being selfish and swearing that she was not going to run his life.

Peg decided to seek help from a counselor. She wanted Frank to go with her, but he refused. He figured a counselor would just tell Peg what she wanted to hear and make Frank into the bad guy. So she went alone, finding a listening ear in an older woman counselor.

Peg talked about her guilt and confusion and the counselor assured her that wanting to create her own sense of family apart from Frank's was not wrong, unusual, or bad. Many young couples have to work hard to create a boundary and balance between their families of origin and themselves, she explained, adding that each and every family and culture is different in this regard. In some cultures it is expected that children remain very close to their families of origin. In others, space and distance are valued more highly.

The counselor offered that as long as Frank remained so defensive, resolution would be difficult. She suggested that Peg assure Frank that she was not asking him to give up his family, just balance things better. Peg felt better after her counseling session, but couldn't get Frank to talk.

Peg decided to write him a letter. She figured she might at least get him to *read* about her concerns, even if he couldn't listen.

Dear Frank,

I feel sad and hurt that we can't work this out. It's been a month now since you went to your mother's, and I miss you. I want you to know that I am not trying to take you away from your family. Your family has been like a new family to me, and I love them dearly. I just wish you'd understand that I want a better balance between the time we—Meg, you, and I—spend together, and how much time we are with your family. I don't feel that this should be a contest. I believe there is plenty of time for both.

I guess I feel that I take second place to your mother, and I need to know that I don't always come last. If you would just listen and we could talk, I know that we could resolve this better. I do not want a separation. I love you, and I want to work this out and bring our family back together.

Love,

Peg

After getting Peg's letter, Frank started to have second thoughts. He realized how much he missed Peg and thought that maybe his strong stance had already taught her a lesson. Frank called Peg about getting together and trying to work things out. Unfortunately Frank did not want to compromise or change. He simply wanted his way.

They set up a time to meet alone. The conversation went as follows:

PEG: Frank, I'm glad you read my letter and decided to talk. I really do want to work this out.

FRANK: So do you think that you can see *my* side of this now?

PEG: Yes, I can see your side, but can you see mine?

FRANK: My family is no big deal, and they're not a threat to you at all. They all love you and Meg like you are their own.

PEG: Frank, I know that already. I think the real problem is how your time is divided between them and us. I hate to be angry with you and them over this. I think we need to get a general idea of how this time should work and then maybe come up with a schedule or something.

FRANK: Do you really think it's necessary that we come up with a schedule? I hate schedules.

PEG: I think it will help if we look at what your idea of time spent with your family means as opposed to mine.

Frank and Peg each came up with a plan for how family time would be divided. Peg's plan called for more time alone with Meg, Frank, and herself, mostly on weekends. Frank's schedule showed many more days with his family. They were both disheartened. They seemed to be pretty far apart.

Peg acknowledged that Frank's schedule made time for her and Meg, but she didn't share her great disappointment that Frank still seemed to be more loyal to his mother and family of origin than to her. He was clearly committed to Meg, but not nearly as much to her.

Frank, meanwhile, was feeling better about the schedule idea and was talking about returning home. It was his perception that he had managed to convince her that he was right, and she was backing down from her rigid position.

Peg was excited about his returning home, but she was concerned that they hadn't made any progress and that Frank didn't really hear her concerns. She began to think about the future: if Frank couldn't hear her over this, he would never hear her on other issues of importance to her. She wanted Frank back but had real reservations.

Peg shared her dilemma with her counselor, who then asked Peg to see if Frank would agree to come to one of her sessions. Peg was feeling a little more optimistic these days, but she was still surprised when Frank agreed to go.

Frank and Peg's Counseling Session

COUNSELOR: Frank, I'm glad to get a chance to meet you. Peg and I have had some sessions. Many of these focused on communication between you and her. Peg is concerned about how decisions are made between you. I know you have been separated for a short while and are working on a compromise on time spent with Peg and Meg and time with your family. I also understand that you are preparing to move back home, and Peg feels she needs to be clear about what you are agreeing to.

FRANK: (*looking uncomfortable*) Yes, that's pretty much it, but I think we have worked this out pretty well and don't really have to talk about it much more.

PEG: (*anxious and uncomfortable*) Frank, I'm so pleased that we're talking and trying to work this out. I'm also glad you came today, (*long pause*) but I'm scared. I know you think we've resolved something about this, but I'm not all that trusting yet.

COUNSELOR: Peg, do you feel OK about raising this issue again with Frank?

PEG: No! I'm afraid that if Frank doesn't hear what he wants to hear then he'll leave again.

FRANK: (*looks angry and irritated*)

COUNSELOR: Maybe we should talk about some guidelines on how you communicate and argue with each other. It sounds like Peg doesn't feel safe to say how she really thinks and feels and is concerned about you, Frank, leaving.

The counselor spent some time speaking to Frank and Peg about their communication process and how important it is not only to talk and listen, but to solve problems as well.

The counselor pointed out that this process was not just about their conflict over time spent with Frank's family, but about how well they respected each other, listened, validated each other, and shared decision-making power. The counselor talked about how often conversation does not address people's underlying feelings and assumptions. The best communication involves taking responsibility for your feelings, thoughts, and opinions, but also creating a safe place where your partner can share him- or herself fully.

At first Frank found himself resisting, but then things began to make sense. Albeit in a limited way, he began to see how he tended to overpower Peg and not really hear her side. He knew down deep that he was afraid of having to give up his position. He even felt a little embarrassed that his wife had had to go to a counselor just to be able to talk to him. Frank was quiet the rest of the session.

The counselor stressed the fact that they needed to share the space and time when they talked. She taught them the importance of listening and not necessarily having to *agree* with each other. She explained that the more insecure one partner is with his or her position, the more that partner will try to control or manipulate the other to his or her side. On the surface, this may appear to work, but it often doesn't and leaves at least one partner feeling misunderstood. She then explained that the more people develop and are OK with themselves, the better they do at understanding and allowing their partners to have a perspective different from theirs. The counselor suggested that in relationships, if one partner believes he or she alone has "won" an argument or gotten his way, this usually means both partners have lost. Relationships work best when both partners feel as if they have been heard and understood and both can feel OK about decisions and issues. Either both win, or both lose.

Frank seemed to understand this and realized how quickly things changed when he became stubborn about getting his way. He agreed to return a couple of weeks later to work on their communication.

That evening, Frank and Peg had the best conversation they had had in a long while. Peg felt that Frank was making an effort to listen to her, and this made a lot of difference. Peg said over and over that her issue with his mother was not just about spending time with her but more about their (Frank and Peg's) relationship. Peg said she needed to know that Frank and she were a unit. She even shared how violated she felt when Frank went to his mother and told her about their conflicts.

For the first time in months, Frank looked sad as Peg talked. He could feel that his own stubbornness had taken him too far. He realized how much Peg did love him and was committed to him and how he may have taken this for granted. That evening Frank and Peg felt very close. They acknowledged that it felt strange that there was no new resolution about Frank's mother but that somehow just this talking from the heart seemed to bring them closer. They once again held hands, hugged, joked, and talked about themselves and their relationship. Frank asked whether this was what the counselor meant by intimacy.

What Changed for Frank

Frank came from a close family in which support and open communication were valued, but he realized during the counseling session that he was not doing his part to make it safe for Peg to openly share. He realized that he thought he was winning the power struggle when in fact he was losing Peg. The fact that Frank was open to talking and counseling as well as looking at himself was a bold and courageous step in his self-development. In reality Frank probably already knew how to do this, he just didn't apply it to this issue of time spent with his family.

That night, Frank also became weepy talking about his parents getting older and dying someday. He wanted so badly for Peg to understand how he felt. When Peg acknowledged Frank's feelings and said she understood, Frank became tearful again. He admitted that he felt a great deal of pressure from Peg regarding his family and hadn't realized the stress it had created for him. From this better place in their relationship, Peg and Frank seemed able to reach at least a tentative agreement on helping each other with their respective issues. Frank really appreciated and began to understand how important his contribution and time was to Peg. Peg was willing to accept how Frank's connection to his extended family was something he would not give up. Each brought more empathy, understanding, and cooperation to this issue. (See Negotiation Exercise, page 309.) Peg wondered whether this would last.

Frank and Peg continued counseling for a few more sessions. The focus was on reducing conflict and learning to communicate from an OK–OK place. Frank began to look forward to the sessions and enjoyed the fact that he and Peg were improving their communication process.

Over the next months, Frank seemed to do a better job of balancing time between Peg and his mother. Peg was honored that Frank had learned something and that he seemed to have renewed his commitment to her. By learning to share openly with Frank, Peg allowed herself to express inner feelings that had never come out. The same went for Frank.

Every so often Frank and Peg got into a power struggle again. This seemed to be a pattern in their relationship. Some of these were over real or perceived violations by the other, including Frank's time with his family. But over time they both experienced a renewed confidence in their ability to talk through conflicts. Peg always remembered what her counselor said about conflict: "Fighting and arguing are not problems in and of themselves, as long you are both confident in your ability to *eventually* talk, listen, and understand." In fact, as Frank and Peg discovered, ongoing struggle can sometimes allow two people to better define their selves and their relationship.

Over time, Frank and Peg slowly began to understand their communication process and how to fix it when it broke down. They realized that this was one of the most important skills to have. They also learned that breakdowns are necessary, as long as there is a way to repair them.

Through their brief separation, this couple learned to appreciate each other more and to improve listening and talking as well as to further develop compassion and empathy for each other. Each realized that what they wanted, they had to *give*. Perhaps it was the fear of losing each other that drove this couple to grow.

With the help of counseling, Frank and Peg continued to create clearer boundaries and to equalize power regarding decision making. They learned to limit conflict when it became destructive and to talk and listen to each other, all the while remembering that compassion and empathy often create the space in which they could reach compromise and resolution. They learned that these are attributes and skills that must be practiced and refined.

With their small breakthrough, Frank and Peg have started down the path that makes relationships work. Their newfound ability to talk to and hear each other formed a foundation on which to build a healthy relationship. This is what I believe to be the golden bridge woven by the golden rule between partners in a relationship. By learning to talk, listen, and understand, Frank and Peg strengthened their partnership.

How Frank and Peg Decided to Stay a Couple

Frank and Peg made a decision to stay together, but only after months of making some fundamental changes in the way they communicated. This shift was by no means easy. It started with conflict and an impasse that appeared unworkable. After a brief physical separation, Frank and Peg learned to make adjustments and undergo a psychological separation from a way of relating that no longer worked for them.

During their psychological separation, they each learned to better define and express what they wanted and expected. Thus their separation became therapeutic. From this new place, Frank and Peg were not only able to renew their commitment to each other, but each felt more loved and understood than they had before their separation. This did not mean they would never get stuck again. In fact, they have become stuck many times and will continue to do so, but they now have a method for becoming unstuck and continuing to grow. Both have renewed their ongoing investment in making this work.

EXERCISE

See Ground Rules for Talking, page 17.

1. Can you identify with Frank or Peg?

2. Do you think Peg was justified in asking Frank to spend more time with Meg and her?

3. What seemed to make a difference for Frank that resulted in his beginning to listen to Peg?

4. What seemed to be the most important factor(s) in Frank and Peg's reconciliation after their brief separation?

5. Are you or anyone you know in this type of situation? What did you or they do?

Couple Situation 13: Mike and Carol: "You Never Want to Have Sex!"

Mike and Carol are in their midforties. This is the second marriage for each, and they have been together six years. They each have a child from a first marriage, Michelle and Judy, both eight years old, and together they have five-year-old Teddy. Both are busy and employed full-time. Carol is a secretary in a large firm, and Mike is an accountant in a small partnership.

Both Mike and Carol are fairly independent and feel they have created a nice blended family life. However, in the last six to eight months, Mike has begun to request and demand more sex.

Carol had always felt she had a healthy sex drive, but it was usually Mike who initiated sex. Sometimes Carol didn't feel like having sex and said no. Sometimes she just wanted to hug and snuggle and feel close to Mike without having sex. But most of the time the snuggling would turn sexual and she would give in. Sometimes sex would be okay for her, and other times only Mike would be satisfied. This really started to bug her and in the past few months, she had begun to avoid

Mike more. When he would come up to hug her, she would break the hug quickly and say she was too busy. She found herself going to bed earlier than Mike and at times even acting as if she were sleeping when he came to bed. Her avoidance was because she feared that if she dared to show any interest or affection to Mike, he would interpret it as a sexual invitation and pressure her for sex. The result, of course, was a major drop in intercourse.

Mike did not approach Carol to discuss what was wrong, and Carol did not explain why she was avoiding sex. The distance between them grew wider, and Mike started complaining bitterly about how lousy their sex life was, and how Carol really didn't seem to care much about it. The more openly critical of Carol that Mike became, the more Carol withdrew. They started to fight more often, both exchanging mean, hurtful words. They would always get over a particular battle, but Mike became increasingly obsessed and started threatening to leave. He would say that his sex drive was strong, and he did not want to spend the rest of his life being what he termed "sexually neglected and deprived." Once Mike even left for the night and threatened to get sex elsewhere if things didn't change.

Carol was afraid their relationship was over. But she still refused to have sex against her will; she couldn't stand the feeling that Mike viewed her only as a sexual object, and it totally turned her off. She realized that sex had been a problem in her first marriage, too, but she simply wasn't willing to sacrifice herself this time like she had done the first time around.

Mike started to think about how he could afford to move out on his own. Carol worried that her marriage was over.

EXERCISE

See Ground Rules for Talking, page 17.

Does this situation sound familiar to you and your relationship now or in the past? How is it similar? How is it different? As you discuss this with your partner, try to be aware of your values, morals, judgments, opinions, and feelings, but also try to understand your partner's point of view. You may not agree and may actually take a strong stance against your partner's view, but do make an attempt to at least understand it.

DISCUSSION

If there is a single issue that couples are in conflict about, it's sex. Sex is at least the surface reason for countless separations and divorces. From my experience working with couples, most of the time, but certainly not always, it is men who are dissatisfied with the quantity, frequency, and sometimes quality of sex, while women more often want more passion, romance, and emotional connection.

The partner wanting more sex often feels controlled, neglected, and denied. The partner who is seen as sexless or asexual is often protective and guarded and many times blames herself for the problem. Efforts to talk usually end in conflict. Couples can go round and round with this problem for years without resolution.

Of course, there can be many complex reasons for low sex drive and desire, and our purpose here is not to have all the answers. Our job is to ease the conflict around this issue and get Carol and Mike talking and dealing with the problem individually and together.

What Mike and Carol Can Do

1. The first step for Mike and Carol is to stop and ease the crisis and conflict. One of them has to say, "Let's stop fighting about our sexual difficulties and start talking about each of us as people and about our relationship." It doesn't matter how many times they have started this conversation in the past, if they want to approach it differently, they must begin by easing the conflict and being willing to communicate.

    Because of Carol's experience with her first husband, she is understandably reluctant to let herself be discounted again. But she will have to allow for the possibility of resolution or it will never come.

Mike is frustrated and obsessed because he expects that he is entitled to a certain amount of sex in his marriage. He has little idea that the turn-on for Carol would be listening and showing some empathy for her wants. Mike does not understand that he is in large part responsible for the climate between them. A more inviting climate of understanding and acceptance could allow them to communicate more openly and honestly.

2. After ongoing conflict, all of their issues seem to have boiled down to whether they are having sex or not and little else gets addressed. Mike and Carol now have to work on letting go of their respective positions or sides.

3. Mike must suspend his obsession and anger, at least temporarily. He must begin to see that Carol is not withholding sex but rather is reacting to his anger and demands with resistance and self-protection. Mike must learn to manage his frustration and anger on this. He must stop badgering Carol for sex and try to listen. He must be willing to see that while Carol has her own set of difficulties around this issue, his perception of her is further defining her as asexual in his eyes. This perception is keeping them stuck.

4. Carol must talk to Mike about how she feels and Mike must make it safe to do so. She must share how it feels to know that Mike views her as cold and sexless and what she wants from him instead.

5. A cease-fire, or truce, must be called and adhered to. Some of the same techniques as for time-out can be used. Gaining control of the conflict begins by deciding to end it and continuing to monitor its presence in oneself and the relationship. If a person cannot be around his partner without losing his temper and attacking, then he needs to take space until he cools down. Only then can he proceed to Step 2.

EXERCISE

See Ground Rules for Talking, page 17.

1. Can you identify with Mike or Carol?

2. Why do you think it's so difficult for Carol to talk with Mike about how she feels?

3. Why do you think Carol resists getting emotionally and physically closer to Mike?

4. What might be the trigger thoughts for Mike's frustration and anger with their sex life? What might be Carol's trigger thoughts around her frustrations and avoidance of Mike's advances?

5. What do *you* think they need to do?

What Happened to Mike and Carol

Mike and Carol managed to cool the open conflict with each other. However, this did not automatically make their sex life better. Mike continued to feel deprived and neglected sexually and thought he could get Carol to have sex more frequently by blaming, criticizing, and making her feel guilty about what she was doing. But sex is often a reflection of the larger relationship between two partners. Our degree of sexual satisfaction and freedom is often dependent on our sexual history and experiences, parental messages about sex, and how free we feel to express ourselves in our current relationship.

It has been my observation that the amount of free Child that you have permission to express will determine the way you and your partner will grow in this area of your relationship.

I can remember back to my high school days in the 1960s, when guys tried to get sex from their girlfriends, as if it was all about the boy's pleasure. Even today, I hear stories of women who simply tolerate having sex while their partners are satisfied. Couples can evolve to more mutually satisfying experiences if they are able to think about their partners' wants and preferences.

I have heard that "foreplay for a woman is what happens in the twenty-four hours before you jump in bed to have sex!" Many women want to feel close and loved by their partners. I'll never forget one particular woman who looked at her husband and said, "I don't have sex with strangers!" in reference to her husband wanting to have sex without emotional or verbal intimacy. I have heard women say, "If he knew what a turn-on it is to feel emotionally close to him, maybe he'd make more of an effort to connect with me emotionally."

On the other hand, sex *is* how many men express closeness and intimacy. Of course sex can be experienced by both women and men at a number of different levels, from the mechanical to the recreational all the way to a much higher spiritual level.

So what does all this mean for Mike and Carol? At this point, Carol feels so defensive and attacked for her low sexual drive and performance that she is not sure her body can even relax enough to get into having sex. Although Mike has stopped the open criticism, he does not get the fact that Carol's wounds and the relationship need comfort and repair.

Knowing they needed change, they decided to use some new communication skills Carol had found in a couple's communication book. Each would take turns listening to the other talk about his or her feelings regarding the relationship and their sex life and attempt to explain their understanding.

CAROL: Mike, I'm feeling very anxious and scared as I start talking about my wants and feelings. I'm afraid I will get criticized by you. I don't think I can take much more, I feel so put down and defective sexually at this point.

Carol starts to cry and puts her head in her hands. At first Mike is annoyed with her crying, but then he starts to feel really bad about how critical he had been toward her. He doesn't share this because he believes if he takes any responsibility for Carol's feelings, she will gain an edge on him, and he might never be able to guilt her into sex again. He silently watches Carol cry.

CAROL: All I think about is us breaking up! I live in fear of this all the time. I made a decision a while ago that I would no longer have sex if

I really didn't want to. I think I've decided that I need certain things to be right with us before I can feel OK about sex. For one, I don't feel cared for by you. It's almost like it doesn't matter to you whether we're close or not. Sometimes it doesn't even feel like you know I'm there. But I'm so afraid that if I don't have sex with you, you'll find someone else. So it's either sex or being left. This is making me real anxious even to talk openly about this.

(*waiting for response*) Why don't you say something?

MIKE: (*puzzled and not sure what to say*) I'm still thinking you don't like sex very much, otherwise it would work better for us. I know if I had sex more regularly, I wouldn't feel so angry.

CAROL: Mike, did you hear anything I said about my feelings? I know what you think and feel but I don't think you understand me. Somehow I think that feeling understood by you is the key to getting closer again.

MIKE: Well, I think I've had enough. It's always about you, and I'm still being deprived, right? You are a cold fish, and you'll always be a cold fish. I'm outta here!

CAROL: Wait, Mike, don't leave!

Mike slams the door as he leaves.

Carol once again felt rejected and misunderstood. She had tried to communicate with Mike about how she felt, but Mike just didn't get it. He seemed unable to accept feedback from her on how his behavior and lack of understanding were fueling the problems between them. He couldn't see that mutual understanding is a fundamental factor in any relationship. If you can try to step into your partner's shoes even briefly and communicate that understanding, you can make a connection. Not only is this connection fulfilling and satisfying, but it is crucial to solving problems between partners.

After talking to a close friend, Carol found she was beginning to get angry. Her friend said, "How could you live with that guy when he can't even hear you? He sounds so self-centered." Carol began to really think about that. Up until this point, she had been trying to reach out to Mike as a first step to being honest and open about what was missing in their sex life. Maybe she needed to take a stronger stance. Maybe she needed some space from Mike. As she thought this, she felt anxiety surge up from her stomach.

EXERCISE

See Ground Rules for Talking, page 17.

You can do this exercise alone or with a partner.

1. After reading about Mike and Carol's talk, what are your thoughts about their communication process (*how* they communicate, not *what* they communicate about)?

    What life position (I'm OK–You're OK; I'm Not OK–You're OK; I'm OK–You're Not OK, etc.) do you think Mike is coming from when he communicates? What position do you think Carol is communicating from when they talk?

2. Reflect on your communication process with your current or past partner. What positions were you in when you were discussing important issues in your relationship? How did you feel when interacting with your partner?

Back to Carol and Mike

Carol made several attempts to talk with Mike about her feelings. These talks broke down, with Mike not hearing and usually leaving in anger. Carol saw her options as continuing to try to talk to Mike, going back to having unsatisfying sex that did not meet her wants, or perhaps demanding respect in some other way.

Mike, for his part, still used manipulation and control to try to have more sex with Carol. Mike did not see or believe that Carol desired a better sex life, too. He was not listening to her, nor did he believe that his attitude or behavior had anything to do with this.

Carol decided to tell Mike that she could not live this way and would not continue to be manipulated into having sex. This decision took a long time to reach, and she was terrified about being left alone, but she finally realized that she needed to do something for herself. She explained that if Mike could not learn to respect her as a person and not a sex object, she did not want to live with him any longer.

Mike seemed shocked by Carol's resolve. Even though he had threatened to leave her many times, he became really nervous and upset by her threat. Mike had always figured he could just leave and that would really show her! But now that the shoe was on the other foot, he was not so confident that this is what he wanted. Mike was beginning to feel more helpless and less able to get his way. Even though he was angry, and now fearful, he was still not ready to learn that trying to understand her as a person might be the beginning of a solution.

He had slipped from his fake superior (I'm OK–You're Not OK) position, to feeling less OK and secure within himself. He was secretly impressed but frightened by Carol's determination.

Because Carol took a new and very much needed stand on what she wanted in her relationship with Mike, a shift and change has already begun. Carol is beginning to feel the power to stand up for what she believes is right.

Purposes of Separation for Carol

1. To make a statement for herself and to Mike regarding what she wants and doesn't want in her relationship with Mike.

2. To separate from a pattern in their relationship that was no longer satisfying for her.

3. By respecting herself, Carol begins to send a message to Mike that she wants him to respect her. She believes that the burden needs to shift from being her problem to one that is shared with Mike. Whether Mike will pick this up is yet to be seen.

EXERCISE

See Ground Rules for Talking, page 17.

You can do this exercise alone or with a partner.

1. Discuss how you think Carol's shift in herself made a change in the process of her relationship with Mike.

2. Has this ever happened in your relationship(s), now or in the past?

3. What do you think is the purpose of Carol's separation?

Mike and Carol's Separation

Mike and Carol took a temporary in-house separation, but then Mike decided to take things a step further and announced that he was going to move in with his brother for a while.

Carol panicked, but she remained tough on the outside and said she thought it was probably best for the time being. Mike was taken aback. He thought threatening to leave would scare Carol into giving in. Carol asked Mike to talk about how they should tell the children about their separation. Mike said he didn't think it was appropriate that the children or anybody know that this was about their sex life. Carol agreed but corrected Mike regarding his belief that this was *just* about sex. For Carol this was about how Mike treated her as a person. Sex was simply the issue; what was important to her was their process.

Mike and Carol sat down with their three children and explained that Mom and Dad were not getting along very well lately and were going to spend some time away from each other. They told the children that they loved them and assured them that this had nothing to do with them, and it was not their fault.

Mike's daughter then asked if they were going to get divorced like her biological mom and Mike had. Mike and Carol both saw the fear and sadness in her eyes. Inside, both felt sick from this question, but neither shared these inner thoughts and feelings with the other. They said they couldn't say for sure and were just taking a break so they might get along better. The following weekend, Mike took some of his belongings and moved to his brother's house a couple of miles away. Mike would continue to spend time at the home and fully participate in the usual tasks and childcare. The children liked Mike's brother and their cousins, so they would spend a lot of time over there, too.

The terms of this brief separation seemed quite easy for Mike and Carol. What was not decided was how long it would last. Other than working on the schedules and tasks of keeping the household running and sharing the children, Mike and Carol took both physical and psychological space from each other. Both were scared about what would happen next.

Whether they realized it or not, they had been engaged in a psychological separation for quite some time already. Carol was attempting to exchange her scared and often overly compliant inner Child for a more determined self who was learning to communicate her real wants and requests to her partner. Would this now turn into a longer-term trial separation or perhaps a working therapeutic separation? It was too early to tell. Remember, both were divorced before and did not intend to divorce a second time. There was much at stake.

EXERCISE

See Ground Rules for Talking, page 17.

1. What are the areas or issues of your relationship in which the process between you and your partner break down?

2. Are you able to repair this? How?

3. Can you understand how Carol's work is a psychological separation in their relationship?

More on Mike and Carol

What started out as a brief physical break stretched into a longer separation. Carol struggled with living alone. She missed Mike but didn't miss the criticisms and badgering about sex. She often went to bed worried that her second marriage was over, but she felt she had to learn to survive on her own and was determined not to be treated as a sex object any longer. She battled feelings of anxiety and fear and had to learn to soothe herself and relax all the thinking that created this. These bouts of anxiety were not new but had resurfaced as a result of the separation.

Mike was starting to worry because what had started out as a bit of a bluff was now beginning to backfire. He realized that he missed Carol a lot more than he thought he would. Living with his brother started to grow old after about a month and he wondered how to approach Carol about moving back home without losing face or giving in.

Mike took the plunge and decided to ask Carol where she thought they stood. Carol was surprised that Mike even cared. He hardly ever let on that he was affected about much except their sex life. It was usually Carol who wanted to talk. One night after the children went to bed, Mike and Carol sat down to talk about their relationship.

MIKE: Carol, I need to know where we stand about me coming home again. When I first moved out, it was supposed to be just for a brief time. Now it's been almost a month.

CAROL: Well, Mike, if you remember, I had suggested that we get some space within the home, and you were the one who got angry and moved to your brother's.

MIKE: OK, so I did, but now it's starting to get old, and I want to know where you stand.

CAROL: (*becoming angry*) Mike, the reason for this space is because I'm tired of being criticized about our sex life. I don't feel safe around you even to discuss how I feel. You're obsessed with sex and have no regard for how I feel as a person.

MIKE: I do care about how you feel, but I just need to know that you are working on wanting more sex.

CAROL: Mike, I think we should make an appointment with a marriage counselor. My friend Betty and her husband went to one and are doing much better now. We need to learn how to talk and understand each other better. Look at how much we're struggling just talking about this.

MIKE: (*feeling pressured and more uncomfortable*), What's some counselor going to teach us that we don't already know? But I guess if you really want to go, I'll try it once and see what it's like.

Carol felt a small breakthrough. She proceeded to get a name from her friend and make an appointment. In the meantime, Carol and Mike continued to live separately and managed to keep the conflict down, but there was not much communication either. Carol was hopeful that counseling would help Mike learn how to relate to her better. Mike was hoping that Carol might want him to come home and just maybe their sex life would improve. He thought that maybe the counselor could help them find out why she resisted sex so much.

Carol made an appointment with a male counselor, thinking that Mike might relate better to a man than a woman. The first session was more comfortable than Mike or Carol imagined it would be. The counselor gave them each a chance to tell their side of the story. At first they both found it kind of uncomfortable to talk to a third party—about problems that involved sex, no less!

When Mike started talking about the lack of sex in their relationship, the counselor seemed to understand and Mike felt good about that. Carol also seemed happy that the counselor seemed to understand how important the overall relationship was to her.

The counselor talked to them about common struggles, such as sex, that couples have. Mike and Carol both felt reassured. The counselor helped them go back to earlier years together so they could remember how well they used to get along and what first attracted them to each other. Mike recalled that Carol couldn't wait for him to come home and have sex. Carol emphasized that Mike listened to her and liked just hanging out with her. This made her feel important and special to him. She explained that she really needed this after her disappointing first marriage. She talked about how feeling good about herself and close to Mike was a precondition for feeling more loving and sexual.

Rather than continue to blame each other for their problems, Mike and Carol were learning that they were different and that this was normal and OK. The counselor helped them, and especially Mike, understand that many women want to feel loved and close and have a good emotional connection. He also talked about the difference between affection and sex and the importance of having clear signals about each.

The counselor helped them see the power struggle they were in, with Mike continuing to try to coerce Carol into having sex, and Carol protecting herself. Even in this first session, Mike got a better glimpse into Carol's thoughts and feelings. At times he became angry, but then he found himself really listening. Carol was pleased and very grateful to Mike for trying out counseling.

The counselor felt they should continue to put their sex life on hold for now, and Mike reluctantly agreed.

They made another appointment. Homework involved talking to each other for short periods of time (three to five minutes during which each would talk while the other listened) reflecting on what they heard and how they felt about the counseling session.

They continued to live apart for another two months and saw the counselor for a total of eight sessions. For one of these sessions, the counselor suggested that he and Mike meet alone. At this individual session, Mike expressed his frustration that even though Carol and he were learning to talk more, he felt she was still resisting sex.

The counselor helped Mike see that all the put-downs about her sexuality were undermining what he really wanted. Mike began to see and trust Carol as a real person for the first time in a long time. He started getting in touch with how lousy it had felt when his mother and first wife had criticized him and actually started to feel guilty for what he had said and done to Carol over the past few months. He decided that his goal would be to work on control and to stop taking out his frustrations and feelings through aiming his blaming, judgmental, critical Parent at Carol. Instead he would attempt to be in touch with his feelings and wants and share those with her. Also through counseling, Mike realized that he needed to slow down and give Carol some time to work through her old feelings of mistrust and hurt. Pressure at this point would just set her back even more.

More importantly, he began to see another way to approach her. If Mike wanted Carol closer, then he needed to create a safer, loving, OK–OK climate for this to happen. But first he needed to get this for himself. This was not easy for Mike, but as he worked on it he found that Carol really responded to his listening and softer approach. At times he slipped back to being a bully, but now realized this and learned to manage his behavior.

Carol was impressed that Mike seemed more relaxed and more interested in her than usual. She was still fairly guarded about his criticisms regarding their sex life, but she also realized that Mike was trying, and this made her feel better. Mike actually reached out to her for a hug and kiss on occasion without groping her butt or breasts as an overture for sex. Over time Carol seemed able to relax more.

What Mike got from his sessions with the counselor was a better understanding of how his behavior affected Carol. He began to understand that Carol actually did want an improved sex life. What he had not understood until now was his role and responsibility in making this happen.

It still wasn't easy for Mike to allow himself to feel closer to Carol emotionally. Mike had never been very close to anyone, and he found the thought pretty scary. Without the old mind games and manipulating threats he felt really vulnerable and naked. He thought a lot about his relationship to his mother, stepmother, and first wife and how things had seemed so distant and strained. He had never really shared these innermost feelings with anyone. This whole experience with Carol, he realized, was teaching him more about his self.

He had always acted so strong, she was unsure if he had any sensitivity left. But during Mike's talks with Carol he would often feel sad and at times he even cried a little. Carol found it a lot easier to be around him when he was this open.

Mike shared how lonely he felt living away from her and the children and how he had started to feel really depressed and lost. He told her how much he appreciated her now. It took much courage for Mike to open up like this.

After one of their good talks, in which both Carol and Mike talked more about their positive feelings for each other, Carol embraced Mike. Soon they started kissing each other tenderly. Carol suggested that they move to the bedroom where, to Mike's surprise, Carol initiated the lovemaking.

Both Carol and Mike were eager to tell the counselor about their new intimacy. The counselor asked each of them what turned each other on the most. For Carol the answer was simple. It was Mike's putting in the effort to work on their relationship. When he shared more of his inner thoughts and feelings, and she could actually see his sensitive and vulnerable sides, she felt a lot closer to him. Mike, however, was unsure why he felt so much closer to Carol. The counselor suggested that perhaps it was because he had allowed himself to take a risk and actually share his deeper feelings with her.

That made some sense to Mike. He could see that he often expressed his inner Child feelings of hurt and rejection through his angry, blaming, attacking critical Parent, and how that had backfired on him.

Mike was grateful to the counselor for helping get them on track. Three months ago they seemed destined for a divorce. Now they were actually doing better than before.

The counselor helped them learn that relationships cool down and heat up. He helped Mike see how he could get closer to Carol by learning to talk to her and share more of himself than by just trying to get her to have sex with him. Mike had to learn that just because he felt "horny," he couldn't just assume that Carol would be in the mood, too. They needed to be clear on their signals to each other in regard to sex. And Mike needed to think about where Carol was and what she wanted before he just launched into attacks about their lack of sex.

Carol needed to continue to monitor how Mike spoke and related to her. She became better at giving Mike feedback and not just rejecting him. Carol learned to coach Mike on how to "turn her on" even more. She found sex becoming much more pleasurable. She had occasional orgasms, some stronger than others, but overall the experience even without orgasms was very nice.

Carol felt she now had a way to communicate with Mike and be heard. Both found ways to be heard, which seemed to make all the difference. And Mike felt humbled by all the change. He had to work at not telling himself that he was less of a man (an old childhood and societal message) because he was now sharing more feelings with Carol and was "giving in" to her demands. Even though this was hard for Mike, it actually felt better—and very different. The rewards of a closer relationship to Carol and improved lovemaking certainly made it worthwhile.

After about four months of separation, Mike moved back home. Mike and Carol's counselor warned them about the likelihood of reality settling back in after a second honeymoon or romance period. They had just started down a new road, and both knew they'd have to keep a careful eye on things. But an initially scary separation had actually done them a world of good; in many ways their relationship had never been better.

How Mike and Carol Used Separation Management

1. Carol took the first step by telling Mike she would no longer have sex under the current conditions. By doing so Carol was breaking with her usual pattern of putting up with put-downs in an effort to please her partner. She had reached a point in her life in which both her self-respect and respect from her partner were absolutely necessary for her to continue in a relationship. She moved from Level 1 (fully invested–committed) to Level 2 ("There must be a change") or possibly even Level 3 (confused–ambivalent).

2. Mike agreed to get outside help. This was a major step for Mike, who had always thought he needed to have absolute control over things—until he started losing control over Carol. Mike learned that good relationships have give and take. He also learned that

by giving more and allowing himself to be influenced by Carol, he actually got more of his own wants met. Mike learned that in a relationship that is working both partners' wants and expectations count and can be met.

Mike benefited a great deal from counseling by simply learning to be more of himself and sharing that self with Carol. He discovered a new approach to emotional and physical intimacy through talking and being more open and genuine. It was hard work, but he could see that replacing his bullying, manipulation, and controlling with straight and honest OK–OK talk was a win-win situation: he got to have more sex and on much better terms. He also came to realize that Carol wanted a good sex life, too. She might never want sex as frequently as Mike, but because they were talking, listening, and getting closer, she was turned on to their sex life again and the overall quantity of sex became less important, even to Mike.

3. For Mike and Carol, Steps 8, 9, and 10 seemed to work together. Mike and Carol each identified core issues within themselves that allowed them to grow and change. Through the hard lessons of crisis and conflict, they learned improved ways to be together. Both began to take responsibility over their parts of the relationship so as to improve the whole process of the relationship. Their willingness to open up a new door had rekindled old, loving feelings.

4. Mike and Carol learned that they would have to continue to monitor themselves. Like most couples, they did go through periods of drought, during which there was less connection emotionally and sexually than either wanted.

Their old patterns reemerged, especially during periods of stress. What they learned was that they now had ways to repair the fallout and get their relationship back on track. They realized that the crisis of their separation had actually allowed them to separate from old behavior that was not working and learn new behavior that felt much more fulfilling.

EXERCISE

See Ground Rules for Talking, page 17.

1. Discuss or think about how the issue of sex was caught up with the process of how Mike and Carol related.

2. What changed for Mike? What changed for Carol during their separation period?

3. Can you identify with Mike, Carol, or both?

4. What can you borrow from them to help you?

5. What goals or changes were evaluated that resulted in a decision to stay together?

CONCLUSION

There are at least two parts to any decision: the first is making it, and the second is living with it.

It can be very useful to try on a decision for a period of time—a day, week, or longer—and be aware of how different parts of you (Parent, Adult, Child) think and feel. For example, if you are at the point of deciding to stay in or leave a relationship, perhaps you can act as if you are going to stay. Think of all the positive and negative facets of the decision over time. Be clear on what you had hoped to change during this separation time.

Next, try on leaving and again practice the positive and negative facets of your decision. What seems right and better for you? Attempt to project yourself as far as you can to get a glimpse of what your life might be with both sides of this decision. Many times it is not *what* you decide, but *how* you go into that decision.

Your Parent may be looking at what you *should* do. Your free Child *feels* what you *want* to do. Your compliant Child may feel he has to please others and *obey* the Parent regarding a decision. Your over-rebellious Child may *resist* regardless of what is best for you. Your positive rebel Child may also provide new energy and willpower to make a change.

Your Adult will gather all the information you have learned and attempt to look at the larger picture. A well-functioning Adult will consider the wants and feelings of your Child as well as the opinions, beliefs, and values of the Parent. The Adult will put you in charge of you as you take increased responsibility for your life.

When you are ready to make your decision, remember, a decision does not necessarily mean your work is over. You will continually grow and change. Learning to practice, live with, and strengthen new changes, beliefs, perceptions, patterns, and scripts while being tested by the challenges of life is just as important as deciding to make those changes in the first place.

As you move forward with whatever decision you make, perhaps you will discover that the greatest change of all is the one you make within yourself. The major point of taking space is a more developed you. Trusting yourself and listening to you throughout this experience often forms the basis for a good decision. May you bring that newly turned-on, enlightened self to life and find the courage to express you in all of your relationships!

Step 10 Exercise: Making a Decision About Your Relationship

At this point in our 10-step process, you have experience and information on your side. The criteria and information used to evaluate your relationship earlier and throughout your separation process have created a foundation for making a decision about what you should do next. Let's say you think your communication with your partner has improved. Do you believe this improvement has been tested enough and will make enough of a difference to salvage the relationship? Is this the issue you wanted to work on?

Over time, any changes in beliefs, thinking, feelings, wants, perception, expectations, behavior, understanding, and skills in you and/or your partner can be measured as to whether they are working enough to make a difference in your experience of your relationship. Are you and your partner invested in and committed to continue working on those identified areas that were responsible for a decision to separate in the first place?

As we've seen throughout this book, a decisive factor in whether a couple chooses to stay together or reconcile is often the degree to which they each assume responsibility for renewed investment and commitment to their relationship, whatever their specific issues and problems. When a partner refuses to make attempts to understand, listen, communicate, show sensitivity and empathy, and take responsibility, there is often a much greater likelihood of the relationship ending.

For those individuals who have been left by a partner, perhaps the primary decision you have to make now is how to get on with your life, or perhaps decide to evaluate and change old patterns (your script) in a new relationship.

For those individuals still in a relationship in varying stages of separation, consider the following:

1. Perhaps you have known what your decision has been for a while, and now it is simply time to carry it out.

2. Perhaps you need more time and want to continue learning from your experience until you think and feel more confident. You may need to rework some of the steps of Separation Management. Committing to three to six months more can be useful.

3. Perhaps it is time to renew an investment and commitment to yourself and your partner.

Conclusion

Life's a journey, not a destination.

—Anonymous

Taking Space has been about understanding and empowering your *self*. Whether you are initiating a request for more space, changes, or a separation in your relationship, or you are the one on whom such a decision is being forced, I hope you have been helped to take charge of you and your experience. The ten steps of Separation Management introduced the necessary tasks involved with setting up a structure to contain the often debilitating and stressful emotions that accompany changes in at least one partner's investment in and commitment to a relationship. As you've seen, managing conflict and attempting to restore communication, the first two steps, are vitally important to maintaining stability during an uncertain time. Beginning to understand the purposes of a separation while assessing the differing levels of investment and commitment is covered in Step 3. Understanding the variety of separation options (Step 4) available to couples continues to build a structure from which to learn and function. Step 5 allows partners to be clear about their expectations of each other and whether any mutual agreement can be made regarding efforts to work together on reconciling a relationship. Being clear on family responsibilities during separation periods helps to keep a household functioning when partners may be living apart, energy is low, stress is high, and attention is divided.

Step 6 helped you understand and talk with children to minimize their anxiety and trauma. Step 7 helped you make a plan for handling separation day should one partner leave the home.

Once you can get to some calm, or ease the conflict, the deeper work can begin, if you choose to do it. As you saw, getting physical and/or psychological space from a partner and problematic pattern can often allow you to see yourself, your partner, and your relationship more clearly. Getting distance can allow some new perspective and energy to emerge. Whether you are physically separated or still intact, this work goes to the heart of the separation process, your inner or psychological growth. Separations help us look at and confront our values, beliefs, feelings, wants, and behavior, and how these contribute to our perception, patterns, and levels of satisfaction with ourselves and our relationships. When new energy, in the form of a separation or change, is invested, it becomes therapeutic for the relationship.

It is my hope that by encouraging you to understand *you*, to take responsibility and work on you and your contribution to your relational pattern, these steps have allowed you to break an impasse and make some changes. My purpose was to get you to stop trying to change your partner and to focus on working on your self. I hope this has helped, whether or not you have a cooperating partner.

Taking charge of your self-growth and development, whether you want a change or one is forced on you, is the heart and soul of *Taking Space*. After all, we must learn to know, like, love, relax, strengthen, and empower our selves before we can even truly discern how we want to be treated and treat others in our relationships. The more OK and loving we are with our selves, the more we will want to exchange this with a partner.

As your self-awareness and self-esteem develop, you will be better able to take care of you and meet more of your own wants. This in turn can create a better balance in knowing what you can reasonably expect from your partner. From here you can address such issues as life goals, values, and compatibility. I hope I have provided a good road map for this process.

And now, good luck on your journey.

Reaching an Agreement: A Negotiation Exercise

This exercise can be useful for partners to get clarity and more information on each other's values, wants, expectations, and available options regarding specific issues in your relationship. It might be helpful if each partner reflected and wrote down ideas before attempting to discuss them. The structured communication exercise (Step 2) in which each partner takes turns talking while the other partner listens can help keep your process on track while you work toward making decisions about specific issues and subjects.

1. Identify Your Issues Identify and clearly state what the issue or issues are that you will discuss. Discuss one issue at a time and be clear that this is the issue you want to resolve (i.e., spending time together, making purchases, child discipline, etc.).

EXAMPLE:

Sally wants to talk with Pete about planning more time together as a couple.

2. State Your Positions Clearly state what each partner thinks about this issue.

EXAMPLE:

SALLY: I want more time to talk and be a couple. I sometimes feel many days or weeks go by and we know little about what the other is doing when we are not together.

PETE: I believe we already spend enough time together. I am busy and would resist having to block off more time in my busy week. But I do value our relationship.

Time Sally and Pete Spend Together Now

Weekdays: very little time as each gets home late from work and they have to tend to dinner, children, homework, and other chores.

Weekends: Saturday evening together at home or out with friends. Sunday some alone time together and mostly family time together.

3. Determine What's (Really) Important to You What are each partner's interests, values, and feelings? What's really important to you in regard to your interests, values, and feelings?

EXAMPLE:

SALLY: When we spend time together I feel more connected. I can tell you about my day and how the kids are doing. It's important to know you care, and then I feel emotionally supported by you. Otherwise I become lonely and fearful and sometimes nag you about our lack of time together.

PETE: I worry that I won't have time to do all the family and household chores, spend time with the kids, work out, and have some time to myself. But I want you to feel supported by me and I don't want you to feel lonely. We're in this together.

4. Think of Options List all the possible options. Identify those options that allow both partners to gain something they want, in which both partners can win. Help each other out so each partner's concerns get addressed. Be as specific as possible.

EXAMPLE:

Pete and Sally listed three possible options for spending more time together as a couple.

Option 1: No change in schedule. The current amount of time together will remain the same.

Option 2: Set aside a half hour every night to talk and visit after kids go to bed and one evening at home or out together on weekends.

Option 3: Brief check-ins daily (5–10 minutes) during which each partner can share significant events of their day (before, at, or after dinner). Additional time: a half hour to one hour or more on Wednesday evening to visit and talk; Friday and Saturday nights, a half hour to one hour on one night and a full night out or at home together on the other weekend night; Sunday open for planning family or individual time.

5. Rank the Options Identify the benefits, drawbacks, and positive and negative consequences of the above for each partner. Identify the best option, second-best option, and third-best option.

EXAMPLE:

Option 1: Sally not satisfied with current amount of time together. Until now Pete has been OK with this, but feels conflicted after hearing Sally's wants for more time.

Option 2: Pete objects with too much time crammed into the evening hours as this will detract time from his other activities and chores. Sally is also concerned about being too tired after the children go to bed.

Option 3: This seems to be the best option. Put this option into action and then evaluate to see if this works for both partners over time and satisfies Sally's desire for more couple time. Also, ensure that Pete is finding the time for his own activities and chores.

6. Decide to carry out an option.

EXAMPLE:

Decided to carry out option three beginning the next day.

7. What Else You Need to Help You Reach Agreement if You Haven't So Far You may need one or all of the following: to take time out to think; more information; to consult a third person such as a counselor or mediator. Discuss the consequences to each partner and to the relationship if no action is taken.

EXAMPLE

Pete and Sally have reached agreement and need time to see if their decision is working.

8. Build in Review Time This will let you see if your decision is actually working.

EXAMPLE:

Build in review and evaluation time after one month to see if option three is working for Sally and Pete. If it is working, discuss why and give each other strokes for making a valuable change. If adjustments are necessary, discuss what might make this work better for whomever is not satisfied. Help create solutions so each partner can have his or her concerns heard.

Positive discussion and compromise seem to work best when two partners have a positive climate and process in their relationship. Breakdown and resistance occur during conflict (passive or aggressive). A positive relationship process fosters cooperation for both partners to win from an OK–OK position. Not all issues are negotiable and sometimes the best you can do is truly understand your different positions and learn to live with them (dealing with your feelings or learning to detach or disengage).

APPENDIX 2
Relaxation–Meditation
Exercise

This relaxation–meditation exercise can be done to relax, go to sleep, or get back to sleep. I find it's most useful when it's done for fifteen to thirty minutes at least once a day.

Prior to this exercise, you may want to think of goals or other problem areas you wish to work on. For example, you may want to feel good about yourself and your decisions; to find the strength to get through your situation; to feel more loving feelings toward yourself or another, perhaps a partner. Each time you do deep relaxation, you increase the chances that your subconscious mind will hear you and help you reach your goal.

Find a quiet spot without distractions. Lie down or sit in a comfortable chair. This exercise requires that you close your eyes. You may want to read the exercise slowly out loud or have someone else read it for you onto a tape or CD that you can listen to.

Because there is a tendency to fall asleep, you may want to set a timer or alarm. Once the exercise becomes a habit, I have found you will awaken naturally when the amount of time you usually allow for it has passed. If you awaken during the exercise, simply close your eyes and begin again.

When you end your relaxation, be sure to allow yourself time to sit quietly with your eyes closed for a minute or more. Some people might feel their body or limbs becoming numb or feel they have left their body during the exercise. This is all very normal. If you feel any discomfort or Not-OK feelings, stop the exercise and open your eyes.

1. Begin by taking three deep stomach or belly breaths Only your stomach should move in and out. Your shoulders and upper body should be still when breathing. Close your eyes. Take a quick trip through your body from your head to your feet. Notice tension, stress, and bodily sensations. Move through your head, face, neck, shoulders, arms, upper and lower back muscles, chest, stomach, lower body, upper and lower legs, and feet. Be aware of tightness, tension, soreness, discomfort, and good feelings.

2. Let your mind drift away, either to a real place or to a place you create This is a place to go where there are no responsibilities. Your escape fantasy can be the beach, a lake, a waterfall, woods, or your home in a comfortable chair or bed—wherever you feel safe, secure, and comfortable. You can be standing, sitting, or lying down. Picture yourself as free and relaxed as you can be, without judging. Notice what you see, hear, and especially what you feel in your fantasy. Give yourself permission to feel relaxed and comfortable—just be!

3. Progressive Relaxation—feet to head Next, let your mind drift to your feet. Either pick a point in each of your feet or picture them. Hold this point or picture briefly, then let go by letting your feet just be on their own. Let any tightness, tension, discomfort, or pain drain out through your toes. Some people prefer to tense these muscles before letting go and relaxing. You will continue to do this throughout your entire body.

Now focus on your lower legs and do the same. Picture and feel the tension draining down and out your feet. If any part won't relax, do not force it. You might want to imagine a point in both of your feet where there is positive, healing, soothing, relaxing, and comforting energy. As you continue this exercise, this energy will move up from your feet and replace all the tight, tense energy that is leaving your body.

Focus on your upper legs, tense, and then relax and release. Now focus on your entire lower body, buttocks, and pelvic area.

Next is your stomach. Relax and adjust your breathing. Create a safe, secure place in your stomach, which is the center of your being and confidence. Let all the negative tension and tightness drain away as you become more and more relaxed and let go of stomach tension.

Focus on your chest muscles next, as tension drains down your hips and out. Then your back muscles, and lower and upper back. Drain away soreness and pain. Picture a nice wave of relaxation across the back of your shoulders and neck as the positive energy from your feet drifts into your upper body. Feel more relaxed and heavy. Next let go of tension in the back of your neck, the back of your head, the top of your head, your forehead. Notice or draw a mental outline around any pain or discomfort inside or around your head. Let it go, but don't force it; it will go when it is ready.

Let your eyes get heavy, relaxed, and tired as they lock into place. This is your time with nothing to do and nowhere to go. Give yourself permission to feel good. Relax the rest of your face and lower jaw as you let your body sink into a deep and comfortable relaxed place. Let all that positive energy from your feet expand into your entire body including your shoulders, head, and face. Each breath you take will allow you to go as deep as you choose.

4. Meditation Focus just on your breathing. Remember to breathe deeply and slowly through your nose and deep into your stomach. Inhale and think the number one, and then exhale and think the number two. You could also think "re" on inhale and "lax" on exhale, or a two-syllable word of your choice. Continue to relax and count, one, two, as you breathe. This is all you have to do for the rest of the exercise. What will naturally happen is that your mind will wander into dreams or nonsense thoughts. If and as you become conscious of it, simply direct your mind back to counting, one, two, and breathing.

Bibliography

Bader, Ellyn, and Peter T. Pearson. *In Quest of the Mythical Mate: A Developmental Approach to Diagnosis and Treatment in Couples Therapy.* New York: Brunner/Mazel, 1988.

Belenky, M. F., B. M. Clinchy, N. R. Goldberger, and J. M. Tarule. *Women's Ways of Knowing: The Development of Self, Voice and Mind.* New York: Basic Books, 1986.

Benson, Herbert, Eileen M. Stuart, and associates at the Mind/Body Medical Institute of the New England Deaconess Hospital and Harvard Medical School. *The Wellness Book: The Comprehensive Guide to Maintaining Health and Treating Stress-Related Illness.* New York: Fireside, 1992.

Benson, Herbert, MD, with Miriam Z. Klipper. *The Relaxation Response.* New York: HarperCollins, 2001.

Berne, Eric. *Games People Play.* New York: Grove Press, 1964.

Boston Women's Health Book Collection. *Our Bodies Ourselves: A New Edition for a New Era.* New York: Touchstone, 2005.

Capacchione, Lucia. *Recovery of Your Inner Child.* New York: Simon & Schuster, 1991.

Chodron, Pema. *Start Where You Are: A Guide to Compassionate Living.* Boston: Shambhala Publications, 1994.

———*When Things Fall Apart: Heart Advice for Difficult Times.* Boston: Shambhala Publications, 1997.

Celani, David P. *The Illusion of Love: Why the Battered Woman Returns to Her Abuser.* New York: Columbia University Press, 1994.

Davis, Martha, Elizabeth Robbins Eshelman, and Matthew McKay. *Relaxation and Stress Reduction Workbook,* Fourth Edition. Oakland, CA: New Harbinger Publications, 1995.

Erikson, Eric H. "Identity and the Life Cycle." *Psychological Issues,* Vol 1, no. 1. New York: International Universities Press, Inc., 1959.

Evans, Patricia. *The Verbally Abusive Relationship: How To Recognize It and How To Respond.* Holbrook, MA: Adams Media Corporation, 1996.

Evans, Patricia. *Controlling People: How to Recognize, Understand and Deal with People Who Try to Control You.* Holbrook, MA: Adams Media Corporation, 1996.

Fanning, Patrick, and John O'Neil. *The Addiction Workbook: Step by Step Guide to Quitting Alcohol and Drugs.* Oakland, CA: New Harbinger Publications, 1996.

Fisher, Bruce. *Rebuilding When Your Relationship Ends.* San Luis Obispo, CA: Impact Publisher, 1998.

Goleman, Daniel. *Emotional Intelligence.* New York: Bantam Books, 1995.

Gottman, John. *Why Marriages Succeed or Fail.* New York: Fireside, 1994.

———and Nan Silver. *The Seven Principles for Making Marriage Work.* New York: Three River Press, 1999.

Gray, John. *Men Are From Mars Women Are From Venus.* New York: HarperCollins, 1992.

Harris, Thomas A. *I'm OK–You're OK: A Practical Guide to Transactional Analysis.* New York: Harper & Row, 1969.

Hendrix, Harville. *Getting The Love You Want: A Guide for Couples.* New York: Harper & Row, 1988.

Jack, Dana. *Silencing The Self: Women and Depression.* New York: HarperCollins, 1991.

James, Muriel, and Dorothy Jongeward. *Born to Win.* New York: Addison-Wesley, 1971.

James, John W., and Russell Friedman. *Grief Recovery Handbook: The Action Program for Moving Beyond Death, Divorce and Other Losses.* New York: HarperCollins, 1998.

Jeffers, Susan. *Feel The Fear and Do It Anyway.* New York: Ballantine Books, 1987.

Katherine, Anne. *Where To Draw the Line: How To Set Healthy Boundaries Every Day.* New York: Fireside, 2000.

Kirshenbaum, Mira. *Too Good To Leave, Too Bad Too Stay: A Step-by-Step Guide To Help You Decide Whether To Stay In or Get Out of Your Relationship.* New York: Plume, 1997.

Kübler-Ross, Elisabeth. *On Death and Dying.* New York: MacMillan, 1969.

Kushner, Harold S. *When Bad Things Happen To Good People.* New York: Avon Books, 1981.

Lerner, Harriet. *The Dance of Intimacy.* New York: Harper & Row, 1989.

Luecke, David L. *The Relationship Manual: How to Diagnose, Build, or Enrich a Relationship.* Columbia, MD: The Relationship Institute, 1981.

Markman, Howard, Scoll Stanley, and Susan L. Blumberg. *Fighting For Your Marriage: Positive Steps for Preventing Divorce and Preserving a Lasting Love.* San Francisco, CA: Jossey-Bass, 1994.

McGraw, Philip C. *Relationship Rescue: A Seven-Step Strategy for Reconnecting With Your Partner.* New York: Hyperion, 2000.

———*Self Matters: Creating Your Life From The Inside Out,* New York: Simon & Schuster, 2001.

———*Family First.* New York: Free Press, 2004.

Peck, M. Scott. *The Road Less Traveled: A New Psychology of Love, Traditional Values and Spiritual Growth.* New York: Touchstone, 1978.

Raffel, Lee. *Should I Go or Should I Stay?: How Controlled Separation (CS) Can Save Your Marriage.* Lincolnwood, IL: Contemporary Books, 1999.

Miller, Sherod, Phyllis A. Miller, Elam W. Nunnally, and David B. Wackman. *Talking and Listening Together: Couple Communication I.* Littleton, CO: Interpersonal Communication Program, 1992.

Real, Terrence. *I Don't Want To Talk About It: Overcoming the Secret Legacy of Male Depression.* New York: Fireside, 1997.

———*How Can I Get Through To You? Closing The Intimacy Gap Between Men and Women.* New York: Fireside, 2002.

Ram Dass, Baba. *Be Here Now.* Albuquerque, NM: Lama Foundation, 1971.

Rice, Joy K. *Living Through Divorce: A Developmental Approach to Divorce Therapy.* New York: The Guilford Press, 1986.

Robbins, Anthony. *Unlimited Power.* New York: Simon & Schuster, 1986.

Rock, Maxine. *The Marriage Map: Understanding and Surviving the Stages of Marriage.* Atlanta, GA: Peachtree Publishers, 1986.

Scarf, Maggie. *Intimate Partners.* New York: Random House, 1987.

Sheehy, Gail. *Passages, Predictable Crises of Adult Life.* New York: Bantam Books, 1976.

———*New Passages, Mapping Your Life Across Time.* New York: Ballantine Books, 1995.

Spring, Janis Abrams, with Michael Spring. Ph.D. *After the Affair.* New York: Harper Collins, 1996.

———*How Can I Forgive You? The Courage to Forgive, The Freedom Not To.* New York: Harper Collins, 2004.

Steiner, Claude. *Scripts People Live.* New York: Random House, 1974.

———*The Other Side of Power.* New York: Grove Press, 1981.

———*Games Alcoholics Play.* New York: Grove Press, 1971.

———*Emotional Literacy: Intelligence with a Heart.* Fawnskin, CA: Personhood Press, 2003.

Trafford, Abigail. *Crazy Times, Surviving Divorce and Building a New Life.* New York: Harper-Perennial, 1992.

Vaughn, Diane. *Uncoupling: How Relationships Fall Apart.* New York: Vantage Books, 1987.

Wallerstein, Judith S, and Sandra Blakeslee. *The Good Marriage: How and Why Love Lasts.* New York: Houghton Mifflin, 1995.

Wegscheider-Cruse, Sharon. *Learning To Love Yourself.* Deerfield Beach, FL: Health Communications, 1987.

Weiner-Davis, Michele. *Divorce Busting.* New York: Simon & Schuster, 1992.

———*Getting Through To The Man You Love: The No Nonsense, No Nagging Guide for Women.* New York: St. Martin's Press, 1998.

———*Change Your Life and Everyone In It: How To.* New York: Fireside, 1995.

Suggested Reading

Anger

Ellis, Albert. *Anger: How To Live With and Without It.* New York: Carol Publishing Group, 1977.

Lerner, Harriet. *Dance of Anger: A Woman's Guide to Changing the Patterns of Intimate Relationships.* New York: HarperCollins, 1997.

McKay, Matthew, Peter Rogers, and Judith McKay. *When Anger Hurts.* New York: MJF Books, 1989.

Potter-Efron, Ron. *Angry All the Time: An Emergency Guide To Anger Control.* Oakland, CA: New Harbinger Publications, 1994.

Williams, Redford, and Virginia Williams. *Anger Kills: 17 Strategies For Controlling The Hostility That Can Harm Your Health.* New York: Harper Paperbacks, 1998.

For Parents and Children

Brown, Laurene Krasny, and Marc Brown. *Dinosaurs Divorce,* New York: Little, Brown, 1988.

Chedekel, David S., and Karen O'Connell. *The Blended Family Sourcebook: A Guide To Negotiating Change.* New York: McGraw-Hill, 2002.

Gardner, Richard A. *The Parents' Book About Divorce.* New York: Bantam Books, 1979.

Johnson, Janet R., Karen Breunig, Carla Garrity, and Mitchell Baris. *Through The Eyes of Children: Healing Stories for Children of Divorce.* New York: Simon & Schuster, 1997.

Krementz, Jill. *Helping Kids Cope with Divorce.* San Francisco, CA: Josey-Bass, Inc., 1988.

Neuman, Gary. Helping Your Kids Cope With Divorce The Sandcastles Way. New York: Random House, 1998.

Ricci, Isolina. *Mom's House, Dad's House. Making Two Homes for Your Children.* New York: Fireside, 1997.

Teyber, Edward. *Helping Children Cope With Divorce.* San Francisco, CA: Jossey-Bass, 1992.

Wallerstein, Judith. *Surviving The Breakup: How Parents and Children Cope with Divorce,* New York: Basic Books, 1996.

Sex

Barbach, L.G. *For Yourself: The Fulfillment of Female Sexuality.* Garden City, NY: Doubleday, 1975.

Kaplan, Helen Singer. *The Illustrated Manual of Sex Therapy.* New York: Brunner-Routledge, 1987.

————*Sexual Desires Disorders: Dysfunctional Regulation of Sexual Disorders.* New York: Brunner-Routledge, 1995.

Kleinplatz, Peggy J. *New Directions in Sex Therapy: Innovations and Alternatives.* New York: Brunner-Routledge, 2001.

Love, Pat, and Jo Robinson. *Hot Monogamy: Essential Steps to More Passionate, Intimate Love Making.* New York: Plume, 1995.

Schnarch, David. *Passionate Marriage.* New York: Henry Holt, 1997.

Weiner-Davis, Michele. *The Sex Starved Marriage: A Couples' Guide to Boosting Their Marriage Libido.* New York: Simon & Schuster, 2003.

Resources

International Transactional Analysis Association

2186 Rheem Dr., #B-1
Pleasanton, CA 94588
Tel. 925-600-8110
www.itaa-net.org
(For all publications, videos, and audio cassettes)

The Coalition for Marriage, Family and Couples Education, LLC

Diane Sollee, MSW, Founder and Director
An information exchange on marriage and relationship courses
CMFCE@SmartMarriages.com

Suicide Prevention Hotline

American Foundation for Suicide Prevention
www.afsp.org
Crisis: 1-800-SUICIDE

National Domestic Violence Hotline

1-800-799-SAFE 7233
1-800-787-3224

Visit Bob Buchicchio's Web site at takingspace.com for information about educational courses, training, videos, DVDs, CDs, and more.

About the Author

For over thirty-five years, Robert Buchicchio has been working with couples as a marriage and divorce counselor. In 1990 Bob began developing specific tools couples could use to manage separations. He designed Separation Management as a problem-solving approach that was based on partners' levels of commitment to their relationship and respected the needs of both partners and their children.

Bob has a BA in psychology from the University of Rhode Island and an MSW in clinical social work from Ohio State University. He holds diplomates from the American Board of Examiners in Clinical Social Work and the National Association of Social Workers, of which he is a former Vermont chapter president. He is a licensed clinical social worker in Vermont, where he has had a private mental health practice specializing in couples work for the past twenty-seven years.

Bob has conducted couples' workshops throughout his professional career and has taught at Vermont College and Norwich University. As a professional associate with the American Humane Association children's division and Action for Child Protection, Inc., he has trained child welfare workers nationally and internationally on building therapeutic relationships. He has been the executive director of the West Yavapai Mental Health Clinic and the chief social worker (holding the rank of captain) at the U.S. Army Hospital in Seoul. S. Korea.

Bob is one of the founders of the Hospice Program of Central Vermont, where he continues to teach communication skills to the volunteers and staff.